Knowledge
and Hermeneutic
Understanding

Knowledge and Hermeneutic Understanding

A Study of the Habermas-Gadamer Debate

Demetrius Teigas

Lewisburg
Bucknell University Press
London and Toronto: Associated University Presses

Associated University Presses
440 Forsgate Drive
Cranbury, NJ 08512

Associated University Presses
25 Sicilian Avenue
London WC1A 2QH, England

Associated University Presses
P.O. Box 338, Port Credit
Mississauga, Ontario
Canada L5G 4L8

The paper used in this publication meets the requirements of the American National Standard for Permanence of Paper for Printed Library Materials Z39.48–1984.

Library of Congress Cataloging-in-Publication Data

Teigas, Demetrius, 1950-
    Knowledge and hermeneutic understanding : a study of the Habermas-Gadamer debate / Demetrius Teigas.
        p.   cm.
    Includes bibliographical references and index.
    ISBN 0-8387-5273-X (alk. paper)
    1. Hermeneutics.   2. Knowledge, Theory of.   I. Habermas, Jürgen.
II. Gadamer, Hans-Georg, 1900-   III. Title.
BD241.T38   1995
121'.68—dc20
                                                                93-29989
                                                                CIP

Quotations from *Knowledge and Human Understanding* by Jürgen Habermas are copyright © 1971 by Beacon Press. Reprinted by permission of Beacon Press.

To the memory of my father

Contents

vii

Preface

The "critical theory" of Jürgen Habermas and the "philosophical hermeneutics" of Hans-Georg Gadamer originate in the sixties, a time when, together with the rapid industrialization of the postwar period and the relative stability and comodification of Western societies, the repressive and antihumanist aspects of technocracy, the "one-dimensionality" of projects and aspirations, as well as the depolitization of the individual, had already emerged. In the background of that period the major critical paradigms were psychoanalysis, critical forms of Marxism and, at a more philosophical level, the Heideggerian critique of Western Reason and technology.

The present phase of world history is in many respects different from that of twenty or thirty years ago, which nevertheless, cannot be comprehended without some immediate relation to the past. The present could be provisionally considered as a continuation, development, and reorganization of the past, and, simultaneously, as a result of ruptures from past practices. Today, we live in societies that have not yet solved basic problems which overtly entered the political domain in the sixties and, although production, science, and technology have provided gross benefits to large sections of the world population, high prices have been paid for these kinds of development and particular choices.

Rifts and divisions emerge continually within national boundaries. Global pollution and devastation of earth's ecology, eruptions of nationalism, and lack of dialogue between nations and world outlooks are current disturbing features. An immense gap separates developed and underdeveloped countries. Overpopulation, malnutrition, and starvation for millions has become the (un)accepted norm. Inequality of income encourages the worse faces of racism, mistrust, tendencies of noncooperation, and destruction, which emerge and go beyond our explanatory frameworks and intellectual visions. The everyday Western citizen has been forced into the role of an armchair-spectator of the *simulacrum*, reenacted on television.

Yet, in these circumstances, we can learn from the approaches and proposals of Habermas and Gadamer and in particular, recover critical efforts and critical dimensions which these authors addressed to specific theoretical and practical problems from the perspective of their time. Although I am bound to follow their philosophical exchanges and their philosophical theses, it is the character of their debate which cannot be confined within abstract philosophical boundaries. Their common concern for the human being and for his quality of life ties their philosophical quests to practical issues.

We cannot ignore, particularly today after having reached the ability to avoid dogmatic attitudes, the possibility of knowledge as *critique*. Neither can we disregard the hermeneutic dimension of our understanding of the "other," of history and of our own situation. The philosophical themes which I examine in this work could serve in several other areas; they can provide frameworks for comprehending fundamental processes involved in social/historical understanding, or in aesthetic expressions, of crises, anxiety, despair, and indifference that have become permanent features of the closing stages of this century.

Habermas's and Gadamer's attempts *are not* the only available paradigms of critical thinking. For many, Gadamer would not count as a critical thinker, although I believe his contributions to philosophical reasoning have significantly promoted the historicality of human understanding and its liberation from stagnant positivist perspectives. The views of Habermas and Gadamer offer valuable insights and opportunities that allow us to trace the philosophical backgrounds of these ideas. At present, other critical positions have crossed the discursive boundaries of Habermas and Gadamer, yet many of the practical problems either remain the same or have intensified in new forms.

Do Habermas's ideas of *undistorted communication* and of knowledge as *critique* appeal to us today? Or, does Gadamer's insistence on *dialogue* and fusion of our own horizon with the horizon of the "other" have relevance for the expediency of our situation? In this direction, is there a need to appreciate "tradition," as Gadamer contends? Can the Heideggerian concern for Being be translated into concern for the present human condition under constant threat from an endangered eco-system?

These are questions of wider contextual importance which we are all bound to ask theoretically and emotionally. I will not raise the very practical (moral) questions in my work, neither will I invite any concrete social criticism. My investigation shall remain faithful to the philosophical treatment of the two hermeneutic approaches. Nevertheless, the philosophical positions I examine are motivated by such practical questions and they echo similar concerns. This is the legacy of contemporary Continental philosophical tradition entangled in this kind of approach, never distancing the theoretical quest from practical considerations.

Acknowledgments

As is usual with acknowledgments, thanks and gratitude are expressed to key people who aided in the production of the work, smoothing down obstacles and generally being supportive at critical times. I feel greatly indebted to my wife Hope for her patience and support over many months. I also have to thank her for typing part of the manuscript which, because of its untidiness, required her most patient efforts. I should like to express my gratitude to Prof. David McLellan for his moral support and encouragement as I embarked on the writing of the first chapter of this work. I am also indebted to Prof. Michael Payne for reading the whole manuscript and for his invaluable suggestions which encouraged me to continue with its publication. I should also like to express my thanks to John Bousfield for his support, and for the lengthy discussions which we had on several topics that appear in the present work. My utmost gratitude is for Kahryn Hughes who edited the whole work in an admirable way and who spotted ambiguous passages in need of further clarification. My thanks also go to Kevin Burns and Chris Savill who helped in the early phases of editing. Without their help and encouragement the task I had set myself would have been much more difficult to achieve and would never have resulted in the same product. And, finally, my thanks go to those friends who supported me and eased the strain by their warm understanding.

Introduction

After a short preface, it is customary to introduce the work to the reader, such an introductory piece having at least a dual purpose: firstly, to indicate the context and the boundaries of the topics dealt with and to allude to their significance within a certain discourse; secondly, to provide a preparatory overall view of the scope, aims, and directions of the work. The Introduction, therefore, can be regarded simply as a short hermeneutic exercise (this time directed from the author to the reader), that wishes to establish the horizon of "the whole" before "the parts" are analyzed. And this is exactly what I intend to do, although I am aware of the fact that there are several conscious intentions, reflected in the titles of the chapters, which may not reveal further intentions and orientations (conscious or unconscious). The reader, however, as a result can develop a more comfortable "space" to move within during his own interpretative relationship with the present text.

I came across the writings of Habermas (after my acquaintance with Adorno and Horkheimer) some years ago and was fascinated with his efforts to present a "critical social theory" which claimed to tackle a number of problems, but most importantly, to criticize "ideology," or "ideological discourses"—a subject so dear to the seventies, yet with a contemporary sway. However, Habermas's continual references to hermeneutics and in particular to the philosophical hermeneutics of Gadamer, hindered my comprehension either of Habermas's appropriation of hermeneutics, or of his intentions, which bore evident links with the teachings of philosophical hermeneutics. This led me to study Gadamer and the debate which took place between them in the late sixties and early seventies, continuing afterward with sporadic exchanges.

Habermas is well-known in the Anglo-Saxon academic world for his philosophical positions on matters of social and political interest. He is famous for his innovative writings in the last twenty-five years and for his insistence upon a "critical social theory" which can be seen as a continuation of the "critical theory" of the Frankfurt school. As a member of this school he shares with it certain Hegelian and Marxist views of history, society, and its evolution. He has exercised a significant influence both on the Continent and in the Anglo-Saxon world as a social and political critic and philosopher.[1]

Gadamer, until recently, did not enjoy the popularity of Habermas in English-speaking countries. His philosophical ideas stem mainly from the teachings of Heidegger, although we can identify within his work a strong influence from the mainstream German philosophical tradition, particularly Hegel. Gadamer is principally known among philosophers preoccupied with phenomenology or with the work of Heidegger. However, this picture has changed radically in the last few years with the extensive attention that has been paid to his book *Truth and Method* by an audience interested either in questions arising in "understanding meaning," or in notions of "communication" and "dialogue." His influence is already apparent, ranging from sociology and literary criticism to historical studies and aesthetic theory where the notion of "interpretation" is continually at stake.

Although the debate between Habermas and Gadamer took place in the late sixties and early seventies, Habermas's *Knowledge and Human Interests* in 1968 could be considered as an indirect reply to Gadamer's *Truth and Method* published in 1960. *Knowledge and Human Interests* is also the text in which Habermas presented his early ideas on language and on "scientific hermeneutics." For these reasons I have decided to direct my efforts in the first few chapters to those works which are immediately connected to the context of their exchange. It is also worth adding that Habermas never rejected his early work in *Knowledge and Human Interests* which concentrated on an epistemological defense of his "critical theory."[2]

This present work is an attempt to study and analyze the opposition between the "critical theory" or "critical hermeneutics" of Habermas, and the "philosophical hermeneutics" of Gadamer. It juxtaposes and questions the project of *knowledge as critique* that Habermas proposes, and the *hermeneutic understanding* which Gadamer claims to be present in any knowledge and "truth." The conflict leads to their debate which initially focuses on our attitude with regard to tradition and its authority. Gadamer feels that the study of tradition is indispensable for the examination of the concept of "understanding." According to him, all understanding is embedded in tradition. However, can we trust tradition as a resource of truth, or should we criticize it as a source of ideology? What reasons have shaped the seemingly "uncritical" (and rather welcoming) attitude of philosophical hermeneutics toward tradition? Why does philosophical hermeneutics seek "truth" in tradition? In contrast, following Habermas, should we consider tradition as the source of deception in language, thus placing tradition at the frontline of criticism, to be scrutinized under a rigorous "hermeneutic method?" Are there sufficient reasons why we should consider ideology as *distorted* communication, so that for its abolition we need to apply critical examination in ways similar to those of psychoanalysis?

The point at issue is also the linguisticality of all (cases of) understanding and the universal dimension of hermeneutic experience. How can we conceive of the linguisticality of all understanding that philosophical hermeneutics proclaims? What are the implications entailed by this premise of "linguisticality" and which "critical theory" finds unacceptable? If, for example, we assume that all experience and understanding is ultimately of a linguistic nature, is there a justified fear that we are entrapped within an interpretative mode of life in relation to tradition and the world, which severely undermines any chance for a scientific study of ideology?

Not only does Gadamer's philosophical hermeneutics face a wide range of questions and objections, but the propositions of "critical theory" have become the object of criticism and severe questioning. What reasons permit psychoanalysis to be used legitimately as a model of "critical theory?" On what grounds can the transfer of its methodology and therapeutic results to a "critical theory of society" be seen as a welcome and permissible theoretical exercise? These and similar questions, as well as the constant references (implicit or explicit) made by both Habermas and Gadamer to their works written before the debate, clarify the urgency of studying the two philosophical positions separately at the outset; they form the basis for approaching the debate itself.

To this end, I intend to follow closely Habermas's attempts to construct a "critical social theory," drawing on the epistemological contributions of Peirce and Dilthey in the domain of methodology in the natural and social sciences. My main inquiry will focus firstly, on the mode and structure he proposes for such a theory and secondly, on the foundations upon which, as he claims, a satisfactory critique of ideology can be based. In his effort to present a new critical discipline, beyond the natural and social/historical sciences, he grounds this critical science upon a special interest in self-reflection,which turns out to be an interest in emancipation. To what extent are his claims justified? These questions will lead us to the notion of "scientific hermeneutics" or "depth hermeneutics" which Habermas attributes to psychoanalysis and borrows as an indispensable tool for the construction of his critique of ideology. However, does this critique combine explanatory statements with hermeneutic analysis? Can such "scientific hermeneutics" avoid the hermeneutic circle of textual understanding? A specific question I will raise concerns the limitations of Habermas's attempt by contrast with the picture we receive from Gadamer's analysis and employment of hermeneutics in ways parallel to those of textual understanding. A central argument will be that "depth hermeneutics" can provide knowledge as critique but, besides its explanatory ability and its scientific character, it cannot escape the involvement of hermeneutic (interpretational) understanding and the hermeneutic circle.

In order to appreciate Heidegger's transformation of hermeneutics to a philosophical hermeneutics, a brief study of the development of hermeneutics from textual interpretation (Reformation period) to a theoretical means of understanding history (Schleiermacher and Dilthey) will be essential. Concerning Gadamer's philosophy, I will examine and elucidate what occurs during our efforts to understand a text, tradition, the past, or another person, processes which make us aware of the wide involvement of hermeneutic experience. According to Gadamer any understanding involves "prejudices" (preconceptions). How are we going to confront such "prejudices?" Do they present an inevitable situation for any act of understanding? Can we become aware of our preconceptions? It is important to clarify the ways in which the interpretive nature of understanding is revealed in any possible dimension of theoretical activity or everyday dialogue. In such cases we must pay close attention to the position of the interpreter and to the reasons for which she must be aware of two horizons, her own and that of the text. A successful interpretation can only materialize as long as the two horizons are fused.

Philosophical hermeneutics introduces conceptions of knowledge and "truth" which move beyond the restricted norms of scientific disciplines. It promotes the notion of valid and true knowledge in the human sciences, the arts, and tradition. Beginning with the conception of "truth" as insight, I will attempt to bring to light further consequences that "truth" entails in Gadamer's theory and in particular the way in which "truth" affects us. An opposite example, with a restricted conception of "truth," is the notion of "scientism," refuted by Habermas as a short-sighted positivist belief which identifies knowledge as science. The critical study of "scientism" can serve to demonstrate the distance separating its approach to knowledge and "truth" from the hermeneutic perspective.

Both participants reap the benefits of the category of "reflection." Philosophical hermeneutics employs it as self-reflection aiming at self-transparency and the accquisition of *phronesis* (practical wisdom). However, in which particular way does Habermas employ the category of reflection in his theory? What kind of reflection does he demand from the cultural sciences and what kind of reflection (self-reflection) does he claim to be present in the practice of psychoanalysis and in his theory of "distorted communication?" These issues require careful attention because of Habermas's conflation of two different notions of "reflection."

Gadamer's and Habermas's views on tradition, exchanged in the debate, appear to be in total antithesis. They present themselves in the form of *antinomies*, a term applied with specific reference to this debate by Paul Ricoeur whose opinions are extensively dealt with in the fifth chapter onward. I will contend, in agreement with Ricoeur, that these antinomies are misleading and that each theory amplifies one aspect of tradition only. Tradition, I will argue, is inhabited by both "truth" and "untruth." Instead of being drawn into irreconcilable antitheses, the two hermeneutic paradigms, exemplifying "critical consciousness" and "hermeneutic awareness," can be brought into dialogue (not a merging) and each one can learn from the other's limitations. One of my concerns in the debate is to show that philosophical hermeneutics can be seen as endowed with critical abilities and not simply as a "recollection of tradition."[3] Philosophical hermeneutics can be considered a critical enterprise for the examination of our prejudices and can be capable of projecting humanist ideas. Into this area of discussion I will introduce the suggestions of Ricoeur who adopts a similar attitude to the potential critical ability of philosophical hermeneutics. In the second part of the debate I will claim that the universality of hermeneutic experience holds true and cannot be refuted, at least by Habermas's arguments. I will additionally claim that philosophical hermeneutics, by its ability to point to the "openness" of the hermeneutic circle, can always put at risk the claims of "critical theory."

The debate and the issues presented in it have forced me to look further, beyond the apparent controversies, into underlying beliefs and orientations shared by Habermas and Gadamer. Both value humanistic ideas inherited from the Enlightenment (universal projects of emancipation and freedom). The introduction of *critique* and *emancipation* by Habermas, or the ideal of *phronesis* (practical wisdom) by Gadamer, show the strong convictions of the authors. Nevertheless, are these ideas valid today? Can projects to freedom and emancipation for the reappropriation of the human subject as the center of the universe be accepted unquestionably? Or, as I will try to show, can they be challenged by Heidegger's critique of "humanism" and technology? For Heidegger "humanism" and technology are both parts of Western metaphysics and the concerns of "humanism" (seen here as a philosophical category) do not provide an alternative to technological rationality. Heidegger's critique of "humanism" can question the projects of both Habermas and Gadamer, particularly those aspects either referring to universal emancipatory projects, or bearing relations to deeply embedded teleological views of history. The emancipatory and universalistic aspirations of the Enlightenment have been rigorously questioned by French critical thinkers and both Habermas and Gadamer were forced to engage in the defense of their positions.[4] In particular they needed to answer the charge that they were reproducing the narratives of "emancipation" and "speculative unity of all thought."[5] By presenting these critical challenges to the projects of Habermas and Gadamer, we can more capably judge the validity of their positions and initiate dialogue with further critical viewpoints and concerns.

Recapitulating, the main aim of the present work is to grasp the two hermeneutical paradigms in their conflict, but also in their dialogue, and to suggest ways in which each benefits from the other. This can provide valuable insights into what we can gain from both "critical theory" and philosophical hermeneutics. Apart from the immediate philosophical benefits, with such insights we could possibly address new questions about the scope and understanding of the human sciences, as well as their radicalization by philosophical thinking.

The importance of the debate can also be seen in a wider context which registers a *conflict* taking place between sciences and humanities,[6] a widespread and well-discussed presumption which has been adopted by many critical theorists in this century. The picture of knowledge and truth which hermeneutics provides, is in sharp antithesis to the picture offered by the methodical sciences. Gadamer's philosophical hermeneutics makes it mandatory for us to become aware of and appreciate our horizon in any attempt to understand (and know) the past, the text, the other person, or the historical "object." Similarly, we must also pay attention to the horizon of the text and "apply" it to our own by fusing the two horizons. Such claims are unique in the wider area of the arts and humanities, as well as in the human sciences.[7] Unlike Gadamer, Habermas undertakes the application of hermeneutic procedures within the specific area of social/historical disciplines in a critical-scientific manner. Nevertheless, these disciplines are led by a (cognitive) interest in communication and they amply display the hermeneutic dimensions of *understanding meaning*. This contrasting appreciation of the role of hermeneutics by Habermas constitutes one of the fundamental reasons for which the two writers became engaged in a debate. A further significant difference central to the debate is that, although "critical theory" makes use of "hermeneutic understanding," it wishes to disassociate itself firstly, from the linguisticality of all understanding, secondly from a conservative attitude toward tradition, and thirdly from the ontological conclusions of hermeneutics.

One prevailing conviction among many philosophers and cultural critics is that the concepts of knowledge and truth, originating in the humanities, are on the defensive when faced with scientific claims.[8] Notwithstanding this belief, the humanities promise a "better" and more thoughtful consideration of life than the sciences have already permitted being, as they are, enclosed within their technological rationality. In this direction the two hermeneutical paradigms (of Gadamer and Habermas) pursue questions of "reflection" and "critique" which are of paramount importance for the quality of life and for its practical (moral) dimensions. They provide the space and vocabulary for addressing critical questions and upsetting what has been accepted as normative, or what conceals social injustices, or what imposes a neglect of personal reflective capacities. However, in our efforts to take sides on these conflicts between science and humanities, one main fundamental question still remains: can we convincingly argue that the "truth" disclosed by hermeneutics is *significant* for practical life?

I believe that the following chapters will confirm the view that the questions raised between "critical theory" and philosophical hermeneutics retain their value for the present. Furthermore, time has put us in a privileged position: We can examine the views of Habermas and Gadamer more critically than previously and from a larger variety of perspectives.

The first chapter will deal with Habermas's critique of "scientism," which he considers to be the main orientation of positivism, and also to reveal the character of "technocratic consciousness." This chapter explicates the critical climate in the sixties, encountered by Gadamer, who often repeats his attacks on the "instrumentality of knowledge."[9] I will devote the second and third chapters to the philosophical hermeneutics of Gadamer, examining the linguistic and ontological implications of "hermeneutic understanding." The fourth chapter will explore Habermas's search for foundations of knowledge and for a cognitive interest in emancipation which can lead to a particular kind of knowledge as critique. Having examined the philosophical positions of both participants, I will analyze their debate in detail in the fifth and sixth chapters and draw conclusions concerning our attitude, firstly toward tradition and its values, and secondly toward ideology as distorted communication. The scope of my study will also extend to the possible dialogue that can be promoted between the two hermeneutic paradigms. Finally in the last chapter, alongside a review of the most important conclusions drawn in this work, I will seek a further evaluation of the debate by questioning the underlying aims and orientations of both participants *vis-à-vis* Heidegger's critique of humanism which, as a larger and more powerful philosophical critique of metaphysics, can act as a metacritique of the humanistic aspects of Habermas's and Gadamer's philosophical projects. More detailed introductory remarks are presented in the opening paragraphs of each chapter.

Knowledge and Hermeneutic Understanding

1
The Critique of "Scientism"

In this initial chapter I will examine the main criticisms Habermas levels against the particular conception of knowledge he refers to as "scientism" and which he believes illustrates the overall orientation and attitude of positivist tradition with regard to knowledge. The critique of "scientism," advanced by Habermas, is rooted in the critique of "instrumental reason," a concept utilized by the Frankfurt school in its own "critical theory." For Habermas the critique of "scientism" appears to be a preparatory exercise in order to refute the implications of "scientistic" beliefs and move us on to a more comprehensive idea of knowledge based upon specific human interests. The possibility of human interests in the background of scientific knowledge enable him to reexamine and approach anew the connections between theory and practice.

Apart from its roots in the Frankfurt school, the critique Habermas levels against positivism originates within the context of the German philosophical tradition which not only revolves around the Kantian philosophical enterprise, but also includes the Hegelian philosophy and its critique of Kant. Moreover, Marx has been seen, particularly in the eyes of the Frankfurt school, as the thinker who inherited and transformed Hegelian thought into a materialist critique of capitalist society. Habermas belonging to the same philosophical tradition, embarks on a reading of Kant, Hegel, and Marx with the aim of showing the possible theoretical reasons which permitted positivism to spread unhindered. To start with, I will trace these views of Habermas, before examining his actual critique of "scientism." The penultimate part of this chapter will complete the picture of the way in which positivism has exercised its grip upon the sciences. Habermas's refutation of positivism is a prerequisite in order to understand what he means by the loss of "reflection" and his efforts

3

to recover this category with the help of his projected "critical social science." Finally, I will refer to Habermas's views on the separation between theory and practical life and the enormous difficulties this separation imposes on any attempt to introduce the normative concept of the "just and good life."

"Critical Theory" and "Instrumental Reason"

Habermas's critique of positivism was presented in his book, *Knowledge and Human Interests,* though he had expressed similar ideas in earlier publications.[1] In the same book he also attempted to look for a satisfactory grounding for "critical theory" which was initiated by his predecessors in the Frankfurt school a few decades ago. Habermas's project could be considered in many ways as a continuation, at least of the aims, of the Frankfurt school's critical attitude. Therefore, a brief introduction to the aims of the school and its concept of "instrumental reason" seems to me to be indispensable in acquiring some valid notions for a comparison with Habermas's views.

"Critical theory" was conceived, at least by Horkheimer, as a theoretical project which would be able not only to analyze and understand current capitalist societies in a cognitive fashion, but also to criticize and disclose what appeared to be repressive, dominating, and a source of unacceptable quality of life for the human agent. Although the "critical theorists" (e.g., Adorno, Horkheimer, and Marcuse) in the course of their writings followed a number of different approaches for the critical understanding of society, Horkheimer's essay "Traditional and Critical Theory," excellently summarizes the aims of the members of the Frankfurt Institute for Social Research.[2]

According to Horkheimer, "critical theory" relativizes the separation between the individual and society upon which the limits of activity of the individual are set and accepted by him as natural. Critical thinking insists that the overall framework of society originates in human action and thus it could be a "possible object of planful decision and rational determination of goals."[3] Referring to those individuals who accept the critical attitude, Horkheimer argues that they find themselves in "tension" with society. They conceive society, in its economic aspects as well as in its social and cultural dimensions, as the product of will and reason but, paradoxically, it appears to them that this same society is on a course of nonhuman, almost natural processes. The examples of cultural forms of war and oppression that Horkheimer mentions do not appear to come from "a unified, self-conscious will. That world is not their own but the world of capital." The tension, then, for those individuals adopting the critical attitude remains but, in a tone echoing the *Critique of Political Economy*, they know that

> the critical acceptance of the categories which rule social life contains simultaneously their condemnation.[4]

Horkheimer believes that such a society which "lacks reason" must emancipate itself. "Critical theory" then fits within the boundaries of a theoretical frame which could promote the emancipatory attitude aiming at the alteration of society as a whole.

We must also bear in mind that the aims of "critical theory" follow the same lines as the ideas of the humanist tradition of the Enlightenment. It is through this tradition that the members of the Frankfurt school utilize the concept of critique "as oppositional thinking, as an activity of unveiling, or debunking."[5] Marx's writings and the Marxist tradition were similarly seen by them as belonging to the same spirit of Enlightenment, even though they abandoned the *Critique of Political Economy* and consequently the importance of the working class as the axis of their theoretical activity.[6] Instead the central concept which the critical theorists (especially Horkheimer, Adorno, and Marcuse) introduced for an effective critical understanding of societies was the notion of "instrumental reason."

The concept of "instrumental reason" originates in Weber's work and is equivalent to the Weberian thinking of "means-ends" rationality. It was introduced and established as a major critical concept during their poswar writings. According to David Held there are two aspects in Weber's concept of *rationalization* that the Frankfurt school incorporated in its own critical approach to society. The first concerns the extension of the model of scientific practice in the natural sciences to all sciences and furthermore the extension of this rationality to the conduct of life itself. Such an attitude corresponds to what Weber called *intellectualization* or *disenchantment* of the world. The second feature shows how this new conduct of life, or "secularization" of life, results in the growth of a "means-ends" rationality since practical ends are sought by methodological accuracy and precise calculation of means.[7]

It is in this appropriation of Weber's writings that Horkheimer reflects upon the lost autonomy of reason in the political sphere. Ideas about justice, equality, happiness, and democracy supposedly sprang from reason. However, the reduction of reason almost to the level of an industrial process set "the ground for the rule of force in the domain of the political."8 He then continues with the bleak idea of "instrumental reason."

> Having given up autonomy, reason has become an instrument. In the formalistic aspect of subjective reason, stressed by positivism, its unrelatedness to objective content is emphasised; in its instrumental aspect, stressed by pragmatism, its surrender to heteronomous contents is emphasised. Reason has become completely harnessed to the social process. Its operational value, its role in the domination of men and nature, has been made the sole criterion.9

Therefore, for the Frankfurt thinkers, the technological and technocratic inspirations in the industrial societies of the West dominate almost the whole landscape of everyday life. Reason has been adapted to successful operations, applications, and control similar to the applications of technological knowledge. Reason, then, has been seen and used as an *instrument* to such ends.

After this uncompromising critique of capitalist organization in terms of the "critical theory," it follows that such a rationality does not allow room for any critical reflection. The world is accepted by the individual, under the premises and ideals of technocracy, successful implementation of "scientific" achievements, and a corresponding notion of progress. Habermas will not follow this almost entirely pessimistic attitude nor will he accept the fact that the concept of "instrumental reason" reveals the whole context of modern industrial societies.

From a Theory of Knowledge to a Philosophy of Science

In the first several chapters of his book *Knowledge and Human Interests*, Habermas presents an overall view of the way in which the philosophical theory of knowledge, introduced by Kant as a *Critique of Pure Reason*, was finally criticized and rejected by the Hegelian phenomenological critique of knowledge. The final blow to the idea of a theory of knowledge was delivered by Marx who, according to Habermas, misunderstood the epistemological significance of Hegel's critique. Finally, Positivism (with the advance of the natural sciences) met favorable conditions in which to establish a philosophy of science as the norm, instead of a philosophical theory of knowledge.

Habermas undertakes this brief excursus in classical German Idealism (Kant and Hegel) and its critical epigone Marx, in order to show the successive steps of the dissolution of epistemology in favor of Positivism and its normative discussion on sciences and their methodology. However, the "target" is Marx, since Habermas wants firstly, to retain certain characteristics of Marx's materialist critique of Hegel (especially the notion of the self-constitution of the species),[10] and secondly, to offer a reassessment of Marx's conflation of critique and the natural sciences.

Hegel, according to Habermas, subjected the critical philosophy of Kant to an unyielding critique from the standpoint of his phenomeno-logical self-reflection of the Spirit.[11] Hegel demonstrates that the epistemology of critical philosophy is caught in a circle. Initially, the cognitive faculty sets the conditions for all possible knowledge; however, if our knowledge is to be trusted, one has to investigate the cognitive faculty, which is knowledge itself. How can one arrive at such knowledge (of the cognitive faculty) prior to any knowledge at all? That is, there is no escape from some initial presuppositions in such consistent epistemological procedures. In his attempt to over-come this problem, Hegel introduces "sense-certainty" as his start-ing point, which he then transcends with phenomenological experi-ence and self-reflection. This initial point is given empirically and does not fall into the previous circle of the Kantian critique. In Habermas's view, Hegel thought that his philosophical enterprise had finally overcome even his own radical critique of knowledge. Never-theless, although the culmination of the *Phenomenology of Spirit* is Absolute Knowledge, Hegel never demonstrated such an achievement "according to the criteria of a radicalised critique of Knowledge."[12] What Habermas means is that Hegel always presupposed a knowl-edge of the Absolute and never put into question his own presupposi-tions in terms of his radical critique. Thus, Hegel stops short of com-pleting his project which he intended as a radical and total critique of knowledge.

Habermas continues with the presentation of three implicit presup-positions that lay at the beginning of Kant's program and which Hegel revealed with his own phenomenological critique. Firstly, Kant took a specific category of knowledge (actually physics and mathematics) and established it as the normative concept of science. From then on Kant could use any valid principles in these disciplines and incorporate them in his theory of the cognitive faculty. Second-ly, Kant's subject of cognition is "a complete, fixed knowing subject or, in other words a normative concept of the ego."[13] Finally, the third presupposition is the distinction between theoretical and practi-cal reason which Kant introduced as self-evident. However, if true it would mean that the critique of knowledge is separate from the cri-tique of rational action. Habermas feels that such a conclusion is problematic. In fact, all these three normative concepts in Kant's philosophy were later denounced by Habermas in his attempt to formulate a "social theory of knowledge."

Turning our attention again to Hegel we learn that his identity theory (where the *Idea* meets itself in Absolute Knowledge) suffered a catastrophic setback for the following reason. Hegel while advancing his philosophical views, ascribed to philosophy the status of "universal scientific knowledge," that is, he conceived of philosophy as providing the most general type of knowledge, which can incorporate any particular knowledge reached by other disciplines. In effect, this conclusion reduces the importance and sets aside the knowledge produced by the methodical sciences. Their knowledge in comparison to Absolute Knowledge can only be of a limited nature. However, such a claim was overtaken by the progress and development of the sciences and thus this new factual situation provided Positivism with its first stronghold.

After the synopsis of Hegel's critique of Kant, Habermas moves onto the *metacritique* of Hegel by Marx. The argument in this case proceeds in such a way as to show firstly the materialist grounds of Marx's theoretical comprehension of Hegel and history and yet secondly, a serious flaw and an ambivalent position in his social theory. The flaw concerns the lack of a synthesis, which Marx was unable to achieve between two major categories —"work" and "interaction"— although his writings revolve around them. But let us follow each theme one at a time.

In Habermas's opinion, Marx demythologizes the *Phenomenology of Spirit* by introducing the idea of the self-constitution of the species through labor. Therefore, the movement of the Idea is now transformed into the social stages of the history of the species. Labor— which actually is viewed by Marx as a transhistorical condition of human existence[14]—is directed, out of material necessity, toward nature for its mastering and appropriation. Nature, however, is no longer an alienated externalization of the Mind as it appears in the *Phenomenology*. Instead, with Marx, it preserves its facticity, its epistemological priority and is mediated by social labor. In addition, labor forms a basic epistemological category, since it refers to the main activity constituting the "objectivity of the possible objects of experience." In other words, labor establishes the main framework within which the "reality" and "sensuousness" of the world are revealed[15] to human beings.

Apart from the materialist and critical reading of the *Phenomenology*, Marx, according to Habermas, is in line with Hegel's attitude toward the Kantian *critique* of knowledge. The notion of the "self-reflection" of consciousness, forming the basic feature of its phe-nomenological advance, is still retained by Marx. Although he never incorporates it in the philosophical premises of his materialism, yet "self-reflection" presents itself in his theory at two different levels. At the first level, the "forces of production" establish the area where "instrumental action" is totally at work; that is, as activity which is governed by technical rules and based upon empirical knowledge.[16] The development of the forces of production become the force for abolishing one form of social life and moving to another. In contrast to Hegel's reflective activity of consciousness, it is labor which moves life from one social stage to another. Reflection then, which helps consciousness for a similar movement in Hegel's philosophy, appears now, in Marx's theory, to be *reduced* to labor activity.

At the second level, the "relations of production" signify the dimension where the institutions, norms, laws, and attitudes regulat-ing the exchange of labor-power are at work. All these simultaneous-ly belong to the space of cultural tradition and communicative inter-action. Yet, in this space, the manifestations of consciousness appear as ideology. Marx retains the notion of reflection in this sphere as critique which can reveal and dissolve ideology.[17]

To establish his point, Habermas performs two readings of Marx's writings—the first through *Capital*, the second through the *Grun-drisse*. He attempts to submit textual evidence that, in one direction of analysis, Marx reduces reflection to labor and in another he retains reflection at the level of (communicative) interaction. With regard to the first reading, Habermas concludes:

> *Marx conceives of reflection according to the model of production.* Because he tacitly starts with this premise, it is not inconsistent that he does not distinguish between the logical status of the natural sciences and of cri-tique. (Habermas's italics.)[18]

What he wishes to convey in this passage is that, for Marx, the stages of reflection have been transformed into the stages of different social forms of life brought about by the development of the forces of pro-duction (in accordance with his Historical Materialism first present-ed in the *German Ideology*). It is in this sense that the concept of reflection is "reduced."[19] There is, however, a second implication in the previous quotation pointing to a serious conflation. We under-stand that Marx uncritically equated the idea of the natural sciences with his critique. Although he accomplished the work of *Capital: A Critique of Political Economy* (which Habermas accepts as a "science of man in the form of critique and not as a natural science"), Marx nevertheless, always compared it to the natural sciences. This is the reason why he never deemed necessary "an epistemological justification of [his] social theory."[20]

From his second reading of *Grundrisse,* Habermas reaches the conclusion that Marx in this new version, typical of his social theory, understands the self-constitution of the species taking place not only at the level of instrumental action, but also at the level of power relations (institutions) which regulate interaction and relations between human agents. However, institutions, norms, and laws, comprising the organizational level of the interrelations of human beings are subject to social forces, that is, the power one class exercises over another. Thus, the notion of social classes and their antagonism enters at this level of Marx's analysis and is combined with a different notion of reflection, absent at the level of instrumental action in the first reading. The process of this reflection is to be found within the class-struggles and in the manifestations of consciousness resulting from these struggles. Accordingly, the institutional transformations which occur in society can be seen from this new angle, as the outcome of class antagonisms and no longer as regulating adjustments for the promotion of production alone.

After these two readings Habermas proceeds with his charges against Marx. The latter is accused of having failed to formulate a critical science which would have been a continuation both of his critique of Hegel and of the foundations of his social theory. To be more specific, Marx did not provide "a science of man," that is, "a critical science"; his philosophical understanding (drawing from the critique of Hegel) was restricted to production, as we saw earlier, so he failed to combine (in a mode of synthesis) the results of instrumental action and communicative action.[21] Because of this restricted philosophical understanding and a lack of reflection upon the methodological presuppositions of his social theory, Habermas concludes that Marx was unable to separate empirical science from critique. That would have prevented him from conflating his critique (of Political Economy) with the natural sciences.

Habermas then lays down his idea of how such a critique "ought to be." In agreement with Hegel's critique opposing Kant's subjectivism, a critical science has to be a "radical" critique of knowledge. The progress of reflection, on materialist grounds, must accomplish the rewriting of the history of the self-constitution of the species (Habermas calls it "reconstruction"[22]), because, unlike Hegel's phenomenology, the stages of reflection are manifested in the history of the species.[23] This critique of knowledge is at the same time a *social theory,* but differs from Marx's social theory which remained at the phenomenological level, employing a phenomenological critique of ideology. Habermas proposes his social theory as a self-reflective mode of thought.

> Social theory, from the view point of the self-constitution of the species in the medium of social labour and class struggle, is possible only as the self-reflection of the knowing subject.[24]

In the manner described in this exposition of the philosophical inadequacies of Marx's understanding, Habermas justified what he had said at the beginning; that Marx contributed to the *liquidation of reflection* by allowing his critique to fall to the level of the natural sciences. Epistemological reflection on the initial presuppositions of his theory was not considered necessary and the door was then opened to positivism, which one-sidedly propelled the advance of scientific methodology.

"Scientism"

Positivism makes its appearance in the nineteenth century and dominates the scene by replacing the existing tendency toward a theory of knowledge with a philosophy of science. The latter is concerned with the methodological development of sciences and the normative criteria regulating their process and research. Habermas rejects positivism as such, especially its "blindness" in reference to the "self-reflective"[25] steps which were the norm for any theory of knowledge. When setting the aims of his effort in the preface of *Knowledge and Human Interests* he emphatically says: "that we disavow reflection is positivism."[26]

Though the positivist understanding of sciences dislodges completely the concerns and legitimacy of the theory of knowledge, the situation before was quite different. The theories of knowledge which had emerged before had never been restricted to the demands of the methodologies of sciences; they were concerned with the questioning and critique of knowledge in its broader aspects. The spectrum of questions could extend beyond the methodological concerns of the scientific disciplines. For example this was the case with Kant, who directed the basic question toward the necessary conditions for all possible knowledge. Theories of knowledge had not yet been identified as philosophies of science.

Habermas criticizes positivism in order to recover, as he argues, the forgotten and repressed experience of (epistemological) reflection. Restoring the abandoned steps of reflection will later prove invaluable to him in revealing the connection between interests and knowledge.

According to Habermas, there are at least two reasons which do not permit scientific knowledge to be viewed as just one category of possible knowledge. The first reason is a consequence of the Hegelian influence. In the Hegelian philosophical system all knowledge tends to be subordinated to the notion of Absolute Knowledge. All knowledge then is to be considered under one category. This was true in the aftermath and in the immediate influence of the Hegelian philosophy, but has ceased to be the case, since philosophical reasoning has moved away from this concept. It is more important for us to consider the second reason that Habermas offers and calls "scientism." As a belief it is located in the premises of scientific research itself and represents science's own self-understanding.

> "Scientism" means science's belief in itself: that is the conviction that we can no longer understand science as *one* form of possible knowledge, but rather must identify knowledge with science.[Habermas's italics.][27]

In my opinion, Habermas's remarks refer to a distinct, as well as definable attitude and practice rather than to an isolated belief only. Scientism can be regarded as the *nucleus* of a broader net of positivist beliefs and orientations of an epistemological nature (e.g., the exclusion of the knowing subject from the cognitive process, or the suppression of any critical questioning directed to the presuppositions of scientific research). At this level of analysis scientific views represent the attitude and practice of the "scientific community."[28] Nevertheless, Habermas arrives at another picture of science concerning its position in the social context. In his own theory of "social evolution" he recognises the fact that science has become the most significant productive force in the evolution of the species.[29] In this environment, scientistic ideas of what science is, or how theoretical knowledge can orient action, or what scientific progress consists of, play an extremely significant role in the social fabric of education and research. These ideas penetrate and direct learning and rational action in all possible areas of cultural life. Wherever solutions to practical problems of life or their discursive understanding is sought, on the basis of scientific information, the scientistic convictions direct their outcome toward technocratic ideals. Scientism then can easily leave its mark on social life and on its practical decisions. In this respect a critique of scientism also acquires political consequences.

What is important here is to evaluate how essential this category proves to be for Habermas and what its relationship is to the notion of "instrumental reason" of the Frankfurt school. Could it only be seen as a fruitful critical category on epistemological questions concerning the sciences, or is it a critical concept allowing social criticism? Habermas uses it in both ways, though the latter case is the more predominant. These two "readings" of scientism across his texts, correspond to the two levels of analysis that he employs: one philosophical, the other sociological.

To appreciate further the importance of the critical concept of scientism we must understand its relationship to technocratic rationality, especially when the latter supplies the norms of practical life. For this we can follow Habermas's reasoning. He believes that if there is to be a critique of science, which is identical with a critique of scientism, it should be twofold. Firstly, such a critique must show that "scientism has not done justice to the research practice of the historical and social sciences."[30] The communicative foundations of these sciences, which orient action rather than produce knowledge on a technological level, have been suppressed. As a result, they have not been developed in this direction of orienting action. Consequently, the social sciences are unable to guide the immense power of contemporary science as a productive and social force.

The second part of the critique must demonstrate that scientism, as an ideology, establishes a paradigm of science in accordance with the natural or empirical-analytic sciences, as Habermas calls them, that provide technically exploitable knowledge. Such a model of sciences justifies and favors technocratic solutions to practical problems of life, excluding with equal force possible rational procedures (like discursive clarification and rational formation of consensus). Continuous attachment to technocratic inspirations then yields norms which can extend, as mentioned earlier, to the whole spectrum of cultural life.

We should not forget however, that Habermas gives elsewhere a comprehensive sociological account of the forces, processes, and interests that lead to the adoption of technocratic orientations and the "depolitisation of practical issues."[31] His commentator Thomas McCarthy says:

> Science and technology in the form of the "technocratic consciousness" fulfil the ideological function of legitimating the exercise of political power over the heads of a depoliticised public.[32]

The key to this quotation lies in comprehending the implication of the concept of scientism in its sociological reading; scientistic ideas, ultimately, serve the demands of economic and political powers. In Habermas's view, this happens because such ideas allow the formation of a new ideology whose central notion is the *"elimination of the distinction between the practical and the technical."*[33] These last points enhance the conceptual picture of "scientism" and of the way it is articulated, not only at a philosophical level of analysis, but also in the overall theoretical approach of Habermas to social issues.

We can now acknowledge the fact that the critique of scientism is a transformed and extended version of the critique of "instrumental reason."[34] It allows Habermas to investigate the epistemological foundations of the sciences and then claim the rehabilitation of the social sciences on their communicative grounds. While "instrumental reason" was considered to be the main rationality and attitude in late capitalist societies, Habermas, in his critical view of society, succeeds in bringing forward further relationships of the formation of "technocratic consciousness." Unlike the Frankfurt school, which would see reason used only as an instrument for the domination of both human beings and nature, Habermas would see scientism (as practice and ideology) to be at the roots of "technocratic consciousness" and technocratic rationality which cover the "life-world." In a sense, scientism shows the rationality upon which the instrumentality of reason is achieved. This new scientistic rationality is totally biased toward technocratic orientations and most importantly, promotes the legitimation of political power and domination, not directly, but by depoliticizing the realm of the practical.

Positivism and the Sciences

One of the main areas that Habermas has been interested in since his early writings is a critical approach to, and an assessment of, the separation of theory and practice, especially the inability of reason to address the normative and important idea of a "just and good life." In order to examine his approach to this topic I will briefly bring together further views he holds on the sciences within their positivistic horizon.

Returning to his book *Knowledge and Human Interests*, we observe that the concept of "scientism" is used mostly in its epistemological context; criticism of this notion is supposed to reveal the presuppositions and restricted views of positivism. However, I must stress here that such a critique does not mean that Habermas is leveling a total assault against the idea of science. On the contrary, he would view favorably scientific projects, as far as their self-understanding and aims do not fall victim to scientistic beliefs. In the spirit of neo-Kantian tradition (especially following Dilthey[35]) Habermas distinguishes two sets of scientific disciplines. The *empirical-analytic* sciences, which are in fact the natural sciences, and the *historical-hermeneutic* sciences or cultural sciences that encompass all social, political, historical, and economic disciplines.

The empirical-analytic sciences provide the model of proper methodological procedures that can guarantee the knowledge at which they arrive. Habermas also adopts the thesis that these sciences share something in common with early philosophical thought: both wish to disassociate themselves from the "disturbing" interests of life and devote themselves to a theoretical description of the universe in its lawlike order. By this he means the early Greek philosophy, which close to the character of cosmology intended to describe the universe in a straightforward manner, "as it is"; this is true of early philosophy on the assumption of "mimesis" as I will discuss later.

This attitude and devotion of the sciences to the theoretical description of the world are, in fact, a form of *objectivism* with which Habermas, following Husserl, charges the sciences and in particular the natural sciences. Objectivism must be seen as a result of positivism; the latter, having avoided reflection upon its own presuppositions, "conceals the problems of world constitution."[36] Habermas refers here to the unanswerable epistemological problem with which the "observer's paradigm"[37] of cognition is confronted, questioning the constitution of the world we come to know. Is it, as in the commonsense view, that our knowledge mirrors reality, or is it that our conceptions shape the world? Kant, asking similar questions, postulated the second possibility together with the acceptance of the "thing-in-itself." Positivism, in abandoning this question, permits the naive idea that knowledge describes reality or that there exists an isomorphism between theoretical statements and matters of fact. Habermas calls this attitude *objectivism*.

Nonetheless, a few remarks should be made about this concept and what Habermas means by it. His charges are directed at the description of early positivism—which is apparent in his criticism of Mach—and are in line with Husserl's phenomenological critique of sciences and their objectivism.[38] In his own positivist orientation, Mach applied general systems of reference (scientific categories and measurement operations) to reality, and adopted the view that reality is organized in this form. Mach, in other words, projects upon reality a number of cognitive devices, rules, and concepts and considers them to be the ontological features of the real. As Habermas says:

> This procedure can be justified only if we presume from the beginning that
> the model of sciences, about whose scientific character consensus prevails,
> adequately describe reality as what it is. This is the basic assumption of
> objectivism.[39]

Thus, the whole process is but a methodical *objectification*[40] of reality and in the end access to it is restricted to the specifications, dimensions, and prohibitions of the scientific system of reference.

However, the objectivist belief of science, in a lawlike ordered
world which can be described more or less successfully, is not
unfounded. In Husserl's critique, its origin lies in the prescientific
world of beliefs and self-evident indications of what is a possible
object of scientific analysis. In this view, the everyday prescientific
and primary life-world[41] influences the origins of science, as their
transcendental a priori basis. Although some modern, postpositivist
philosophical theories of science might reject this charge (especially
claiming that the new "constructs" which the sciences put forward as
new objects of research have nothing to do with everyday beliefs of
the natural world), from a phenomenological point of view Husserl
correctly shows that the background of all basic and general scientific beliefs, or their transcendental origin always lies in the prescientific world.

Finally, the frame of reference of the empirical-analytic sciences,
in Habermas's view, provides rules and normative criteria "for the
construction of theories and their critical testing." This frame consists in the orientations and expectations shaped with respect to the
technical control of reality. Within this frame Habermas also
emphasizes two major aspects of the natural sciences. Firstly, their
predictability is based upon lawlike hypotheses and secondly, the
meaning of such predictions coincides with their technical
exploitability. It is fair to say that Habermas's view of the natural
sciences is restricted to the early notions of the postwar period and
does not consider at all (at the time of writing his inaugural lecture
at the University of Frankfurt[42]) the new ideas, such as Kuhn's,
which had just begun to emerge and which form the climate of postpositivist tradition. Nevertheless, his critique of the sciences is rea-
sonable considering the prevailing convictions of their practitioners,
especially on the aspect of predictability. This is a fair judgment for
Habermas, even if the aspect of technical exploitability may not
characterize unequivocally the basic legitimating factor of the natural sciences today.

Concerning the second set of sciences, the "historical-hermeneutic"[43] ones, Habermas does not hesitate to contrast them with the nat-

ural sciences. This is because of the different methodological procedures of these sciences which do not rely on observation (of facts) and their aim is not to collect exploitable knowledge of successful operations as in the empirical sciences. On the contrary, they rely on their *understanding of meaning* in their approach to their objects of study. This conception of the social/historical disciplines—fundamental to the sociological tradition called *Verstehenden* sociology—indicates a very basic and formal distinction between the natural and the social sciences developed at the beginning of the century within the neo-Kantian movement.[44] The ability to understand cultural phenomena, artifacts, or historical texts, depends on the understanding of their meaning. Any social or historical phenomenon involves the activity of social agents. Such activity expresses certain meanings and their deciphering and understanding are essential. Yet, human activity is embedded in certain historical and social contexts and thus the deciphering of its meaning presents further obstacles for the interpreter. The emphasis here is upon the recognition of the importance of "meaning" present in cultural phenomena and subsequently upon the aim of the social/historical disciplines to understand such "meanings," unlike the previous set of empirical-analytic disciplines. This distinction, separating the two sets of sciences, is essential for the whole argument Habermas develops and is the reason why he adopts the hermeneutical procedures capable of "understanding meaning" as well as the establishment of these procedures in the social/historical disciplines.

As mentioned earlier, in the natural sciences the meaning of possible statements is organized around the frame of technical control. In this sense, theoretical accounts follow the model of hypothetico-deductive connections between propositions. As a result this model allows the deduction of lawlike hypotheses with empirical reference. For Habermas, however, the historical/hermeneutic sciences exhibit a different organization. The meaning of the validity of their propositions does not rely upon the frame of technical control but upon communication and mutual understanding. He also believes that the strong attachment to the understanding of meaning reveals the existence of a practical interest toward forms of mutual understanding for the possibility of the orientation of action. These are topics which I will examine in the following chapters. However, my aim here is to show how Habermas conceives the influence of positivism even upon the historical/hermeneutic sciences. This should help us to understand his rejection of positivistic claims in the social sciences and of the way he carefully pilots the demands of his "critical theory" away from such a positivistic scope and framework.

While Habermas recognizes the hermeneutic dimension of the second set of sciences he charges them with an objectivist illusion of pure theory, that is, a situation corresponding to the positivistic orientations in the natural sciences. He argues that although the historical-hermeneutic sciences may not follow the same methodological procedures of the natural sciences, they exhibit a similarly *scientistic* belief with regard to methodological advances. In addition, they borrow their own sets of methodological rules from hermeneutics. In the hermeneutic tradition such procedures have been developed in the interpretation and understanding of texts. In his own words:

> The verification of lawlike hypotheses in the empirical-analytic sciences has its counterpart here [in the historical/hermeneutic sciences] in the interpretation of texts. Thus the rules of hermeneutics determine the possible meaning of the validity of statements of the cultural sciences.[45]

The historical/hermeneutic sciences with such methodological equipment finally form (under the prescriptions of positivism) the belief (and practice) that the description of a structured reality is possible and can be held independently of the knower. In fact, such disciplines are permeated by a naive idea that historical, social, or cultural phenomena are given or revealed directly as far as one follows the proper hermeneutic procedures for the understanding of their meaning. This is similar to the equally naive idea that in the case of a text the interpreter can simply situate herself within the horizon of language from which the text derives its meaning and then arrive at a "successful" understanding, without questioning her initial presuppositions that are essential to the understanding produced. This attitude which Habermas calls *historicism* and in his eyes comprises the positivist attitude in the historical/hermeneutic sciences, actually erases the interpreter's preunderstanding at the time she enters the process of interpretation and understanding.

In conclusion then, we can argue that the grips of positivism upon the historical/hermeneutic sciences appear both as "scientism" in the form of methodological ideas and predictability and as "historicism," which could be thought of as the corresponding notion of "objectivism" in the cultural sciences. These two orientations, characteristic of a descriptive attitude toward cultural life, conceal the process which takes place simultaneously within any hermeneutic inquiry. As just mentioned, following hermeneutic methodological procedures alone is not enough to produce credible meaning. Phenomena of cultural origin are not given in advance so that one cannot simply approach them and understand their meaning from a position in which the perceiving subject is "empty" and unbiased as the Lockean tabula rasa. Cultural phenomena can actually be singled out and discussed because they are already understood and communicated in the "world of traditional meaning," as Habermas calls it. This is the reason why the interpreter tries to mediate between her own world and the world of traditional meaning, that is, the world where all current available meanings lie. In this world of traditional meaning she will have access to what forms her preunderstanding: the basic convictions, concepts, and meanings of their object of study exist prior to her investigation. The world of traditional meaning also includes the current conceptions of the interpreter's own activity. These remarks indicate how important it is for the interpreter to approach the horizon of traditional meaning in order to clarify her position and furthermore to become aware of the preunderstanding at her disposal. This process constitutes the first step in any hermeneutical inquiry. All these Habermas summarizes in a notion borrowed from Gadamer: the interpreter must "apply" tradition to herself and to her involvement.

Finally, to disassociate his own "critical social science" from the positivist environment and yet remain close to his initial position of a "theory of society with practical intent,"[46] Habermas recalls that the systematic social and political sciences, under the influence of positivist understanding, orient themselves in producing knowledge of *nomological* nature, that is, descriptive knowledge of lawlike social processes. A "critical social science," Habermas contends, cannot remain only at the level of judging propositions which describe lawlike regularities occurring in social action. He has in mind the process of self-reflection I referred to earlier, which, if triggered by a "critical science," can bring about changes in the unreflected consciousness of the social agents. Considering that the "unreflected consciousness" is one of the major reasons of the reproduction of lawlike social regularities, a process of self-reflection can at least make such laws inapplicable. Because of this extra power attributed to self-reflection, we can begin to understand why the new framework which establishes the legitimacy and assures the overall "meaning" of Habermas's "critical social science" revolves around the concept of *self-reflection*.

Theory and Practical Life

When discussing the Frankfurt school in an earlier section, I referred to the particular interest and aim of the school regarding the promotion of an emancipatory attitude in our present social reality which exhibits processes of exploitation, of alienation, and of the hypostatization of everyday experiences. In the same spirit of critique Habermas's efforts are always aimed at the recovery and justification of a similar emancipatory interest among social agents, pointing to the normative aim of a "good and just life" (of individuals and citizens). This concept signifies, in a condensed form, the ideal of an emancipated and "rational society"—that is, a society which can freely attain its commitment to reason. Habermas has in mind the notion of reason that has not been shrunk in accordance with the prescriptions of positivist thinking assigned either to the verification of hypotheses or to the sociotechnical control of behavioral patterns. The concept of a "good and just life," which Habermas wants to reintroduce, has been adopted as a normative idea by the project of modernity envisaged in the Enlightenment and in the years of the French revolution.

Usually, the possibility of the realization of the "good and just life" has been thought of in terms of *theory* which can connect with and virtually guide practical life. The importance of the relationship between theory and practice became paramount when Habermas was formulating his "critical theory" in a direction including a "practical intent," in the sense of providing radical changes to or the abolition of present institutions of social life. However, what kind of theory could claim to inform human activity of such aims? Would it be possible for critical reason to achieve contact with practical life especially in the conditions of technocratic rationality that Habermas was arguing about? Presented with these and similar questions he proposed his intention for a systematic investigation of this relationship[47] between reason and practical aspects of life.

In Habermas's opinion, the crisis for the relationship between theory and practical life occurred in the nineteenth century, when, with the advance of the natural sciences, any previous acceptance of such a connection disappeared. Prior to this, the dominant paradigm of the bond existing between theory and practice had descended from the ancient Greek world. For the Greeks, the ordered notion of *kosmos*, with its harmony and faultless proportions, was revealed in *theoria* which was conceived as the contemplation of the world. The individual (philosopher) confronted with the perfect harmony of the *kosmos* directs his choice to an "imitation" of this harmony. Through *mimesis* the individual transforms himself and attempts to lead his life in accordance with the proportions of the *kosmos*. Thus arises the concept of *bios theoretikos* (theoretical life), that is, the notion of the individual life guided by theory, and Habermas believes that this particular concept of theory and its impact on life has shaped philosophical thinking since its beginnings.

A significant division occurring in the notion of "theory" in the Greek world must be clarified here by following McCarthy's comments on theory as *epistemi* and theory as practical knowledge.[48] Theory as *epistemi* (metaphysics, mathematics, and physics) was very distant to practical life, since it was about the eternal and the divine; it was the apodictic knowledge of the order of *kosmos*. Theory as practical knowledge, that is, knowledge achieved through the *practical sciences* of ethics and politics, was directed to the guidance of action and was not of exactly the same character as *epistemi*. Rather, it referred to rules that "more or less" indicated constant patterns in the contingent character of life. These two types of knowledge were quite distant and the most *epistemi* could supply directly to practical knowledge was some presuppositions of the latter. As an example, McCarthy mentions a theory of "human nature" which has as its basic presumption the belief that "human nature" is composed of natural and nonnatural parts. Such a theory, supplied by *epistemi*, becomes a fundamental presupposition to practical knowledge concerning ethical and political activity.

Nevertheless, this enormous distance of reference of the two types of knowledge, one preoccupied with nature and the other with practical life, converged in the "mimetic" appropriation of the *kosmos*. The individual could transform the theoretical account of the *kosmos* into theoretical wisdom for the direction of his life. Moreover, the aim of the "theoretical life" was the formation of virtuous character that could promote the interests of the Greek *polis* toward "the good and just life" of its citizens. In this version of ancient Greek life ethics and politics promoted the cultivation of the virtuous character that could guarantee political wisdom and corresponding judgment and action.

Ethics and politics, then, remained within this scope and attitude of the classical doctrine of practical knowledge up to the nineteenth century, as Habermas suggests. By that time, classical politics had transformed itself in the mould of the new "scientific disciplines" and become a monological discipline[49] that could achieve, as a practical science, prescriptive and "scientifically grounded" knowledge. The aim was no longer the cultivation of the individual in the ideal of the Greek *polis*, but the exact study of political systems, decisions, and whatever other factors could organize a "successful" political administration of society. At this point, however, we must remind ourselves that the rupture between theory and practice was not a sudden event, but a result of a process that started as early as the seventeenth century with Hobbes, who set the foundations for the scientization of politics.[50]

Habermas's references to the past configuration of theory and *praxis*[51] help him to extract at least two basic features of positivism, which, he contends, elucidate the way it stands in relation to early philosophical tradition. Firstly, he argues that positivism shares with early philosophy the illusion of "pure theory." In Greek philosophy the idea of "theory" as contemplation of the world had freed itself from the immediate interests and links to practical life. Modern sciences, according to Habermas, share the same conviction. The knowledge they seek is "pure theory" distilled from all "impurities" (e.g., unjustified directions, biased choices, and partial subjective understanding) that the problems of practical life could inject in it. Although this conviction does not affect the practice of the modern sciences it represents their self-understanding. For Habermas such an attitude of the modern sciences amounts to an illusion because there are always (concealed) *interests* that direct "theory" and its subsequent knowledge. Even in the case of Greek cosmology the interest was the theoretization of practical life. Secondly, in *contrast* to the ancient world, modern sciences have rejected any claim that the knowledge they produce has as its principal aim the cultural upbringing of the individual; "the conception of theory as a process of cultivation of the person has become apocryphal."[52]

There, therefore, appears to be a gap, or an irreconcilable distance, between knowledge and practical life since the abandonment of the "mimetic" appropriation of nature and the accompanying aim of the cultivation of the individual. Nevertheless, this is only apparent, as the sciences, besides their objectivism and scientistic beliefs, are in contact with practical life, though in a different way. Instead of the introduction of dialogic processes for the solution of practical problems, technology takes over and is supposed to solve the same problems without dialogical agreement. In addition problems and difficulties of everyday life have also been objectified and objectivated, so that they are imagined to be accessible to technocratic solutions. We have reached a point where there is no distinction between the practical and the technical. It was in this context of contemporary life—as Habermas saw it in the sixties and seventies—that the notion of critical theory could rescue what had been rejected and repressed by positivism and its scientistic rationality.

2
Text and History

In these two chapters I will present and discuss the basic elements of the philosophical hermeneutics of Gadamer, with principal reference to his writings in *Truth and Method*. After some introductory remarks on the notion of "understanding," I shall single out a few issues that Gadamer considers significant concerning the development of hermeneutics and its employment in comprehending history. These themes originate in the older hermeneutical tradition of understanding the Scriptures and also in the works of Schleiermacher, Dilthey, and Heidegger. The ideas of these writers have influenced Gadamer's work, particularly in following the theme of hermeneutics and they form his starting-point. I will begin with some preparatory thoughts on the hermeneutic approach toward "understanding" and the significance this notion has for Gadamer. I will then briefly review the development of hermeneutics and the specific ideas that have attracted both the attention of Gadamer and his critical remarks. These topics include the employment of textual interpretation for the understanding of history by the Historical school, and later, Dilthey's attempts to provide methodological foundations for the historical sciences with the help of hermeneutics. My examination will continue with Heidegger's hermeneutics of *Dasein* (or existentialist hermeneutics) which is the primary source of Gadamer's ontological commitment. Finally, I will analyze and study the basic hermeneutic notions of the "rehabilitation of prejudices," the "historicity" of any understanding, and the way in which we can comprehend the "application" of tradition, of the past, or of the text to the interpreter. All these will illustrate how "understanding" is possible, as well as the range of its dimensions according to philosophical hermeneutics.

Focusing on "Understanding"

Gadamer, in his *Truth and Method*, develops a theory of "understanding" that surpasses the customary conception we meet within the methodical sciences which, in principle, rely upon the notion of explanation. In the area of methodical sciences, if a proper explanatory account of a natural phenomenon is given, we claim that we have understood the phenomenon. However, for Gadamer, the act of "understanding" and of the correct interpretation of what has been understood is a problem that cannot be addressed within the available methodical sciences.

We can think of a few examples if we recall familiar situations. For instance, when we look at an historical object, perhaps a monument, or a work of art, questions such as: "What is it?" "What does it mean to us?" "What is its relationship to us?" "Is it significant for our own conduct of life?" "Does it contain any 'truth'?" arise. We then find ourselves approaching this object in order to provide answers to these and similar questions, which hopefully will enable us to "understand" the "object" in question.

One further familiar example is that of a presented text. We automatically assume that each text bears a meaning that we can reach by understanding it, that is, by understanding what the text "says." We usually have to begin by interpreting the specific meaning embedded in each particular sentence of the text. Later on we confront the task of continually accommodating these "pieces" of meaning to the overall meaning of the text, if such a meaning arises. Thus, we can assert that we have understood what the text "says," or what it "conveys," or what its meaning is. Similarly, we declare that we understand an utterance of another person when we are convinced that we have grasped the meaning of what has been said. As this occurs in every communication or discussion so rapidly and repeatedly, without presenting any obvious problems, it is almost unnoticeable. Only when we have problems in understanding another person, is our effort to grasp the meaning of what is said noticeable to us.

These trivial, everyday examples of understanding, suffice to show that it cannot be dealt with, as the methodical sciences would claim, through the notion of explanation. A similar situation arises in the social sciences where meaning is present, although the understanding of such meaning is curtailed whenever the ideal of methodical cognitive procedures similar to those in the natural sciences is adopted. In order to understand human activity, norms, beliefs, artifacts, institutions, and so forth, we must follow processes leading to the *understanding of their meaning* and not to the explanation of their presence.

To this end, the understanding of textual meaning, as just described, provides the essential and fundamental basis of any attempt to discover and understand meaning in areas beyond the text.

Textual understanding gave rise to hermeneutics in the reformation period as the art or technique of interpretation which had to be applied to the Scriptures if they were to be understood in their proper theological spirit. It is not difficult to imagine that the notion of the "correct interpretation" arises as a guiding norm, particularly in theological or legal interpretations. This occurs because the possibility of different interpretations always appears to accompany any attempt to understand the text. A given text presents a "provocation" for the faculty of our understanding, particularly when faced with the problem of multiple interpretations. For Gadamer the understanding and interpretation of texts is not an activity that a scientific discipline can deal with. For him, as we shall see later, "it is part of the total human experience of the world."[1]

Although the hermeneutic experience Gadamer describes is not concerned with any particular method of understanding which would result in guaranteed methodical or scientific knowledge it is, nevertheless, bound up with an orientation towards *knowledge* and *truth*. Gadamer obviously has in mind a notion of knowledge and truth different from the one established by the scientific disciplines, as for him even a work of art or a play possesses knowledge. Rather, for him this knowledge must be conceptualized in terms of insights of a pedagogical character and which are impossible to reach via any scientific approach.

The importance of the notion of "understanding" seems to be paramount for Gadamer, for whom it characterizes all human relations to the world. He is not alone in this argument. He detects a growing resistance to subordinating understanding to a methodical principle by theorists in all regions of human sciences. "Truth," he believes, can be experienced in areas (e.g. art, literature, and philosophy) which lie beyond the normative boundaries and the control of scientific method.

> The human sciences are joined with modes of experience which lie outside science, with the experiences of philosophy, of art and of history itself. These are all modes of experience in which a truth is communicated that cannot be verified by the methodological means proper to science.[2]

However, one needs further legitimation for these modes of experience. Gadamer is of the opinion that this legitimation can be provided philosophically. His theory of the phenomenon of understanding is intended to yield secure philosophical positions which enlarge the concept of knowledge and truth derived from other modes of experience not addressed by the methodical sciences.

In *Truth and Method* he begins by focusing his attention on art and on the aesthetic consciousness; he then demonstrates the notion of truth experienced in art and the mode of understanding involved in attaining this truth. Having done this he moves on to the human sciences,[3] in order to recover the notion of truth from their practice. The human sciences, in his terminology, investigate different aspects of our historical tradition. Through this exposition and analysis, from aesthetic consciousness to human sciences, Gadamer's main preoccupation is "to present the hermeneutic phenomenon in its full extent." The last part of his book elevates the notion of understanding within language and establishes the hermeneutic phenomenon as a basic ontological position of human beings. However, he warns the reader that, although his reflections concern the phenomenon of understanding, he does not provide a technique or method of understanding. On the contrary, his aim is to show "what is common to all modes of understanding"[4] and thus to correct our idea of what the human sciences truly are. Gadamer argues that such an awareness can bring back to life an invaluable insight. The natural order and historical tradition in which we are immersed cannot alone provide a full picture of the unity of our world; "the way that we experience one another, the way that we experience the natural givenness of our existence and of our world, constitutes a truly hermeneutic universe, in which we are not imprisoned, as if behind insurmountable barriers, but to which we are opened."[5]

Always eager to dispel misconceptions about his aim and scope, Gadamer, in his Foreword to the second edition of *Truth and Method,* repeats that his concern is a philosophical one, to show "what happens to us over and above our doing."[6] With equal force he denies that his concern was to refute the necessity of methodical work supplied by the social/historical sciences as the present phase of technological civilization actually requires this practice. Neither did he want to revive the old dispute between the natural and social sciences. For him "the difference that confronts us is not in the method, but in the *objectives* of knowledge."

The Development of Hermeneutics

At this point I would like very briefly to add a few introductory remarks concerning the development of hermeneutics and then to examine the position of Gadamer in relation to Schleiermacher, Dilthey, and Heidegger. Gadamer's views have been enlarged and reinforced by the critical attitude he has displayed towards these thinkers and I believe that an awareness of his position contrasted with theirs is essential for an overall perspective of his work.

Hermeneutics as the art or technique of understanding and interpretation can be located within the Reformation period. However, we must appreciate two separate branches of it:[7] theological hermeneutics which is concerned with the reading of the Scriptures, and literary critical hermeneutics which is concerned with the revival of classical literature, a humanist claim in itself. The reformers had to promote their own reading of the Bible, since, in their opinion, the understanding of it had been dominated by the dogmatic attitude and tradition of the church. As far as the literary tradition is concerned, it had been absorbed by the Christian attitude, so it was in need of reformulation. Thus, both hermeneutic attempts were preoccupied with the rediscovery of some initial "original" meaning that was embedded in the texts of the Bible and of classical literature. This orientation to the original sources of meaning in both traditions generated the study of Greek and Hebrew in contrast to the picture we have of the Latin language as the standard written language of the Middle Ages.

Luther and the reformers established and developed the universal principle of textual understanding. They had argued that understanding the Scriptures does not need to rely upon reading it in the context of tradition. The meaning of the Scriptures is to be discovered in a literal reading. However, individual parts and passages must be understood with reference to the meaning of the whole while, simultaneously, the whole can be reached from the cumulative understanding of the parts. Therefore, this initial formulation of the principle of textual understanding displays the circular approach that is involved. Nevertheless, apart from these modifications, Gadamer claims that Scriptural understanding was still dogmatic. Its basic assumption that the Bible constitutes a unity remained unchanged; such a presupposition did not permit "any sound individual interpretation of scripture that takes account of the relative context of a text," its purpose, and its composition.

This particular employment of hermeneutics was altered later in the eighteenth century when the dogmatic idea of unity was abandoned. The Scriptures could be considered to be a collection of historical documents, as pieces of literature which invited an historical interpretation. The first transformation of hermeneutics, then, permits the principle of textual understanding (which relates parts to the whole and vice versa) to liberate itself from "the dogmatic unity of the canon" and orient itself toward the historical conditions and environment in which each document was supposed to belong.

At this juncture, we can observe two further significant changes which affected the reception of hermeneutics. Firstly, since the differences between the Scriptures and literary texts concerning their interpretation were abolished, hermeneutics could be considered as a *unified* discipline. Secondly, it became indispensable to historical research. Hermeneutics, with its ability to focus on interpretations of meaning, was necessary for the interpretation of past literary sources residing in the hands of the historian. In addition to these changes the following significant parallelism took place between text and history. I mentioned earlier that the individual parts of the text are dependent upon the context. In her research the historian appears to give equal attention to both the individual historical "objects" or "events" upon which she focuses, and upon the historical context to which they belong. Thus, the historical context defines itself as a whole giving full significance to individual historical "objects" or "events"; conversely, this historical context can be reached by understanding the individual "objects." For example, we could think of our efforts to understand cultural/historical objects from Greek or Roman antiquity. The significance of a drawing on a Greek vase or of a sculpture of a Roman emperor must be understood in relation to the corresponding historical contexts of those periods. Conversely, the historical sciences have already formed these contexts utilizing the available individual "objects," texts, and testimonies. In this change of roles, in which hermeneutic understanding of history utilizes textual hermeneutic procedures, the body of hermeneutics can now serve as a "historical organon" which, according to Dilthey, is its true nature. Gadamer then, commenting on the transformation just described, leads to the main conclusion.

> History is, as it were, the great dark book, the collected work of the human spirit, written in the languages of the past, the text of which we have to try to understand. Historical research sees itself according to the modes of literary interpretation of which it makes use.[8]

The important point to notice here is the notion of the "text" expanding beyond its traditional image in literature. The *text* becomes the significant example and the basic model for historical research. This idea and practice is undoubtedly the foundation of Dilthey's "historical view of the world."

Hermeneutics, according to Gadamer, moves away from the concept of technique in the direction of a discipline which is more and more concerned with the fundamental question of the relationship between understanding and meaning. Before Dilthey, this attitude was taken up by Schleiermacher who employed it in his own theory of hermeneutics. He acknowledged the fact that there was always a more severe problem of *misunderstanding* rather than understanding. Preoccupied with such thoughts, he began examining the systematic presence of basic elements which hinder understanding and must be removed. Therefore, he defined hermeneutics "as the art of avoiding misunderstanding." What Gadamer recognizes as significant in Schleiermacher's attempt, is his effort to produce a *methodical* discipline that can stand on its own and confirm the results of its methodical procedures, without any need to rely on occasional arbitrary insights.

There is also another shift in Schleiermacher's hermeneutics which needs particular attention. He expands the space of understanding not only to the written text but also to speech. In the region of speech, the *individuality* of the speaker is essential for understanding the uttered word and thus, the speaker (as a person) must be understood. Correspondingly, as far as the understanding of the text is concerned, the author too must be understood. Gadamer considers this aspect of Schleiermacher's theory to be an introduction of *psychological interpretation*, which is the latter's contribution to hermeneutics. This kind of interpretation "is ultimately a divinatory process, a placing of oneself within the mind of the author, an apprehension of the 'inner origin' of the composition of a work, a recreation of the creative act."[9] The insistence on the individuality of the author and the belief that the original thought of the author can be re-created or grasped, is what characterizes Schleiermacher's hermeneutics as *Romantic hermeneutics*.[10] For Schleiermacher, a text is the result of "free creation" and the "free production" of the individual, in the same way in which speech is considered free creation. Furthermore, this holds true independently of the context of the text. Following this line of reasoning, Schleiermacher accepts that whatever is cast in language, speech, or text, to be "expressions of life" through which the interpreter can reach the author or be at the same level with him, independent of the content of the text. He can then reproduce the original meaning of the author. History, similarly, is a free creation, the result of a divine productivity.

Overall, in Gadamer's opinion, Schleiermacher freed hermeneutics from two dogmatic rules which meant that either the preservation of the truth of the Scriptures is most important, or that the imposition of the classics as the normative model has to be followed. Nevertheless, Schleiermacher led hermeneutics in another direction beyond Gadamer's interest; Schleiermacher was mainly concerned with the problem of the "Thou" rather than the understanding of history.[11]

The Understanding of History

The person who further transformed hermeneutics with a real concern for the understanding of history and for the adoption of a proper methodology for the social/historical sciences is Dilthey. He based his studies upon both the Romantic hermeneutics, which had elevated the interpretation of the text, and the assumptions of the Historical school (Droysen and Ranke), which was interested in the understanding of universal history.

The course taken by the Historical school was to reject the dogmatic and teleological views on world history. Its representatives distinguished themselves from the Hegelian notion of history which they regarded as an a-prioristic construction. As a matter-of-fact, they viewed the unfolding of the Hegelian "Idea" as always occurring imperfectly in history. They were convinced that philosophy, unable to perfect the "Idea," has to give way to historical research, which in a more satisfactory way could provide "men" with knowledge about themselves and their position in history. The Historical school also had recourse to Schleiermacher's Romantic hermeneutics and his concept of individuality; this concept alone could resist the Hegelian notion of world history.

Gadamer makes another point which, in my opinion, helps in understanding the affinity between hermeneutics and history. He claims that Schleiermacher's concept of individuality provided the historical sciences with a methodological orientation and an aim similar to that of the natural sciences. Thus, the concept of research in the historical sciences emerged. What Gadamer means here is that historical knowledge can be gained by approaching and understanding *individual* agents in history, instead of the meaning and significance of their activity (conceived in a framework of imposed general historical categories), which would indicate that one is still trapped amid the Hegelian philosophy of history. As a consequence of this attitude history can be understood from within itself, that is, from the historical tradition with which we are acquainted. For Gadamer, this is precisely the claim of literary hermeneutics, that the meaning of a text can be understood simply from itself. Accordingly, hermeneutics is the basis for the study and understanding of history. This, I believe, gives a glimpse of the continuous involvement and development of hermeneutic theory in understanding history during the nineteenth century, and also of the basic and rather simple literary ideas concerning textual understanding, which accompany hermeneutics.

Dilthey, who approved of the aforementioned orientations of the Historical school, proposed a more ambitious project: to provide the historical sciences with methodological foundations equivalent to those of the natural sciences. In a sense, he proposed a critique of *historical Reason* in parallel terms to those of Kant's *Critique of Pure Reason*. In this way he hoped to provide the philosophical grounds for historical knowledge, as Kant did for the knowledge of nature.

After the dissolution of Hegel's philosophy of history, the latter no longer appears to be the manifestation of Mind. In order to understand history we need to rely upon certain categories in a way similar to that in which Kant presented his categories as necessary for the knowledge of nature. Dilthey, however, extracted his basic categories from *life philosophy*, utilizing Misch's philosophical positions. *Lebensphilosophie*, or philosophy of life, was developed by Misch as the science of mental contents that give meaning to life.[12] The categories which are central to Dilthey's thinking are "experience" and "expression," providing an introduction to the way in which Dilthey conceptualized history and to his attempts to establish sound foundations for the human sciences. The category of "experience" constitutes his basic starting-point for the acquisition of historical knowledge. He was convinced that "experience" is an empirical, demonstrable category coming from "real life," and does not constitute an a-prioristic one.[13] According to Dilthey, whatever we understand is an "expression." This concept stands in opposition to the causality sought in the natural sciences. Human life, individual activities, the character of the individual, customs, or any aspect of human relationships and activities, are always expressed in certain forms or manifestations that can be understood.

I am not concerned here with a detailed account of Dilthey's theory; instead, my concern is with, primarily, the presentation of his main aim. His target and preoccupations with the methodology of the social/historical sciences are significant in the history of hermeneutics. Dilthey's convictions have influenced the adoption of interpretative (*Verstehenden*) sociology by Weber and the introduction of similar methodological approaches to the rest of the social/historical disciplines. His ideas also constitute well-established themes in sociological tradition which Habermas follows. Furthermore, Dilthey's attempts serve as a clarifying stage for Gadamer's thought when the latter levels a critique at Dilthey.

Gadamer argues that Dilthey is as totally committed to the beliefs of the Enlightenment as Kant. For the first time, there appears the possibility of applying "sciences" and the capacities of understanding in order to produce knowledge of social and historical reality. While life had appeared before as chaotic, inexplicable or incomprehensible, now the human sciences can yield clear knowledge of it. For Gadamer this completes the historical Enlightenment and at the same time, such knowledge provides protection and certainty. However, if the historical Enlightenment is the ideal aim, the Cartesian concept of sciences that Dilthey imposed upon the human sciences, beginning from "expressions" of life (as just mentioned), proved to be an impossible task. He could never put the human sciences on the same level as the natural sciences. The objectivity shared among the natural sciences could not be understood as the model of objectivity for the human sciences. In a simplifying analogy, the "subject to object" epistemological relationship firmly established in the natural sciences could not do justice to the "subject to subject" relationship attained between the interpreter and the historical tradition in the human sciences. If this were the case, the *historical nature* of "experience" would be concealed. This constitutes Gadamer's first objection to Dilthey.

The second point, which is more crucial for Gadamer's critique, concerns the reading of history as text by Dilthey. The latter borrowed the concept of hermeneutics from his Romantic predecessor, Schleiermacher. The object of understanding is the text which has to be "read," deciphered, and finally understood. As we saw earlier, Romantic hermeneutics assumes that the total understanding of the original meaning of a text is possible, as far as one can place one's self on the same level with the author. If this condition could be met, the total understanding of a text or of a person would be possible. Similarly, the human sciences can thrive upon this "reading" of meaning which, for Dilthey, constitutes the legitimation and the superiority of the hermeneutic method in these disciplines. Gadamer detects in this borrowing of Romantic hermeneutics by Dilthey the inability of the latter to probe into the historicality of the experience of understanding. According to Gadamer, hermeneutics for Dilthey is not only a means, or an instrument of the mind, but

the universal medium of the historical consciousness, for which no longer exists any other knowledge of truth than the understanding of expression and, in expression, life. Life and history have meaning like the letters of a word. Thus Dilthey ultimately conceives the investigation of the historical past as a deciphering and not as an historical experience.[14]

Thus, Dilthey arrives at a methodical hermeneutics that accepts history as a pure text which simply has to be *deciphered* in order to be understood. One major consequence of this attitude was the reduction of history into intellectual history. As any approach to a text would ultimately be an encounter with the author's spirit (mind), similarly, deciphering history as a text constitutes an encounter with a broader intellect.[15]

Heidegger's Hermeneutics of Dasein

Dilthey's hermeneutics does not provide the "correct" approach with respect to the whole phenomenon of understanding, entrapped as he was amid the epistemological dilemmas of the social/historical sciences. It was Husserl who first introduced a new basis for phenomenology and later Heidegger who provided a new beginning, overcoming epistemological problems via phenomenology and by elevating understanding to an ontological position within philosophical tradition.

Husserl introduced the concept of "life-world," which according to Gadamer brought phenomenology back to life and avoided the very narrow path Dilthey had followed with his inquiry into the methodology of the human sciences. The "life-world" is the everyday world in which we encounter ourselves and conduct our lives. We are immersed in it and all our activities take place in it; it is the world which precedes any theoretical account of, or philosophical reflection on, reality and its nature. The "life-world" becomes an object of investigation through a reflective consciousness that can transcend the immediacy of experience and can consider it as an object of study. The "life-world" constitutes the basis of all of our experiences and is given in advance.

According to Gadamer, Heidegger could utilize this rich phenomenological concept provided by Husserl, instead of the limited Dilthean approach. It appears to me that the appropriation of the Husserlian concept of "life-world" by Heidegger is evident in the formation of the concept of *Dasein* (the specific being of human existence) in its initial condition of *"Being-in-the world."* *Dasein* finds itself "thrown" into the world, an event preceding any subject/object distinction, reminiscent of the way in which we encounter ourselves within the Husserlian "life-world." Nevertheless, with the notion of *Dasein* in *Being and Time*, Heidegger goes beyond Husserl and introduces the specific mode of existence characteristic of human beings which does not relate to the previous concerns of ontology such as "what exists," or "what there is." *Dasein* is a specific mode of Being and therefore, Heidegger's whole effort can be seen as concentrating on the major question of Being that he wanted to rescue from oblivion.

It is beyond the scope of this work to trace Heidegger's phenomenological approach to Being and his inquiry into the Being of *Dasein*. However, it is important to stress the fact that Gadamer's development of hermeneutics originates in the Heideggerian initial positions concerning the ontological character of understanding. It would obviously require separate research in order to determine exactly which features of Heideggerian philosophy Gadamer appropriates as his starting-point and as possible projects of his own inquiry.[16] Nevertheless, I would like to add a few further observations which appear important to the elevation of hermeneutics to its ontological significance.

As just mentioned, Heidegger's efforts concentrate upon the introduction of the question of Being and we are shown that any question about Being (Being in general, Being-in-the-world) can only begin from and through *Dasein*. This indicates the significant position *Dasein* holds in Heidegger's philosophy and that a proper *ontology* must begin from the study of *Dasein* itself, instead of being a well-structured branch of traditional philosophy. However, there are further consequences: if *Dasein* is involved in understanding its own Being, and also the meaning of Being (in general), this activity necessitates the *interpretation* of such meaning. Therefore, philosophical reflection upon Being, as phenomenology, is directed toward hermeneutics which is the proper body that deals with interpretation. These thoughts, I believe, can facilitate the understanding of Heidegger's conception of the phenomenology of *Dasein* as being hermeneutics.

> The logos of the phenomenology of the *Dasein* has the character of *hermeneuein*, through which the understanding of Being appertaining to the *Dasein* itself is informed of the essential meaning of Being and the fundamental structures of its own Being. Phenomenology of the *Dasein* is *hermeneutics* in the original meaning of the word, according to which it denotes the business of interpretation.[17]

Hermeneutics here moves away from Dilthey's use of it as a methodological concept, or from its initial use as the corpus of rules of interpretation. In Heidegger's approach, hermeneutics "turns out to be an original attitude towards the peculiar structure of the *Dasein*."[18]

One important feature which should also be mentioned here is that Heidegger's equation of phenomenology with the hermeneutics of

Dasein has been achieved through the transformation of Husserlian phenomenology. Heidegger considered Husserl's phenomenology to be rather restricted and lacking in concreteness. It was mainly situated around the concept of "intentionality" and the subject-object relationship, thus unable to orient itself toward the question of Being. When Heidegger poses the question of the meaning of Being, he firmly believes that this task must be achieved through phenomenology, although on new premises beyond those of Husserl. For Heidegger phenomenology, since it can deal with the "things themselves," provides the proper methodical approach for the question of Being. Even if his etymological insistence on the interpretation of the word *phainomenon* may be questionable,[19] one of his main aims concerning phenomenology was to show how the phenomenology of *Dasein* can be grasped as a process of interpretation. Given that *Dasein* enters interpretation in order to learn about its own Being (and about Being), we can argue that, for Heidegger (and also for Gadamer), understanding is the original character of human life itself.

Paul Ricoeur adds his voice at this point reminding us of the new significance of Heidegger's transformation of phenomenology. The *Verstehen* of Heidegger, Ricoeur claims, must be considered as a response to that initial position of *Dasein* (we can think here of any human being), thrown into the world and trying to achieve its way through by *projecting* its own possibilities. This account represents the primary ontological situation of the human being, and Heidgger entrusts the business of interpretation to hermeneutics. According to this line of argument, understanding, as a main feature of *Dasein's* everyday activity, becomes part of the ontology of *Dasein*. Thus, understanding acquires an explicit ontological character. "The subject-object relation—on which Husserl continues to depend—is thus subordinated to the testimony of an ontological link more basic than any relation to knowledge."[20] The hermeneutics of *Dasein*, in such a context, also constitutes the main starting-point for Gadamer, although in his philosophical hermeneutics he promoted mostly the notion of our being and predicament in language. He did not follow Heidegger's project for the reinstatement of the question of Being as the central task of philosophy, nor did he embrace later Heidegger's critical position on the end of philosophy as metaphysics.

Apart from this ontological character of hermeneutics there is a larger area which has acted as a strong pole of attraction for Gadamer's philosophical hermeneutics. It is the realm of language as it is thought of in the second phase of Heidegger's philosophical itinerary. In the previous notes on Heidegger I stressed the significant position of *Dasein* in revealing primarily the interpretative character of human existence. That was the theme in *Being and Time*. Later, in his "Letter to Humanism" Heidegger declares the priority of Being over man.[21] It is Being which reveals itself to the human subject and Heidegger's whole philosophical effort focuses now upon Being rather than upon a philosophy of human existence. Thus, the later Heidegger visualizes the new ontological relationship between Being and human being and affirms that their common meeting place is language. We can still hear the echoes of his famous statement: "Language is the house of Being. In its lodgings dwells man."[22] The elevation of language to a new significant position in which Being reveals itself is the second crucial teaching from Heidegger which Gadamer incorporates into his theory of understanding.

On "Prejudices"

In his previous attempts at hermeneutics, the lack of attention paid to the interpreter and the incorrect views held for her and her historical position, were considered entirely unsatisfactory by Gadamer. I mentioned earlier how the "understanding" of a text was once considered capable of revealing the author herself; or how the task of understanding was thought to be simple deciphering. The historical situation of the interpreter, and in consequence the *historicality* in which any understanding is embedded, forms the nucleus around which Gadamer weaves the structure of the notion of "understanding." He begins with the act of understanding historical tradition in order to study the notion of the historicality of understanding and subsequently elevates this concept to the status of a hermeneutical principle.

Following Heidegger, Gadamer believes that if the structure of *Dasein* as "thrown projectiveness" (in its attempt to realize its own being) is finally understanding, this has also to encompass the act of understanding in the *human sciences*. The latter should display the same structure as *Dasein*; what holds true of *Dasein* has to be true of the understanding of the historical tradition. There are a number of reasons why Gadamer, after his study of understanding in the arts, chose as his subject the human sciences in order to amplify his study of understanding. Firstly, he is in a position to take advantage of Heidegger's studies on "historical hermeneutics" and to retain as his initial point of departure Heidegger's basic teaching of the fore-structure of understanding. Secondly, and in my view this is the most important reason, since Gadamer's final aim is to elevate the notion of understanding to an ontological position, he actually does justice to the Heideggerian notion of *Dasein*. The projection of its own possibilities, which *Dasein* carries out, are in accordance with its own potentialities: *Dasein* cannot go beyond its own facticity. This is the lesson from Heidegger. Thus, Gadamer argues that the facticity of *Dasein* has to be thought of in concrete terms and this task can be accomplished best within the historical tradition in which *Dasein* is situated. Tradition is the space of *Dasein* which also precedes, further revealing the limits and boundaries of *Dasein*'s being. "Everything that makes possible and limits the project of There-being [*Dasein*] precedes it, absolutely. The existential structure of Therebeing must find its expression in the understanding of historical tradition as well."23 In other words, what we are, what our preconceptions are, and the way we are all formed, have to be discovered within historical tradition.

A third reason for Gadamer's interest in the human sciences, to which I will refer later, could be seen as a methodical one in the sense that analyzing understanding which is focused on an object in history, can reveal more easily and sharply the fore-structure of understanding in an historical context. It can reveal the role history has played in producing this fore-structure.

Heidegger raised hermeneutics to its prominent position following above all his own preoccupations with ontology. The historicality of understanding is not to be found in a developed form in Heidegger's writings. It was Gadamer who put it forward as his first aim. The initial idea that he takes over from Heidegger is the circular structure of understanding, which is best explained in the case of the text. When attempting to read and understand a text, as soon as a minor, perhaps insufficient, initial meaning appears, one *projects* this meaning onto the whole of the text. This suggests that there is an anticipation of meaning and the reading continues within certain expectations. The continuation of reading may bring new revisions to the meaning projected and new projections can take place in the course of reading. Thus, new expectations and articulations of meaning may repeatedly arise. In the older tradition of hermeneutics this circularity was mainly thought of as an interplay between the parts and the whole. The particular meanings of the parts would determine the meaning of the whole and vice versa. However, Gadamer claims that the Heideggerian notion of the *hermeneutic circle* involves notions of *projection* and *anticipation* that have further consequences for the theory of understanding. While for Heidegger "the circle" had an *ontological* significance, for Gadamer it shows the interplay of projection and prejudices. The understanding of a text always starts with certain preconceptions which, with the help of new projections and anticipations of meaning, are constantly replaced by more satisfactory ones in the process of interpretation. "This constant process of new projection is the movement of understanding and interpretation."[24] I consider it entirely legitimate to say that no reading of any text commences without certain assumptions (fore-meanings) that the reader holds. The notions of "life-world" and "tradition" exemplify the way in which all individuals confront themselves as constructed through certain preconceptions, meanings, and expectations that Gadamer calls fore-conceptions or *prejudices*. This means that we cannot conceive of any blank, empty starting-point in the intellectual capacities of the individual and his sharing of fore-meanings. We discover ourselves in an historical continuum and social environment sharing opinions, beliefs, and meanings of activities—in other words, the cultural tradition available at the time. Each one of us moves within his own *horizon*[25] of meanings, preconceptions, and understandings.

Gadamer specifically chose the concept of "prejudice" aware that, since the Enlightenment, it has acquired a negative meaning. In fact, it signifies a judgment accomplished before concrete gathering of all information concerning a situation has been achieved. The negative meaning of "prejudice" is well exemplified in jurisprudence, where prejudicial judgment is to be avoided and vilified. During the period of the Enlightenment prejudices had been seen as originating either in authority (transmitted by the state, its institutions, family, or language) or as being the products of ignorance, misjudgment, and miscalculation. The criticism was usually directed against the notion of authority, which, with its own power and force could impose its own prejudices in unfounded judgments. The critique against prejudice developed by the Enlightenment was also directed against the religious understanding of tradition and aimed at understanding tradition without prejudice. This is exactly the idea that Gadamer questions: could there ever be any understanding of tradition, of a text, or of a society, devoid of any preconception or fore-meaning? If this were true, reason would constitute the ultimate source of authority without any historical limit imposed on it; reason would become Absolute Reason. Even Kant, according to Gadamer, had to restrict "pure reason" only to the a priori matrix of categories related to the knowledge of nature. Furthermore, this position appears unsustainable, particularly in the case of understanding history and acquiring historical knowledge. Any historian, involved in understanding history, is already immersed in a given context that supplies her with the first conceptions of her object of study. She sees an historical "object" from a certain perspective which provides its own foreunderstandings. The view of understanding history and tradition without preconceptions cannot be supported.

At this point I must stress the fact that Gadamer considers prejudices in a positive way. The concept of prejudice has also been chosen in order to refute the prejudice of the Enlightenment, that is, its belief in the removal of all prejudices. Gadamer, with forceful and convincing arguments, points out that prejudices accompany us always and therefore, if we want to do justice to our finite, historical mode of being, we should accept their unavoidable presence. It is true that the concept of "prejudice," as it is used today, is somewhat overloaded with negative connotations. Nevertheless, we should familiarize ourselves with its Gadamerian dimension in order to follow Gadamer's theoretical project. There are also occasions when "prejudice" could indicate even more than a preconception we hold, for example, on "freedom," "justice," "antiquity," or a preconception of cognitive value, "heavy," "straight," "volume," and so forth. It could refer to an extended perspective characterizing the bias of a theoretical attitude or of a scientific project, or it could indicate the popular orientation of an historical period. In these terms we could consider the attitude of the Enlightenment toward reason as the absolute seat of judgment as an example of "prejudice." Similarly, we can view as prejudice the way in which scientific programs and their technological implementation operate under old convictions of "mastering" and "exploiting" nature for the benefit of humanity.

Gadamer's message is that all understanding, in one way or another, involves preconceptions or prejudices. As soon as this position is accepted a number of important consequences follow; they can be seen both in relation to the reading of a text and also in relation to their philosophical significance. The understanding of a text is not arbitrary and accidental. The continuous misinterpretation of a word or a sentence will unavoidably affect the meaning of the text as a whole. The same effect will arise when stubbornly applying our own fore-meanings or prejudices to the text. If they must be replaced by other meanings revealed in the process of reading the text, one cannot arbitrarily hold onto them. Although one cannot immediately abandon the preconceptions with which one begins understanding a text, it is important that one becomes aware of one's own prejudices, so that one can be in a position to accept the new conditions and meanings the text imposes. The same is true of conversation when, beyond one's own prejudices, an openess is required with respect to the other person.

But this kind of sensitivity involves neither "neutrality" in the matter of the object nor the extinction of one's self, but the conscious assimilation of one's own fore-meanings and prejudices. The important thing is to be

aware of one's own bias, so that the text may present itself in all its newness
and thus be able to assert its own truth against one's own fore-meanings.[26]

If the task of the interpreter or the reader or the participant in a discussion, consists in becoming aware of his own prejudices this
process has a philosophical counterpart. In my opinion, the philosophical importance of prejudices can be seen in the following way.
Prejudices appear to exhibit a double role. They are a primary means
of approaching the text or an other person and yet, when aware of
them, they become resistant to adequate understanding and inhibit
the text from yielding further meanings. Thus, in order to overcome
possible misinterpretations, or limited understandings imposed by
our prejudices, there emerges the task (in the act of interpretation) of
overcoming their restrictive role by being aware of them and dissolving their boundaries by adopting new positions. This is the first
instance of *reflective* activity of which the individual is capable.
However, since we are talking here of individual awareness, the category we must deal with is "self-reflectivity," a notion that hermeneutics shares with the phenomenological tradition.

The Historicality of Understanding

We now have reached the point which Gadamer continually brings to
the center of his discussion. It is the concept of the *historicality* of
understanding and we must realize the important consequences it
bears for hermeneutic theory. The historicality of understanding can
be thought of from several different angles. For example, it would be
adequate to assume the "historicality of understanding" as referring
to any understanding and its inescapable belonging to a certain historical time. Furthermore, the "ability" of understanding and its
range of "openness" toward its objects (e.g., a text, an historical event,
another person in conversation, or a work of art) are also historically
located. This happens because, as I will explain in due course, historical "objects" release their "effects" upon understanding through history. These are the aspects which Gadamer wishes to highlight; if
understanding could be aware, so to speak, of its own historicality, it
could execute its task without gross misunderstandings and could
take care of its own historical dimensions. This awareness, when considering the notion of the "historicality of understanding" seriously,
opens new dimensions for hermeneutic theory.

I discussed earlier the notion of prejudices that inhabit any understanding; these prejudices arise in time, they play the role of valu-

able starting-points in any attempt at understanding, and they are transmitted via what Gadamer calls *tradition*. We can provisionally conceive of tradition as the "space," or network of all current beliefs, norms, customs, social activities, and preferences that constitute the cultural, intellectual, and practical environment in which we are situated. We develop within tradition and are influenced by it. Traditions are located in time; for example, we can distinguish between the tradition of the ancient Greek *polis* and the tradition which arose in the Enlightenment. Thus any understanding, beginning inevitably with prejudices, is itself situated in a specific historical time and a specific tradition. We share the prejudices of our tradition.[27]

For Gadamer, hermeneutics does not provide a methodical procedure of understanding but instead clarifies the conditions which accompany any act of understanding. To this end, he introduces the concept of "temporal distance" as a means of separating and distinguishing prejudices between "productive prejudices," that help understanding, and "unproductive" ones, which hinder understanding. This concept, besides its role in facilitating understanding, also displays the historicality of understanding from another standpoint. If we try to understand a text, we are immediately confronted with an historical distance that separates us, as interpreters, from the author of the text. Romantic hermeneutics believed that it could reach the authentic, original thoughts of the author and thus provide an even better understanding of the text than the author himself had achieved. Gadamer has rejected this attitude as naive. Instead, we should pose the question: What are we confronted with when we become aware of this historical or "temporal distance?"

A "gap" is introduced by "temporal distance" at the moment at which we notice its presence: it is the gap between our historical time and that of the text. Can this gap or distance be thought of only as an obstacle to be bridged, or does it push our awareness toward a more critical stance? Before answering such questions we need to follow Gadamer's thoughts which illuminate what we really seek in approaching a text from the past. Gadamer insists that, in interpreting a past text, we are not concerned with the individuality of the author (a remnant of the "aesthetics of genius" in Romantic hermeneutics) but with what the text says, with its "objective truth." Obviously, such a notion of "truth" raises new questions and problems about Gadamerian thought which is examined in the next chapter. Nevertheless, we could assume that in a text there is always something said, something that makes a claim to a truthful state of affairs, an insight. It is also true that we reach such "truths" or insights of a text differently at different historical times, that is, there are different interpretations. Yet, what is the role of "temporal distance" if we accept our interest in the "truth" of the text, as Gadamer proposes? "Temporal distance" actually assists us in becoming aware of the prejudices, or the prejudgments, which we hold whenever we attempt to interpret a text from the past or appreciate a work of art from a different era. By revealing that we begin with fore-conceptions and prejudices, "temporal distance" forces us to examine such prejudgments critically. It acts as a filter which can separate and reject those profoundly limited and possibly ill-conceived prejudices entering any interpretation.

The same process in reverse, can be observed in the appreciation of a contemporary work of art, or a literary work. If required to formally judge them, we may experience some uncertainty concerning their importance or what they convey. Gadamer argues that we are immersed in a number of prejudices which, as a result, could give emphasis to these contemporary works in a way which may not be at all in line with their "true content." However, when time has elapsed and the multiple relations of these works to the present have ceased, their "true significance" can arise and become dominant and universal. At this "distance" our judgment has become more secure. Therefore, "temporal distance" should not be viewed negatively in the hermeneutic situation. It urges the clarification and awareness of the prejudices held by the interpreter at the time she approaches a text from the past. Prejudices can be questioned by suspending them. This does not mean that we end our participation in understanding. According to Gadamer we put our prejudices "at risk" by allowing the claims of the text or of the other person to be heard. Such a change in tactics allows new sources of meaning to emerge and enables us to arrive at new messages within the text which were not previously available.

Therefore, we can claim that "temporal distance" serves as a critical-methodical concept which permits the filtration of productive and unproductive prejudices, while simultaneously engaging our consciousness in a self-reflective process. Furthermore, the "temporal distance" between our tradition and a past text demonstrates the fundamental condition that we are all subjected to. Although such a distance may seem unimportant, awareness of its existence in the hermeneutic context specifically reveals the historicality of our understanding. The distinction between the present and the past that "temporal distance" illuminates, stresses once more the inseparable position of understanding from history. Also, the acquisition and accumulation of prejudices appears to be rooted in history. We share these prejudices, at each historical time, with the tradition we belong to. However, further effects of history upon our understanding that show additional aspects of the "historicality" involved, are expressed in the concept of "effective-history."

Gadamer informs us that our approach to an historical phenomenon, to a text from the past, or to any historical object that requires an understanding of its meaning, is not a simple juxtaposition of the interpreter and the object of her attention, or study. History has always established a number of predispositions toward any historical object. We just saw that when considering an historical event, an historical distance develops between the event and ourselves. In this gap the historical object has released its own "effects" which constitute the "effective-history" of the object. For example, previous traditions have studied the same historical phenomenon or historical object and have formed certain opinions and judgments about it. What we presume to be important in the historical object, indicates the operation of the "effective-history" of the object. Gadamer denounces the naive approach to an historical object, which does not inquire into and reflect upon the way in which we are involved with the understanding of its meaning. To claim that there is an historical phenomenon of which we are aware is only half the truth according to Gadamer. What has formed our preunderstanding of it, what orients our inquiry or the matrix of questions engaged in our approach, constitutes the other half. The preunderstandings and shared knowledge of the historical object have been formed in the process of history and constitute the influence the "effective-history" of the object has upon us and our understanding. It would be naive to assume that approaching Homer's *Odyssey* we simply encounter the text, merely ready to read and understand its meaning. What we consider as important in this work, or what must be questioned and analyzed, is the impact of the "effective-history" of the *Odyssey* already made upon us, including opinions formed by historical research.

Let us consider another example. The way in which we focus, at least initially, upon historical research describing some incident in the First World War is in many ways predetermined by what we know about that war. This war has been discussed extensively; its scope, its results, or the way in which it was experienced by its participants have been analyzed, questioned, and portrayed in books, films, novels, and poetry. All this awareness, or part of it, which we may possess or share in the tradition we live in, is the "effect" of the event in history. It *preforms* our understanding of the First World War and subsequently our initial judgment on our historical research. Questions of whether or not the research does justice to the war by being faithful to its details and its character as we know it, or whether it is an important research, are based upon the "effective-history" of the "object" of study.

The notion of "effective-history" illustrates another dimension of the historicality of understanding. In addition to the "prejudices" just discussed, the historian or the interpreter begins her study of an historical object conscious of what has been handed down to her as a *trace* or *effect* of this object through tradition. Our existence in time, in historicity, has compiled "effects" upon us that, in turn, have affected our understanding of an historical object. In this respect when approaching an historical phenomenon, a work of art, or a tradition, we cannot disregard its "effective-history."

> We are not saying, then, that effective-history must be developed as a new independent discipline ancillary to the human sciences, but that we should learn to understand ourselves better and recognise that in all understanding, whether we are expressly aware of it or not, the power of this effective-history is at work. When a naive faith in scientific method ignores its existence, there can be an actual deformation of knowledge.[28]

Gadamer informs us of one aspect of our understanding which usually passes unnoticed: the way in which something from the past "lives" together with us through its "effective-history." The "effects" of an historical object in history should not be viewed in a linear, "cause-effect," relationship. They are the result of the mediation between the object and the traditions which have met and interacted with it at different times. An historical object then should not be conceived as an isolated "object" in the past, as in objectivist thinking; instead, we must recognize in it "both the reality of history and the reality of historical understanding."[29]

Gadamer, talking in terms of "consciousness," has characterized the awareness of our historicality as "historical consciousness." If our awareness extends to include the impact of "effective-history" on ourselves, then we have reached the level of "effective-historical consciousness" (a consciousness that is also aware of what history has handed down to us). But "effective-historical consciousness is primarily consciousness of the hermeneutical situation."[30] We encounter the first signs of what Gadamer means by our "hermeneutical situation." It refers to the position whereby we find ourselves in tradition with the additional urgency to continually understand its meaning, so that one can lead one's own life. A "situation" for Gadamer is "a standpoint that limits the possibility of vision."[31] Therefore, our hermeneutical situation has to be seen within terms of specific limits. Although Gadamer's language is metaphorical, we can easily understand his message: our present, concrete, hermeneutical situation allows an understanding of things ("vision" for Gadamer) that is partial and moves within limits, which have been imposed upon "understanding" by present tradition and by the "effects" which history has transmitted via tradition.

Horizons and Their Fusion

One of Gadamer's major concerns when he investigates the notion of understanding is to demonstrate our position within history, within tradition and our relation to the past. In trying to articulate a representative picture of the individual in history and tradition, he starts by introducing the concept of *horizon*. "The horizon is the range of vision that includes everything that can be seen from a particular vantage point."[32] A horizon can be narrow or broad; it can extend or meet other horizons (i.e., historical horizons, horizons of other traditions, or of other individuals). At the same time, a person aware of the extent of her own horizon is not overwhelmed by what appears to be close to her but can value equally well distant things which lie at the edges of her horizon. The Gadamerian language, with the notion of horizon, also tends to be metaphoric and poetic. However, it manages to convey the notion powerfully, since we can associate the image of "horizon" with the familiar experience of an actual visual horizon.

Tradition for Gadamer can be conceived in terms of expressing itself within a particular historical horizon. As a consequence of the fact that our efforts are attuned to understanding tradition, the historical understanding that Gadamer analyzes is given a new task: it must reach and extend over the horizon of tradition so it can understand tradition in the fullest possible way. In this task, it appears that there are two horizons: the horizon of the interpreter and the horizon of tradition. Here Gadamer strives to avoid the danger of (historical) objectivism that appears as soon as one attempts to understand and judge the horizon of tradition separately from one's own horizon. But, are they two hermetically closed horizons that do not bear any relation to each other? For example, if we try to reconstruct the historical horizon of a past text, recognizing it as an alien past horizon, at the same time putting aside our own horizon, then Gadamer thinks that we do not allow the text to claim truth for what it says. This happens because when we think that we have reconstructed the historical tradition of the text, then what the text says has a meaningful content and truthfulness only for that tradition and not for our own. In these circumstances, we put aside our own horizon of prejudices and prejudgments. We keep the two traditions distinct and separate. In this way, we appreciate the "otherness" of the text, but we do not go any further. We do not really allow the claim to truth in the text to reach us.

The same result will occur in conversation, when, while trying to understand the other person, we reconstruct her own horizon, but do not involve our own. If we keep the standpoint or the horizon of the other person continually present in what she says, we manage to make her sayings intelligible. At the same time however, we do not agree with her and also keep our own standpoint removed and out of touch with the other. There is no agreement with what she says. We cannot really follow her claim to truthful statements since we have kept the two standpoints apart. We restrict any claim to truth of the other person if we think what she says is valid within her own horizon and not in ours. Nonetheless, is this the way of the hermeneutic approach to a text or to another person? Is our own horizon formed in such a way that would impose this closeness and inability to open up to another horizon? Gadamer rejects any notion of closeness of horizons.

> Just as the individual is never simply an individual, because he is always involved with others, so too the closed horizon that is supposed to enclose a culture is an abstraction. The historical movement of social life consists in the fact that it is never utterly bound to any one stand-point, and hence can never have a truly closed horizon. The horizon is, rather, something into which we move and that moves with us. Horizons change for a person who is moving. Thus the horizon of the past, out of which all human life lives and which exists in the form of tradition, is always in motion.[33]

There always seems to be a connecting link between the interpreter's horizon and the horizon of tradition. We can imagine that this happens because our present is formed from the past. On the other hand though, there is a tension between the present and what comes from the past. The difficulty of approaching a past text or tradition, as the horizon coming from the past, presents us with the basic hermeneutical situation. Thus, the hermeneutic approach needs to make this tension explicit and to find ways of overcoming it. However, what is the relationship of our present to the past? Why is the past important?

Thinking of our present horizon, it is for the most part determined by the prejudices that structure our own understanding. Nevertheless, this is not a permanent situation; it is not a fixed horizon that does not allow reflection upon the prejudices or the approximation of other horizons. On the contrary, our present horizon is in constant change and involved in actual "testing" of prejudices, especially when we come into contact with the past, and its traditions. Prejudices can either be retained or rejected according to whether they help or obstruct the understanding of the past.

If we consider the present to be formed from the past, the understanding of tradition appears to be imperative to understanding the present. The horizon of the present cannot be formed without the horizon of the past. How is then the approach to the past possible? Gadamer says that we need to have a horizon in order to approach the past. I take him to mean that in having a horizon we are aware of our own boundaries and the particularity of our own position. Equipped with this awareness, it makes sense to talk of our ability to distinguish and to approach a different past horizon. Nevertheless, such a task does not seem to be a simple positioning of ourselves in an alien horizon. Studying, for example, a number of historical pasts, or historical horizons, it would appear that we should transport ourselves to an equal number of alien horizons. Gadamer rejects this idea, which is the methodology of the historical sciences, because it amounts to self-alienation; in such circumstances we lose sight of our own present horizon.

Our historical consciousness, Gadamer believes, needs to be in touch with the present, and in its transposition to the past it needs to "see" its own present. We must "place" ourselves in the horizon of the past or the horizon of tradition. It is important here to make clear what Gadamer means by such an hermeneutic approach. If, for example, instead of the horizon of tradition we consider the horizon of another person, we can say that we "place" ourselves in the other's position. This "placing," nonetheless, should not be achieved through "empathy," nor, on the other hand should we impose our own criteria and judgments upon the other person's position. Instead, this "placing" should involve our own historical consciousness in an effort to overcome our own as well as the other's particularity and reach a higher universality that can do justice to both positions. The same applies to the effort of our historical consciousness in its task to approach the horizon of tradition. Avoiding a one-sided approach, we must reach a higher level of consciousness in which we can equally well understand the past and the present surpassing the particularity of both.

What Gadamer is driving at is the concept of the *fusion* of horizons that allows the meeting of the past with the present. In such a *fusion* there is a special condition which is kept intact. Our "historical consciousness" is aware of the tension between the present and the past; it is aware of the otherness of the past horizon of tradition. Yet, it recognizes itself as part of that changing tradition and tries to combine the past with the present. A conscious hermeneutic approach, in its efforts to approach and understand a past horizon of tradition, must *project* this historical horizon which is different from our own; otherwise, we would attain a naive assimilation of the past. "In the process of understanding there takes place a real fusion of horizons, which means that, as the historical horizon is projected, it is simultaneously removed."[34] This is possible since our "historical consciousness" can distinguish between the past and the present. The projected past horizon is then "removed" because it is absorbed by our own historical consciousness which merges with it.

We could now reach some additional conclusions which appear to be part of the Gadamerian analysis.

(a) I mentioned earlier that the horizon of the present is continuously formed and that we continually test our prejudices in our encounter with tradition. The horizon of the present *cannot* be formed without the past. This shows the falsehood and *naïveté* of an isolated formation of a horizon of the present without recognizing and acknowledging the necessity of knowing tradition. However, this insistence on tradition by Gadamer has been criticized harshly (as I will mention when examining Habermas's account), but sometimes unfairly. In particular Gadamer's critics come to the conclusion that, with tradition, he introduces a conservative past inhabited by authority and its forces of domination and exploitation. Such insistence on tradition, according to his critics, does not allow any scope for emancipation or for the critique of ideology that resides within tradition. My comments so far have been focused on demonstrating the importance of tradition to the understanding of our present horizon and the reasons for which Gadamer considers its study necessary for the examination of the notion of "understanding." He also informs us of the need to appreciate the past in terms of the truth and significance it holds for us. Nevertheless, I will discuss his failure to raise questions about ideological and repressive elements in tradition in the fifth chapter.

(b) Gadamer shows how the encounter with the past, in the process of the hermeneutic project, involves the notion of the fusion of horizons. However, since our present horizon is constantly reformed, merging with a continually moving and changing tradition, the fusion with tradition occurs continuously on a day-to-day basis and is not a matter of choice. This fusion, as far as I understand it, is part of our hermeneutical position and cannot be ignored. We belong to a tradition and although it changes, we move along with it.

(c) There do not exist totally enclosed horizons to which we are denied any access at all. As there is always a link between the past and the present, the same applies to any horizon we might encounter. Our historical consciousness can establish a link with any horizon of the past.

"Application"

Before concluding this chapter, which focused primarily on an explication and examination of the notion of the historicality of understanding, I will turn to the significant notion of *application* which for Gadamer constitutes a major hermeneutical problem.

Until now we have seen that any act of understanding a text involves interpretation. In addition Gadamer considers interpretation to involve understanding; the two do not constitute separate processes. Interpretation signifies understanding and vice versa.

> Interpretation is not an occasional additional act subsequent to understanding, but rather understanding is always an interpretation, and hence interpretation is the explicit form of understanding.[35]

Any interpretation indicates that an act of understanding has taken place and that the understanding achieved is inseparable from the interpretation performed. Nevertheless, any interpretation is not accidental or free from the historicality of the interpreter. There has to be a mediation between the horizon of the past and the horizon of the present, or between the other person and the "I" if it is a conversation. This mediation and fusion of horizons Gadamer has developed with the help of the concept of *application* which forms another inseparable "moment" in any understanding.

We can get an initial idea of what application might be by following Gadamer's examples from legal hermeneutics, or from theological hermeneutics; both of these areas in earlier periods of hermeneutics were connected to literary and historical hermeneutics. In court, the judge does not simply apply the law arbitrarily to any case. Instead, in order to pass a just judgment, he makes an attempt to apply it in accordance with the particular circumstances of each case. This involves a specific understanding and interpretation of the law in the light of each particular legal case. Similarly, the same process applies in the case of religious sets of rules and ideas concerning the conduct of life. In order for rules to be practiced properly and yet retain their "redeeming" results, they cannot just simply be considered as historical documents, they must each be applied to contemporary conditions and according to each specific case.

However, when we return to literary or to historical hermeneutics, the notion of application appears rather difficult to comprehend. In the case of the text, we have to apply it to ourselves, in our present conditions. But what does this application mean? Initially, it does not seem to be the same as applying either the law or a religious proclamation. It is neither a case of arriving at a just judgment nor binding ourselves to rules of conduct. The interpreter faced with the text, has not only to reproduce what is said by one of the partners in discussion (Gadamer thinks of such a case as a discussion, where the "voice of the text" takes the place of one of the partners); but also "to *express* what is said in a way that seems *necessary* to him considering the real situation of the dialogue." He is in the position of a translator, knowing both languages, that of the text and of the present, so that he can bring to the present language the claims and significant points of the text. In other words, in the case of a past text, the interpreter has to "translate" it in the terms of contemporary conditions. If the translator also understands what is said in the text's own actual conditions, in the past, he has to retain in the translation or interpretation such insights or significant points or "truths." We need to *apply* the text to the present, so that we can understand it and its truth.

The similarities between the application of the text and the application of the law start to emerge. As the judge applies the law to the present—by "translating" or "reading" it into present circumstances, norms, and behavioral patterns—so it is the case with the text; one "translates/reads" or applies it to current norms and expectations. In contrast to this notion of "application," a naive attitude would be a word by word interpretation (transliteration), without paying attention to what is significant, worth saying, and for what reason.

A few more remarks, however, should further clarify the notion of "application" in relation to the text. Firstly, the text may possess an original meaning (Gadamer does not deny the existence of an *original meaning* in a poem, in a piece of music, etc), but in each historical time the interpreter *cannot* bring about the same meaning, or perform the same interpretation; "in the human sciences, understanding is essentially historical, i.e., in them a text is understood only if it is understood in a different way every time."[36] This is a result of the changing situation of the interpreter and of his historical position. As an example we can recall the different ways in which the antiquity period has been understood during the Renaissance, during the Enlightenment, and today. The three different interpretations show that there isn't any original meaning that can be grasped, only that there is something significant to *return to* or to *appropriate* in view of the present.

Secondly, at the moment of application, it is the interpreter with her own historicality who has to *admit* her own condition in approaching the text. Awareness of her historical position dictates to her that she cannot understand the text, in the terms of the text, by forgetting herself, her prejudices, her matrix of norms, expectations, and horizon. She *applies* the text to her historical condition, not in order to judge (as in legal hermeneutics) or to follow a religious dogma, but instead *to present before her* that piece of history (the text), or the partner in discussion (the text), and to allow its corresponding horizon to join with her own, by fusing the two horizons. Application then is a *fusion of horizons.*

From what I have said until now it follows that application is accompanied by *awareness* of what is involved. Consequently, application erases the forgetfulness of the methodical disciplines concerning their own historicality. This conclusion Gadamer uses as a criticism even against the human sciences which do not take into consideration their historicality which is involved in the formation of the knowledge they represent. Thus, finally, we can say that an application of a text to the interpreter yields a *specific interpretation* and a *specific meaning* of the text, because the application has brought the interpreter to an awareness of her own historicality which in turn affects the interpretation. The interpreter has fused the two horizons consciously, in order to arrive at a specific and satisfactory meaning. Although the meaning arrived at is *situational*,[37] the truth of the text should have been transmitted to us.

The conclusion which follows from the previous pages is that all understanding involves application. The notion of interpretation alone is not sufficient to throw light on the whole structure of understanding. Awareness of the historicality of understanding dictates the mediation between the past horizon and the present horizon, or between participants in a dialogue and this is achieved through the fusion of horizons and *application.* The involvement of the interpreter proves to be significant for any interpretation reached. If the interpreter is aware of her hermeneutic situation, she should overcome an explicit forgetfulness of the historical immersion of consciousness. This actually represents the condition of "effective-historical consciousness," that is, the consciousness which is aware of all the dimensions of its own historicality. The resulting interpretation of a text, or the knowledge achieved in a hermeneutic approach of a text or of an historical object or an historical phenomenon, is of a *situational* character.

3
Linguisticality and "World"

Continuing the presentation and examination of Gadamer's philosophical hermeneutics, I come to the last part of his *Truth and Method* which is devoted to the linguistic nature of understanding and the ontological significance of language. Pursuing these themes we will encounter his efforts to reposition language to its primary ontological status that allows access to Being. I will begin by examining the basic notion of understanding as interpretation and then move to the linguisticality of all understanding, which permits Gadamer to demonstrate how we "have world"[1] through language as well as to present our hermeneutic existential position. In order to achieve a closer acquaintance with his notions I will examine what can comprise his theory of language, especially that which he draws from Humboldt's philosophy of language. Gadamer's conception of the connection between "word" and "object" will provide the opportunity to expand on his notion of "truth" which initially appears difficult to understand but is also rewarding. I will then conclude with the notion of philosophical hermeneutics as a practical philosophy that Gadamer proposes, which is in line with his conception of "truth."

Understanding and Interpretation

Before embarking upon a study of Gadamer's claim that all understanding is linguistic in nature, it is necessary to examine his conclusion that "all understanding is interpretation," or that "the mode of realisation of understanding is interpretation." How are we going to understand these statements? Anticipating the difficulty of comprehending these propositions, Gadamer provides us with the examples of translation from a foreign language and conversation as, for him, both practices illustrate the notion of interpretation. The translator is faced with the task of bringing over what he understands from the foreign language to his own language. It is obviously not the case of translating word-for-word with the expectation of arriving at a coherent meaning. For example, it would be impossible to render the meaning of an idiomatic expression simply by translating word-for-word. Instead, the translator must render the meaning understood in the foreign language plausibly and, as far as possible, accurately in his own language. In this example the translator is faced with the problem of *highlighting*: if something appears significant to him in the foreign language, it must be noted and given concomitant prominence in the translation. At each moment the translator is aware of the gap between the original text and himself. What is important here is that the translation has involved interpretation, that is, rendering of the meaning of the text to another language. This is a familiar occasion when, in a translation of a text from another language, one can see the distance from the original and especially the lack of certain literary virtues which exist in the original possibly lost in the translation process. A similar case can be seen as occurring within conversation.

In conversation we are faced with two or more people geared toward understanding each other. It is not an activity in which each one simply "enters" the other person in order to understand her as an individual (e.g., her psychological buildup, or her feelings), but, rather, each attempts to understand what the other person "says." Yet, Gadamer argues that an almost imperceptible translation takes place between the two partners during discussion. Each one translates the other's views in order to understand them from one's own position. Conversation, similar to translation, involves interpretation in a *common language* to which both partners try to arrive in order that they can both reach "agreement"[2] on the views expressed. The example of conversation can also be used in the case of understanding a text, in that the text can be thought of as the other partner and the conversation itself (or the understanding of the text in our case) becomes hermeneutical because of the interpretation involved. The interpreter of a text finally expresses in her own language the meaning of the text.

What Gadamer wishes to promote is the notion of interpretation that is inevitably bound up with all understanding. The examples of translation and conversation as presented, lead toward this conclusion. When there is understanding there has been an interpretation. We must not regard understanding and interpretation as separate moments of a process but rather as one and the same thing; for an interpretation to be accomplished something has been understood and understanding something involves interpretation. The consequence of Gadamer's conclusion is that *the universal mode of understanding is interpretation* and all other possibilities of understanding conform to this mode.

So far as it concerns textual understanding or the understanding of the meaning of cultural phenomena, Gadamer's claim appears to be well supported. Firstly, his theory does justice to our empirical experience as readers or partners in discussion. Secondly, in the realm of social/historical sciences (and especially for those theories which do not identify their methodology with that of the natural sciences) understanding is constantly connected with the elaboration of interpretative accounts. Objections, however, have been raised about the way in which explanatory understanding is employed in the natural sciences. A great number of philosophers concerned with the philosophy of science would consider explanatory understanding to be the major paradigm proper to natural sciences and, for some of them, to social sciences. In contrast to Gadamer's position, an explanatory account of a natural phenomenon, or a natural process leading to the understanding of this process, does not amount to interpretation. The (causal) explanatory statements produced within the reasoning of scientific disciplines, sufficiently guarantee the understanding of the natural phenomenon. This argument sounds stronger, if the advocate of this position retains an underlying correspondence between the terms of the explanatory account and "reality." However, such a situation is more suited to a rather naive realist approach to sciences. It also suggests the most radical separation between explanatory and hermeneutic understanding.

Nevertheless, instead of introducing a strict correspondence between explanatory statement and reality, we could think along different paths. As in conversation, where any interpretation is imperceptible, the mode of formulating explanatory statements in sciences, so far as it remains unchallenged, is taken for granted and "hides" behind itself those interpretive steps bound to it. One does not usually question the construction of explanatory accounts (connecting causes or causal conditions with effects), and the way in which they render intelligible, within language, those "matters of fact" which they denote. Furthermore, one does not question the scientist's choice (almost unnoticed) of the theoretical terms which are used in the explanatory statement, as well as their availability (formation). According to this line of thought, an explanatory account could be thought of in terms of the Kuhnian notion of "competing paradigms"

in "normal science," or in terms of Popper's notion of "conjectures."[3]
These later positions are close to Gadamer's standpoint and could
admit the explanatory account itself as an interpretation, since they
do not involve a "correspondence" theory of truth. In the Kuhnian
view the explanatory account based on an accepted "paradigm" is
one possible way of looking at a natural phenomenon until the scientific community stops to consider the "scientific paradigm" correct.
Or, in accordance to Popper's views, a theory is upheld as valid until
a way for its refutation can be proposed. Besides the similarities
which might be found between Kuhn, Popper, and Gadamer, I think
Gadamer's position makes the boldest claim by insisting that any
understanding is interpretation.

For Gadamer, even the attempt to understand a natural phenomenon via a concrete explanatory account, as is usually the case in the
natural sciences, constitutes an interpretation. It is *one possible way*
of looking at things within a given frame of available concepts (the
available linguistic horizon) and historical boundaries. Gadamer's
position will become clearer later when I will examine his views on
the linguistic constitution of the "world" and our hermeneutical position in it. This raises questions and indicates standpoints that are
obviously connected with the well-known problem of the distinction
between the natural and the social sciences, or between "explanation" and "understanding" of meaning that each set of sciences utilizes in pursuing their object of study, a distinction which has relent-
lessly attracted lengthy epistemological exchanges.[4]

The Linguisticality of Understanding

Gadamer, before arriving at the center of his philosophical theses
concerning our hermeneutical existence and the significant position
of language as the ontological basis of our being, reflects upon the
explicit or implicit involvement of language in every understanding.
We are already familiar with what he considers to be a linguistic
interpretation. When trying to understand a text, we saw that a
fusion of horizons occurred and that the notion of application was
apparent in the effort to bring into our own language the meaning of
the text. Moreover, the act of understanding as interpretation was
accomplished within language and the whole process was linguistic
in nature. Inevitably, any textual understanding engages language
for its operation.

However, Gadamer, extends the *linguistic* form of interpretation to
any other form of interpretation. If this is true then all understanding
is of linguistic nature. He states that

linguistic interpretation is the form of all interpretation, even when what is
to be interpreted is not linguistic in nature, i.e. is not a text, but is a statue
or a musical composition.[5]

I consider this to be a bold statement which needs further explanation
as, in many cases, it certainly runs counter to common sense. For
example, on what grounds could we say that a musical performance
involves a linguistic interpretation? The same applies to an artistic
reproduction of a statue Gadamer discusses. The writings of
Gadamer on this topic concerning the linguistic form of understanding include a certain ambiguity. The two poles of ambiguity appear
by formulating the following questions. Does the form of any interpretation *resemble* the linguistic form of interpretation? Or, *is* every
interpretation a linguistic form of interpretation? I will argue that it
is the second case that Gadamer proposes.

Let us take the example of a musical conductor, or a soloist "studying" a musical piece in order to deliver a performance. It is certain
that each one of them needs to understand the piece of music in order
that they can perform a new production (re-production) in which the
meaning(s) included in the musical piece will be manifested. Highlighting certain areas show that *an interpretation* of the piece has
been achieved by the soloist, or by the conductor, revealing how each
one understands the musical piece. This demonstrates the first aim
of Gadamer, which is to show that any performance of music or play
or act, is always an interpretation which goes hand in hand with the
understanding of the musical piece, the play, or the "role" (in a play)
that was reproduced. However, the main question I earlier posed
remains: in what sense does the linguistic form of interpretation
reveal itself? The ambiguity of Gadamer becomes evident when, initially, he argues that this interpretation (the performance of a play) is
a modification of linguistic interpretation and later, that it presupposes language. We are not sure whether we are confronted with a
resemblance of linguistic interpretation or with straightforward linguistic interpretation.

The same question applies to other situations Gadamer discusses.
For example, the demonstration of the existence of a common theme
by placing two pictures alongside each other or the drawings of an
artist reproducing an old master. Each example for Gadamer presents a form of linguistic interpretation, even if the visual demonstration initially appears to have nothing in common with such an interpretation. The similarity of these examples is the notion that
language underlies the ability to distinguish the common theme
between the two pictures, or the ability of the painter to understand

and reinterpret (reproduce) the original painting. If we return to the case of the soloist, we certainly hear him saying that he performed in the way he felt what was worth bringing forward in the meaning of the musical piece. The soloist is unaware of any linguisticality involved in his understanding. Therefore, this example strongly indicates that Gadamer's position (since other alternatives cannot be logically sustained) is the following: what the soloist felt was impossible to be grasped by him without the mediation of language. The soloist's ability to distinguish what is essential, or what needs highlighting, is based upon certain knowledge and experience he possesses but which has been transmitted to him linguistically. It is language that has allowed all knowledge from experience, or "demonstration," from communication, or tradition, to be received by the individual soloist so that he can judge and provide his understanding of a musical piece. I must also note that Gadamer stands against any romantic theory suggesting the immediacy of approach of an artistic object which is the "aesthetics of the artistic genius."

We can reflect upon a similar situation if we put ourselves in the position of the audience before which the soloist performed. If we are able to understand the highlightings, the exaggerations, the weaknesses perhaps, of the performance, this happens because we have knowledge of similar cases and this knowledge has been attained via language. Language has allowed us, the audience, to achieve familiarity with such artistic forms and *our interpretation is possible thanks to language*. This becomes more evident in the event of our desire to communicate our understanding of the performance. Then we must put in language-form—even in a restricted way and always less satisfactorily than our inner thoughts and feelings—the interpretation of the performance that we have reached. Similarly, an artist reproducing an old master's painting arrives at an interpretation made possible by language. Although his interpretation appears to him as immediacy and as intuition, the experience of the colors, the forms, or the subject, have all been conquered through language and their employment always involves language. My explication of Gadamer's thesis is further supported by his theory of language, which I will discuss later, and by his conclusion that "all experience is linguistic in nature."

What I have examined up to now represents the strongest claim arising of Gadamer's position and concerns the linguisticality of all interpretation. He also adds a weaker claim demonstrating the involvement of language, for example, the possibility of presenting through words the actor's understanding of a play and his subsequent performance. The actor cannot deny this possibility, even if he thinks that a verbal description of his performance can never totally capture the performance itself. But Gadamer believes that this possibility of rendering into words the interpretation reached by the actor demonstrates once more the linguistic basis of all interpretation.

This theme of the linguisticality of all interpretation and subsequently of all understanding has been challenged by Habermas (as we will see in later chapters). However, the point remains whether all interpretation conforms to the linguistic paradigm, or whether there is understanding that does not involve language. We might tend to think that there are prelinguistic experiences, that is, experiences that are lived through without the introduction of language. Even if such experiences were available, in the absence of language they could not be shared (in a dialogue or communication), or be (conceptually) identified. They could never have the same character as those experiences which depend upon language. This, eventually, brings us to the example used by Gadamer of the nonlinguistic experiences of animals forming their habitat. The world the animals share is not the world shared in language by humans.

Here, we are questioning whether all experience is linguistic in nature, or whether there are experiences not dependent on the presence of language for their perception and intelligibility. We could imagine a number of cases in which the presupposition of language for the reception of an experience is debatable. For example, in what terms can we think that the production of a specific note through a wind instrument involves language? The immediacy of the experience tends to suggest that the auditory sensation is a straightforward situation not involving language. On the other hand, many times it is the case that in order to reproduce accurately this specific note, the teacher would insist on a specific technique, perhaps blowing and aiming at a certain distance from the end of the instrument. This suggests that language has been employed to establish the conditions for the reception of the experience. We could also question in our example how the experience and identification of a note with one that we have heard before is possible. This involves previous knowledge (and distinction) of what we call a "note," and a background of linguistically mediated experiences that allow the identification of the note/sound, its discrimination from other sounds, and also a possible discussion upon the correctness (identity with the previous note) of the reproduced note. Although it seems that the immediacy of a sensory experience is beyond language, upon further reflection language appears to have been involved in the entire process.

Returning to the argument for the existence of prelinguistic experiences that Habermas raises by recalling the epistemological conclusions of Piaget,[6] Gadamer is prepared to answer with a further remark which, I think, provides a strong point for his position. He argues that, even in the cases in which language is absent, he is able to specify a common attitude or a common trait, amounting to what we usually term *reason*. He would even accept other experiences of the world coming through communication systems other than language. For example, bodily movement, or facial gestures, can play this role, or even the very specific and formalized languages of mathematics used in other scientific disciplines. As systems of communication, all exhibit, in Gadamer's opinion, the common trait of "reason." Thus, what Gadamer is attempting is the demonstration of all understanding as a case of reason. This conclusion can be seen as a consequence of the previous position that all understanding involves the linguistic form of interpretation. Reason and language meet in this (form of) interpretation. In the end, he actually reaches the conclusion that "language is the language of reason,"[7] although aware and cautious that such a conclusion almost identifies reason and language. Nevertheless, he believes that reason and language, despite their proximity, are not one and the same thing.

We just saw that Gadamer does not hesitate to call "reason" the common trait that one can identify at the background of prelinguistic experience. Nevertheless, we almost always conceive of reason as being expressed in language and finding its way through it. But does this limit reason within the boundaries of language? According to Gadamer, reason can overcome the limitations set by any specific language. The ability of our understanding to reach the meaning of a text from a different historical epoch through the fusion of horizons, serves as an example, showing that reason can overcome the barriers initially posed by the current language each one of us uses. He reintroduces the example of translation and focuses on what he characteristically calls the "agony of translation." At the beginning, it seems impossible to translate accurately from a foreign language into our own. The words (concepts) in each language seem to have a perfect harmony with the things they refer to. It appears impossible to transfer into our own language what the individual words in the foreign language signify without considerable loss of meaning. Nevertheless, the translation is eventually accomplished without necessarily translating word-for-word, using other means such as paraphrasing, in order to communicate the meaning understood by the translator.

With this example of the practice of translation Gadamer wishes to remind us that reason is not totally at the mercy of language. It can progress beyond the initial and actual limitations of any language. Translation, interpretation, fusion of horizons, all of them indicate this ability of reason. In his words "the thinking reason escapes the prison of language, and it is itself constituted linguistically."[8] This result has been reached after the examination of the hermeneutic experience, that is, the experience of understanding and interpretation. It permits Gadamer to approach language not as an enclosed system of linguistic signs in which we are trapped. On the contrary, language is the space which opens up the possibility of dialogue with others and points to the infinite dimensions of discourse. Instead of a "prison," language is the springboard from which to enter and expand the world. Nevertheless, these conclusions cannot stand alone and Gadamer is in need of a fundamental theory of language able to preserve what he considers the intimate unity of "word" and "object."

Gadamer's Theory of Language

The linguist that Gadamer draws from is Wilhelm von Humboldt whose theory of language has been significantly influential. According to Humboldt every language should be seen as a particular view of the world. Primarily, this formulation appears to suggest that each particular concept and each particular statement expressed in a language is a specific way of "seeing" the world. For example, one language could have developed a concept about "forest" or about "nature" or "natural surroundings" that might be quite different from corresponding conceptions evolved in another language. It is also possible that the second language in our example might never have developed corresponding concepts at all. Through the first language, then, one receives a *different* "view" of the "forest" or of "nature" than the possible "view" one could acquire through the second language. The picture becomes more complicated if we begin examining the grammatical features of each particular language and their effect on the meaning of statements in each language. Grammar is essential in the expression of meaning and provides additional evidence for Humboldt's theory that each language is "a particular view of the world." Gadamer accepts this conclusion with certain reservations. Humboldt's assertion detaches the theory of language from a very limited notion which considers language to be a tool or a simple means of communication; instead, language becomes responsible for our attachment to the world. Gadamer is, however, aware that this conclusion alone could lead to the idealist's camp because Humboldt's conclusion stresses the subjective aspect of consciousness in its encounter with the world. Languages could thus be seen as entirely subjective constructions rather than as retaining a relationship with the world they address.

In addition, Gadamer objects to another theme of Humboldt's theory: the reduction of the linguistic phenomenon entirely to a corresponding linguistic faculty. Obviously, by studying language as form, Humboldt could detach it from any specific content and thus penetrate into the patterns, ways, and processes through which the "linguistic faculty" generates language. These studies, according to Gadamer, consider language primarily as *form*, yet, the hermeneutic experience cannot separate form (linguistic rules, grammatical features, and structures, as well as their relationship to linguistic faculty) from content (the meaning that is conveyed, or what is expressed in language). Thus, for example, in order to study the linguistic tradition in which we belong we cannot simply separate it into form and content; one needs to intergrate both. A study of only the formal aspects of linguistic tradition (form), would entirely miss what is transmitted in it (content). Gadamer, however, would not deny that ignorance toward the formal aspects of the linguistic tradition would hinder its deepest understanding. Therefore, in Gadamer's analysis, one language is not simply *different* from another on matters of form, but also on what it "says."

In my view, we are faced here with a conflict between the interests of a "scientific" approach to language and the interests of a philosophical theory of language. The latter commonly finds the vision of the former restricted and unable to foresee the philosophical implication of its own studies. Nevertheless, Gadamer willingly borrows certain conclusions from Humboldt that enable him to support his own philosophical hermeneutics. We can follow Gadamer on the question as to whether there would be a *human* world without language, to which Humboldt gave a negative answer. Gadamer welcomes this conclusion and adds:

> Language is not just one of man's possessions in the world, but *on it depends the fact that man has a world at all.* For man the world exists as world in a way that no other being in the world experiences. But *this world is linguistic in nature.* This is the real heart of Humboldt's assertion which he intended quite differently, that languages are views of the world. (italics mine.)[9]

Gadamer's assertions and conclusions must be read carefully as a number of misunderstandings have followed their interpretation. Habermas, for example, in opposition to Gadamer's phrase that "the world is linguistic in nature," or that "all experience is of linguistic nature," proposes the categories of "domination," "power," and "work" which, he argues, provide a clearer and more coherent picture of the world and of our experiences of it (we will meet these categories in later chapters). Is this, however, what Gadamer suggests? A "weak" picture of social reality that could be replaced with a collection of more concrete social categories that Habermas proposes?

We must track Gadamer closely in order to grasp more accurately his assertions on the linguisticality of the world and of experience. Following Humboldt, he believes that the language of a linguistic community stands above and, in a certain way, independent of, the members of the community. Thanks to this language, each member of the community is initiated into the world, "learns" the world, and develops specific relationships with it. It is obvious that when Gadamer says "the world is linguistic in nature" he does not suggest that language *creates* the world *ex-nihilo* or that there would be no physical world without language. He simply encourages us to reflect upon the fact that what we know, or what is presented to us, has come through language or, at least, that language is the necessary condition for the world's existence for us. As an example, we can consider familiar sensory experiences and then question the presence of language for their reception. There is no doubt that animals which do not share a (human) language do have sensory experiences. However, it is also true that these experiences do not register in the same way as those which the human agent encounters and communicates. Human experience is registered by means of corresponding concepts in language; through them experience is also communicated; from a toothache, or a sound to the visual experience of a painting. At the same time, any experience is registered in a specific way, associated with a grid of interconnections language allows. For example, fire and its destructive consequences is associated via the concept of "fire," with the dangers expected from it, with notions of its causes, ability to control them, and a whole network of relationships (beyond what personal memory of previous experiences can furnish), which are evidently quite different from those in the animal kingdom. It is this "availability" of the world via language that Gadamer insists upon.

However, we must proceed further and explore Gadamer's distinction between habitat (Umwelt), characteristic of all life and world (Welt), applicable to human beings.

To have a "world" means to have an attitude toward it. To have

> an attitude towards the world, however, means to keep oneself so free from what one encounters from the world that one is able to present it to oneself

as it is. This capacity is both the having of a "world" and the having of language. Thus the concept of "world" (Welt) is in opposition to the concept of "surrounding world" or "habitat" (Umwelt), as possessed by every living thing.[10]

World as habitat means the surrounding (environmental) conditions upon which life depends. For humans the situation is different: although we are born in a habitat we can "free" ourselves from it. We can alter the habitat, discover ways to go beyond it, or redefine it collectively (either in beneficial or disastrous directions, one should add), as human history amply demonstrates. I must stress here that the possibility of freedom should be related to the human ability to reflect upon the world and to draw an *attitude* toward it. Such a reflective ability is given via language and is the consciousness of the "I" facing the habitat. This new relationship in which the habitat can be shaped and from which one can achieve "freedom," is the relationship of "having world."

> To rise above the pressure of what comes to meet us from the world means to have language and to have "world" [Sprache haben und Welt haben].[11]

For Gadamer to "have world" underlines the active relationship with the habitat, the continuous possibility of altering it and surpassing its immediacy as well as the ability to reinterpret the past within it, comprehend the present, and project the future. Simultaneously, the world to which we rise is the world constituted by language. With his neologism "to have world," he upsets our perception of it and draws our attention to the meaning he wishes to convey. The notion of "freedom" from habitat, introduced here, describes our ontological situation and is in line with Heidegger's existential positions.

Gadamer examines a deeper level of our ontological position of freedom toward the habitat and emphasizes the importance of language in "having world." Somehow, the world cannot be thought separately from language, a basic standpoint which also applies to our scientific projects and sociological analysis of our situation. Habermas's remarks evoking the categories of "work," "power," and "domination" lie at a different level of discourse with an immediate concern for a critical understanding of the structure of our life and the unearthing of the repressive features, institutions, and mechanisms that dominate us. He confronts Gadamer as if the latter had proposed that language alone creates political domination or that the causes of such domination could be solely attributed to linguistic properties. His understanding of Gadamer on this point is limited. He does not wish to grasp the philosophical discourse of Gadamer on language, fearing that the latter's statement leads to a subjectivist withdrawal into the linguisticality of experience, which in the end neglects the "materiality" of the forces of domination. On the contrary, I would believe that Gadamer's suggestion leaves a theoretical space open to critical/scientific examination of our social life-forms. Yet, he wishes to demonstrate our basic ontological relationship to "world" and "language." This indicates the two different levels of discussion between Gadamer and Habermas, which, in many instances, become apparent in their debate.

In a further clarification of Gadamer's position I return to his remarks which point to the many different cultural worlds that exist today and that members in one world "see" the world differently than the members of another. His efforts concentrate on showing that there is always a common underlying event in the experiences in different cultures: there is a *linguistically constituted world* that presents itself to us. The same occurs with the different "historical worlds" of which we are aware and which differ from our own present world. The assertion that the world we live in is constituted by language must be understood from the stance just discussed. It is not a matter of language creating the world but that what we come to know as "world" is available through language. Furthermore, Gadamer enriches the picture of a linguistically constituted world with the notion of "openness" for further insights and its availability to others (through dialogue, fusion of horizons, and application). We are familiar with this "openness" from one of his statements, presented earlier, asserting that language is not the "prison" of reason. However, our understanding of the notion of "having world" with which Gadamer provides us, would be incomplete unless we arrive at the full extent of the relationship between language and "world" that he has in mind.

For Gadamer "language has no independent life apart from the world that comes to language within it, . . . language has its real being only in the fact that *the world is represented in it*."[12] This statement lies at the center of his theory of language and is characteristic of the whole attitude and orientation of his philosophy. All Gadamerian positions on language I have examined so far demonstrate the continuous promotion by Gadamer of the thesis that, whatever we understand, is of linguistic nature. I mentioned earlier how we can understand the statements that "all experience is linguistic in nature" and that we also live in a linguistically constituted world. But this is only one aspect of his argument. The other half resides in what he views as an essential connection between language and the world. Whatever "comes to language" is part of the "things" themselves. Somehow, the being of the world extends itself within language.

Although at the moment I am forced to employ the language of Gadamer, which in Anglo-Saxon philosophy is in danger of sounding metaphorical, we can at least appreciate the sort of picture from which he distances himself. He no longer considers language and its capacities to generate new concepts, statements, and "views of the world," as an *independent* linguistic system that stands in opposition to the world and is able to describe, explain, or mirror it. This particular view is rather one accompanying the notion of scientific "objectivity." In accordance with this, "being" exists in itself and the world becomes an "object" of knowledge as soon as we require such knowledge. On the contrary, Gadamer claims that "the object of knowledge and of statements is already enclosed within the horizon of language."[13] As far as the world is linguistically constituted, and being has presented itself in language, one looks within the region of language in order to understand the world. These claims are in line with Heidegger's proclamation that "language is the house of being where man dwells."[14] Thus, the basic ontological significance that Gadamer ascribes to language, since being expresses itself therein, is a continuation of the Heideggerian philosophy. However, it is certainly difficult to absorb the Gadamerian insistence that being, things, "objects," have all expressed themselves in language, or (to state it in another way), that the world is *represented* in language (as I have just quoted him, n. 12).

We can gain an indication of what Gadamer means by following his sayings on the connection between "word" and "object." We can look at the example he provides which suggests that changes in the linguistic expression indicate changes in the nature of things. In German, he says, one must find proper words to express the continuance of moral norms in ways that lie away from older established conventions. For example, one can no longer use the old concept of "virtue" (*Tugend*) that has acquired an ironic significance. This process, Gadamer says, reflects reality as a mirror. He means that "virtue," as it was thought of before, does not coincide with recent moral preoccupations and norms. Thus, the linguistic search for some other concepts in order to express "virtue" indicates that social life itself, as it has evolved, sustains moral norms in new ways different than those associated with the concept of "virtue" before.

This I take to be only an instance of what Gadamer has in mind concerning the relationship between "word" and "object." He reminds us that such a view of the representation of the world in language needs to avoid a one-sided approach. It is not the world alone that changes and language remaining inactive (simply recording these changes), but language "itself helps to fashion the relation to the world we live in."15 All these remarks, however, do not provide a clear picture. To make it worse there seems to be a variety of ways that "representation" of the world in language can be thought of, depending on whether one examines a statement, a theory, a linguistic expression, a change of a linguistic habit, and so on.

The idea of representing the "world" in language, which results in the connection of "word" and "object," is a constant theme to be traced within the German philosophical tradition of the last few centuries. It reminds us of Hegel's view on the connection of "concept" and "reality," although for him the preferable vocabulary was "concept," "reason," "thought," and the homogeneity that extends between "concept" and "reality."16 Gadamer, nevertheless, does not follow the same strand; in one sense, language is distinguishable from the world and in another the world is represented within it. What one detects is not an Hegelian identity of "concept" and "object" but, instead, an extension of being within language: part of the being of things extends in language. Language thus acquires a new ontological significance. It is not a simple medium of communication or description but the "space" where the "I" meets the "world."

We should remind ourselves here that Gadamer's view does not invoke any conception of "correspondence" when he discusses the connection of "word" and "object." This would have resulted in a "correspondence theory of truth," a theme that he ascribes to the "objectivist" view of the world. His views are also far removed from the early Wittgenstein's picture of reality and the very strict correspondence of "atomic propositions" to "facts," as it is exposed in the *Tractatus.*17 Still, however, the whole concept of representation is never presented with sufficient clarity and does not satisfy a number of questions that arise in connection with the concept of "truth" which I will discuss later in this chapter. For example, we still need to ask the question: between two views on the same thing, which is true? or what are the criteria for deciding which one is true? Does Gadamer offer a different means by which to respond to these and similar questions? Alternatively, the concept of "representation" appears quite "open" and can accommodate a number of possibilities through which we can appreciate how the world expresses itself in language forms. With this I mean that "representation" is not restricted to a form of strict or absolute correspondence between "concept" and "object."

There are at least two themes I wish to underline here showing the interests and positions of Gadamer.

1. First, because of his insistence on the connection between "word" and "object," Gadamer accepts the fact that each view of the

world or, each particular statement about the world, could be equally valid and representative of the world. We are not forced to accept one view only as correct and the other as false. As he states, the variety of these views of the world does not involve any relativization of the "world." Rather what "the world is, is not different from the views in which it presents itself."[18] Obviously this attitude must not be confused with the position in formal logic concerning contradictory statements. Gadamer would accept that we cannot hold such statements (e.g., "A is blue and green all over"), or simultaneously hold statements which logically contradict each other.

Instead, Gadamer directs us to a notion of truth that has more dimensions than is usually the case in formalized logic. I could provisionally say that "truth," for Gadamer, can reveal itself in a variety of statements. All these statements may equally present different *aspects* of the "world," of a phenomenon, of a process, or of a situation—without of course violating our basic logical rules of reasoning. As just mentioned, there is also a stronger point that he wants to register: all these views, statements, or propositions, do not lead to an unspecified relativism devoid of any notion of truth. On the contrary, he claims that all (valid) views, interpretations, or statements, bring about, reveal, or state different aspects of the "object"; "truth" can be seen, discovered, or presented in all these different approaches. We are presented here with a multidimensional notion of "truth." Truth cannot be captured by this or that statement, neither by this or that interpretation.[19]

This philosophical commitment to "truth" has further consequences for the Gadamerian project. We are immersed in language and we are continually bound within the linguisticality of our experience of the world. Such connection with language, Gadamer concludes, *does not involve an exclusiveness of perspectives*." This is a result of the number of linguistic views available and of the fact that all share portions of the truth of the world. We can understand this claim by thinking that there are a number of languages available (different linguistic views of the world) and all can claim to be truthful of the world they represent. In no circumstances can any language claim exclusiveness of its view of "truth." More than that, as we have seen, we can move from one language to another and share the perspective and views offered in the other language. But if this is the case, as Gadamer argues, between different languages, the same could apply by analogy to one language alone. If within a language there are different approaches toward the same "object," none of them can claim exclusiveness to "truth." Concerning for example an object of study, one cannot claim exclusiveness of perspective

offered by a particular theory or statement. Further statements, or
theories, can present different aspects of the object of study and
reveal additional dimensions of its "truth."

2. The second aspect of Gadamer's preference that I wish to stress
is his undiminished insistence on the connection of "word" and
"object." Even if he doesn't pay much attention to clarifying the representational mode through which being expresses itself in language,
nevertheless, for him the connection that exists between language
and the world is of paramount importance. This view is a consequence of the strong ontological commitment that he shares with Heidegger, namely, that language is impregnated with the "being" of
things it talks about. We can share to a large extent Gadamer's arguments about the linguistic nature of our experience and the linguistic
nature of the world, in the way I discussed earlier. They seem to be
valid positions that are also supported by linguistic studies. However, if one wants to follow Gadamer into the connection of "word"
and "object," it seems to me that, despite a number of good reasons in
its favor, this position amounts to a further commitment which is vul-
nerable to current linguistic theories.

The theory of language that I have in mind is Ferdinand de Saussure's semiological theory. Language in this paradigm is a system of
significations organized around the two basic units of the "signifier"
and the "signified."[20] The "sign" developing inside the system does
not have any immediate connection with any referent (i.e., the
"object" to which the "signified" could refer).[21] Reference is not
necessary and if it exists it is not essentially connected with the articulation of language and with communication. The chain of *signifiers*
and the chain of *signifieds*, through a network of differences and
exclusions, provide the total available area for the constitution of
meaning. The Saussurian paradigm excludes "reference" which is a
specific relationship of "word" and "object."

Although "reference" is not the particular way in which Gadamer
considers "word" and "object" to be connected, and it would also
seem inappropriate to contrast the Saussurian view of language with
Gadamer's, Saussure's theory is, nevertheless, the major theoretical
paradigm that rejects any special connection between "word" and
"object," even that proposed by Gadamer. However, the juxtaposition of these two rather incompatible views of language could
demonstrate the theoretical consequences of a *commitment* to either
of them. Saussure's theory would be classified by Gadamer as a
nominalist theory, descending into modern thinking from a theme
Plato himself inaugurated with his notion of "forms."[22] We can
understand Gadamer's opposition to any nominalist view of lan-

guage since such a theory would more or less result in Humboldt's idea that "each language is a particular view of the world." In this respect, any particular language-system would produce its own reality. The world would be of as many versions as the particular languages available. This, for Gadamer, amounts to an "absolute relativism" and the notion of "truth" he has put forward could not be sustained.

Although we may question the extent into which Gadamer's connection of "word" and "object" is justified, we can at least appreciate two areas that he opposes. One is the aforementioned "absolute relativism" and the *indeterminacy* that appears with it, potentially resulting in serious inability to secure (valid) knowledge and insight. Even the aesthetic conception of "truth" in art could be seen as failing to fulfill its recovery of "truth" in a mimetic way, as Gadamer thinks of it. If "absolute relativism" is upheld such "truth" could never be located.

The second notion which he opposes is that of "being-in-itself," cultivated and promoted, as he says, as *an objectivist attitude* in the modern sciences (especially in physics). According to this view, the world of the natural sciences exists on its own and does not depend on the will and imagination of the human agent, yet science claims to know this world (as an object of its investigation). We are all familiar with this picture of the "world" of science since it constitutes the commonsense view of the "world," accompanying the teaching of sciences in all grades of education, its popular appreciation in research, and its presentation by the mass media. With Gadamer, however, we have come to recognize the linguisticality of the world and the priority of our linguistic experience of it. How is it then possible that there is a "world-in-itself," as this conception suggests?

Gadamer argues that the world we know through language does not possess a being-in-itself; "it is not being-in-itself, inasmuch as it does not possess an objective character and can never be given in experience as the comprehensive whole that it is."23 According to Gadamer modern sciences and especially physics, projects a world that is certainly not the totality of what exists; they produce the false idea of it as the absolute object to which all living things relate themselves. It would be more accurate to say that the world of science corresponds to a particular mode of will and desire for domination. We can observe here that Gadamer, together with his rejection of the objectivist "being-in-itself," also embraces the idea that "the knowledge of all the natural sciences is knowledge for domination."24 This was, at least, his position as regards the sciences in *Truth and Method*.

Gadamer attempts to alter the universal impression of the "objec-tivist" picture of the world that we are accustomed to through the sci-ences and their domineering role in the last few centuries. Instead, he wants to show that, as we live within language, we "have world" and this does not permit the universal picture of the "object-world" with which physics provides us. We cannot step outside language, as physics does, to observe an objectified reality. It is impossible to see the linguistic world we live in from "outside"; our experiences come from the world in language. For Gadamer, the world could only become an "object" of investigation from within language.

I have strived to examine and analyze Gadamer's philosophical position on language and simultaneously underline the problems and difficulties associated with his conception of "word" and "object," either as representation or expression of being in language. Further-more, I considered it to be important that his approach rescues our reasoning from absolute relativism and objectivism. These positions are in accordance with his main conclusion concerning language and ontology which is my next topic.

The Ontological Importance of Language

The link between "word" and "object" upon which Gadamer insists leads finally to his major aim of introducing the "universality of understanding" and the major ontological significance of language. According to Gadamer,

> we can now see that this turn from the activity of the thing itself, from the coming into language of meaning, points to a universal ontological struc-ture, namely to the basic nature of everything to which understanding can be directed. *Being that can be understood is language.* The hermeneutical phenomenon here draws into its own universality the nature of what is understood, by determining it in a universal sense of language, and its own relation to beings, as interpretation. . . . *That which can be understood is language.* (Italics mine.)[25]

Language, by including and expressing within it the being of things, is the only region in which we meet the world. Thus, our "under-standing" in order to approach any being must orient itself within language. However, Gadamer presents us with a stronger claim: that which we *always* understand is language. One needs to unravel this claim as it can attract confusing interpretations. For example, when expressing in theoretical terms the presence of a "natural law," what do we understand? A feature of the world as the law itself dictates, or the meaning of the statement the law is expressed in? This question can be plausibly raised by people who are trained to see a reality beyond thought and language, in the objectivist manner I described earlier. Despite the fact that we start from linguistic expressions, Gadamer endeavors to reveal that we are not entrapped in them. What we can understand is what the statement (formulation) of the "natural law" says; that is, its meaning. Concurrently, following the connection of "word" and "object," which Gadamer proposes, we become aware of the "natural law" itself, although not in an objectivist manner. The statement which expresses what that law is about must be considered as presenting one part of the world, an aspect of its being. The "law" does not necessarily cover the whole range and multiplicity of relationships of that aspect of the world it refers to (as it many times has been the case in physics and other sciences). Our perspective within language can eventually encounter further aspects of the "law," possibly reformulating it. Thus, Gadamer's assertion, "that which can be understood is language," must not be interpreted as if we are prisoners within language, unable to know the world at all beyond our linguistic constructions. Instead, his claim must be evaluated from a notion of language which allows us to speak and know of Being expressed in it.

Nonetheless, despite my effort to render Gadamer's propositions intelligible, one could still question him further on this topic. His approach suggests that, in order to understand anything in the world, we are bound to do it in language. It appears that although this claim is extremely strong, it needs clarification when considered in conjunction with what Gadamer says concerning the "word" and "object" connection. The question which arises is whether *all* statements, propositions, and theories represent or express something of the world, or whether they are not expressions of things in the world at all. Is it not possible that certain statements can simply be false without expressing any being at all? Are there criteria that could guarantee the representational content of statements and obviously their truth? These are questions to which Gadamer does not give any clear answers and I shall return to them when I examine his notion of "truth."

After having observed the linguisticality of human experience, the linguistic nature of all understanding and the ontological aspect of language, as Gadamer unfolds these positions it becomes evident that language is transfered to the center of focus and attention and it is the ground par excellence upon which we must search for the basic ontological features of human existence. The hermeneutic phenomenon Gadamer traced within the arts and historical studies, especially in the interpretation of texts, ultimately acquires universal dimensions.

We must also bear in mind that we are always members of linguistic communities and language is not simply a means or tool of communication which only aids understanding, as would be the case in artificial or mathematical languages. Communication "is a living process in which a community of life is lived out."[26] Gadamer believes language is able to promote human communities in its ability to *disclose* the world. In communication between humans the world disclosed by language is the common ground which all participants recognize.

If we question our own existence, in the perspective unfolded by the Gadamerian project, we discover that we are bound by the linguistic horizon we inhabit. Any process of communication and understanding the world and others occurs within this linguistic horizon. These conclusions are straightforwardly presented by Gadamer when he writes:

> Philosophical hermeneutics lays claim to universality. It bases this claim on the fact that understanding and interpretation do not mean primarily and originally a methodically trained approach to texts, but are the form in which social human life is achieved—that life which is in its ultimate formalisation a language-community. From this language-community nothing is excluded.[27]

We understand the world and others primarily within language, because of the linguistic nature of all experience, and this understanding inevitably involves interpretation. According to this line of argument we are interpretative beings and the hermeneutic attitude is a universal feature of our existence.

On "Truth"

A subject central to Gadamer's position is the notion of "truth." This concept is always located at the center of philosophical theories and determines, to a great extent, their successful or unsuccessful reception. Moreover, in the case of Gadamer's writings, there are at least two additional reasons requiring a closer examination of "truth." Firstly, it is his opposition to the univerzalizing attitude of the natural sciences, or to *objectivism,* as he terms it, and to the possible notions of "truth" that have developed along such lines. Secondly, there is a need among the social and historical sciences, which in their practice adopt certain hermeneutic conclusions, to have a clear perspective of Gadamer's approach to the notion of "truth" through his philosophical hermeneutics. It should be eventually possible to determine whether his remarks are helpful to those disciplines, or whether they belong to a philosophical discourse removed from the practices and experiences of the social sciences.

There are many passages in *Truth and Method* in which Gadamer talks of "truth," of the "truth of reality," and of tradition as well as the "claim to truth" that a text, art, or tradition make upon us. How are we going to understand these expressions and what is the core of the notion of "truth" that Gadamer proposes? We receive an initial indication at the end of *Truth and Method* when he categorically rejects the idea that in the sciences method alone can provide well-established "truths." For him, method alone is a limited and partial excursion into the discovery of truth. He says:

> The certainty that is imparted by the use of scientific methods does not suffice to guarantee truth. This is so especially of the human sciences, but this does not mean a diminution of their scientific quality, but, on the contrary, the justification of the claim to special human significance that they have always made. The fact that in the knowing involved in them the knower's own being is involved marks, certainly, the limitation of "method," but not that of science. Rather, what the tool of method does not achieve must— and effectively can—be achieved by a discipline of questioning and research, a discipline that guarantees truth.28

If, however, the methodical sciences are not the sphere where we can discover the notion of "truth" Gadamer pursues, we can turn our attention to the introduction of *Truth and Method*. He proposes to investigate modes of experience which lie beyond the methodical sciences, such as the experiences provided by philosophy, art, and history. Here, one meets *truths* that can be communicated but there is not the slightest chance that they can be verified by any method that the sciences use. One can, Gadamer contends, encounter certain claims and insights in the texts of Plato and Aristotle that one cannot either dispute or transcend in the horizon of the present "historical consciousness." "Claims to truth" are laid down in such texts and this experience cannot be substituted or provided by the methodical ways with which any scientific discipline works.

Before I begin tracing further remarks concerning "truth" in the experience of art it is useful to consult Richard Bernstein's similar attempts to understand Gadamer's notion of "truth." Bernstein arrives at the conclusion that the Gadamerian notion "is a blending of motifs that have resonances in Hegel and Heidegger."29 As in Hegel, "truth" is to be traced and brought to light in experience itself. Experiencing art or tradition or the impact a text exercises upon us, we have the opportunity to understand the "truth" within them. However, here ends the similarity, because Hegel's path leads to the overcoming of the uncertainty of experience by reason, and the perfection of knowledge which is achieved in "absolute knowledge." The Hegelian ascent of reason from experience to "absolute knowledge" results in the abolition of experience as inferior and unreflective, while, at the same time, reason (moving along gradual steps) becomes Spirit (accomplishing complete self-consciousness), within an idealist identity of consciousness and reality.[30] In an entirely opposite way Gadamer believes that "the truth of experience always contains an orientation towards new experience."[31]

The similarity with Heidegger, which Bernstein mentions, revolves around his idea of "truth" as *aletheia* or disclosure. We can grant this view certain validity since any "truth" that is revealed to us highlights aspects of "the world" (or entities in the world which are disclosed to *Dasein*, in case we use Heideggerian language), that were previously unattainable. "Truth" has made them "visible," so to speak.[32] Nevertheless, I do not consider simple reference to the Heideggerian notion of truth—particularly leaving unspecified the notion of disclosure—to render the Gadamerian view clear. Apart from the explicit reference to Hegel and Heidegger, the notion of "truth" we are searching for is difficult to pin down. Bernstein accepts the fact that "the precise meaning of truth in Gadamer's philosophy still eludes us."[33] He then elaborates on Gadamer's notion that, if we hold a view to be *true*, we are able to give convincing reasons and arguments for its validity. Finally adding the basic teaching of hermeneutics, that each member in any community is essentially an interpretative being, Bernstein concludes:

> In effect, I am suggesting that Gadamer is appealing to a concept of truth that (pragmatically speaking) amounts to what can be argumentatively validated by the community of interpreters who open themselves to what tradition "says to us."[34]

This conclusion seems to me to be partially illuminating by illustrating how truths can be arrived at and upheld especially as a result of a lack of criteria in determining what is "true" or "false." It is this side of "truth," how something can be upheld as "true" that worries Bernstein, particularly in view of "scientific truths" at which the scientific disciplines arrive. In this respect, by stressing what is argumentatively validated and shared, his conclusion does not stand at a great distance from Kuhn's proposals for upholding the dominant "scientific paradigm" as "true" or valid.[35] Yet, it also does not do justice to Gadamer's conception, because it does not question what "a truth of reality" could mean for Gadamer, nor does it question the possible relationship that can exist between "truth" and us.

It is not only in texts and in tradition that "truth" reveals itself; this also happens in art. Gadamer analyzes the concepts of "game" and "play" as illuminating examples bearing a similarity to the aesthetic experience of works of art. Art, for him, also retains a representational character through the concept of *mimesis*. He recalls all these findings, specific to aesthetic theory, when attempting to clarify what he means by "truth" in the concluding remarks of his *Truth and Method*. I will briefly mention these notions of "game" and "play" which seem to me helpful in attempting a further understanding of his notion on "truth."

In a game, players must follow the specified norms and rules. Although it is the individuals who carry on the game, nevertheless it is not them, but the goals of the game that mostly dictate the players' actions;[36] thus, in a sense, the goals of the game take over the individual players. According to Gadamer, similarly we can understand the impact of works of art upon their audience. The authority which the game exercises over its players is similar to the (normative) authority a work of art imposes upon its audience. In addition, through this relationship, works of art make a "claim to truth" upon their audience. In Gadamer's view, as we will see in the remaining pages of the present section, this "claim to truth" stems from the fact that works of art are supposed to represent "truth."

Similarly, as in the "game," Gadamer draws the relationships between the play and the actors. The actors here are what the players were for the game. In a game we saw that the players enter a "new reality" of rules and tasks that the game imposes upon them. In the example of the play this "new reality" that the actors perform is the play itself which is finally presented to the audience. However, this "new reality" is "a self-contained and meaningful structure";[37] a play in Gadamer's analysis extends its authority not only to its actors but also to its audience.[38] Thus, through this authority, the play transfers to the audience what it represents or what it is about. According to this view, art has an impact upon its audience ranging from a simple increase of their awareness by permitting other points of view, to challenging the kind of life that people take for granted. In Gadamer's opinion if art has this effect and impact upon its audience this is due to its ability to represent "truth"; it makes "a claim to truth" upon its audience. This claim involves recognition of "truth" but also of a "demand" or impact that the "truth" brings to bear upon the individual.

When we read in Gadamer that art has a representational character we discover that he does not mean that art copies reality. He uses the concept of *mimesis* not in the sense that art can mimic reality "as it is." Instead, he refers to "truths" that art can discern and extract from a number of relationships which may seem barely important or essential. In this way the representations that art offers are not of a photographic nature. In this line of argument Georgia Warnke adds:

> Through mimesis art rather reveals the truth of reality, a truth it precisely does not possess on its own. Hence works of art do not capture reality as it "really" is. They rather extricate their subject-matter from that which is considered to be inessential to it and simultaneously reveal that which is most significant.·39

Therefore, "truth" can be recovered by art and presented to its audience through the authority art exercises upon it.

Let us now move to what Gadamer claims when he moves from the aesthetic experience into the linguistic form of "truth." My aim will be to explicate the similarities which he alludes to and which exist both in art and the linguistic world in their presentation of "truth."

In art, Gadamer appealed to the notion of "play," which he feels clarifies his conception of "truth." Rather than a play, he now has "language games" in which we are immersed.40 "Language games are where we, as learners—and when do we cease to be that?—rise to the understanding of the world."41 In these language games we come to learn the "truth" available within them. As in the relation between play and actors, in which the play imposes what is to be said and performed, similarly in a "language game" we move into the boundaries of the language; language draws its players into itself. "It is the play of language itself, which addresses us, proposes and withdraws, asks and fulfils itself in the answer."42 In this quotation Gadamer draws our attention to the similarity he conceives between play and language. We can comprehend our position in language as in a game or play. However, in our case, it is language which "plays" the game ("a game with words playing around and about what is meant").

I mentioned earlier the representational character of art and its ability to be the locus of "truth." The same happens with language, although, in this case, we no longer encounter the mimetic concept of representation. In language, things (the world) are represented differently: part of their being lies in language; they "dwell" in it. This was the conclusion reached earlier when examining the strong connection of "word" and "object" proposed by Gadamer. Thus, "truths" about things in the world are supposed to be also represented or expressed in language. The notion of "truth," however, remains unclear and rather suggestive. It is difficult to see how and in what circumstances we can expect a statement to show "truth" (or perhaps to be true) with certainty. No doubt, in understanding a statement, we are bound to follow the steps of the hermeneutic experience encountered in previous pages. Nevertheless, by understanding a statement hermeneutically, do we always arrive at a "truth" and are we always capable of differentiating between "true" and "untrue?" These questions present problems to which Gadamer does not provide any concrete solutions. Instead, he insists "that the words that express an object are themselves known as a speculative event. Their truth lies in what is said in them."43 Also "what we encounter in the experience of the beautiful and in understanding the meaning of tradition has effectively something about it in the truth of play."44 We are again presented with the similarity adhering between the "truth" in the play and the "truth" in tradition.

I would suggest that we can more thoroughly comprehend this almost "eventual" relationship between "truth" and our "recognition" of it, by following Gadamer in his suggestion that art, texts, and tradition make a "*claim* to truth upon us." In the arts it is perhaps easier to imagine the situation in which "truths," represented therein, can impact upon the audience (and the way in which they are received by the individual). For example, after the experience of a play, we can conclude that the play is capable of providing us with new "knowledge" which, initially, enables us to understand and then justify, change, or reject certain beliefs we hold as true. This type of impact, gives an idea of what "the claim to truth" is upon us, originating in a play.

However, if we wish to be more precise we must look closely at the Gadamerian phrase that texts and tradition "make *a claim to truth upon us*" (*Anspruch auf Wahrheit*). I think there are two aspects of this statement that bring us nearer to what I just said concerning the example of the play. Firstly, a linguistic statement in tradition or in a text "addresses us" to what it says as true, or it makes a claim that what it says is true. This is, importantly, the point generating problems in Gadamer's presentation, especially when there is a need to recognize and decide whether such a claim can be validated. However, a second aspect of the statement emerges when considering this claim as applying to us. The "claim to truth" is extended, so to speak, *upon us*; it is "brought" upon us. To put it in other words, *truth, when discovered, cannot be ignored.* Closely following Gadamer's approach, we could confidently say that, in the course of understanding, we do not simply arrive at the truth but we must acknowledge the demand that any truth imposes or exercises upon the interpreter. Here we can appreciate the similarity with the impact, or influence, a play usually generates over its audience.

Is this a commonplace assumption? Is it not the case that any truth always influences our decisions, thus having an impact upon us to some degree? Is it not so with "scientific" truths? For example, a new formulation of a statement in physics or in chemistry considered to be true could immediately influence the technological innovations dependent upon it. However, it does not appear to me that such cases are similar to that which Gadamer describes as "true" and the demands such truths impose on us. In this example—even in danger of oversimplifying the network that exist between science and economy—we could imagine the impact of the new "scientific" statement: it could force production to new technological adaptation and to new production methods perhaps less costly and more profitable. We could also expect the adaptation of future research on lines suggested by the new paradigm. Nevertheless, such changes and responses to "scientific" truths do not necessarily alter our beliefs about the conduct of life; they do not make a *demand* on us in the sphere of practical reason. They are simply truths that can still be seen to belong firmly within the rationality of the technological era.

Returning to Gadamer, we come to grasp something that emerges as an interplay between "us" and "truth." Before I expand on it, there is another dimension to be recollected from what Gadamer has argued in a scattered fashion, concerning our approach to tradition and the truth in it that "speaks" to us. I must also recall the conclusions reached earlier concerning the historicality of our being and the nonexistence of a privileged point of view. The "claims to truth" that are made upon us when dealing with tradition, art, or the text do not intend to exhaust truth or present truth as a statement made once and for all time. Such claims can only be parts and aspects of the "truth" they attempt to "disclose." Which truth and which aspect of it we can reach or recognize depends largely upon our own "historical consciousness" and upon the available linguistic (and aesthetic) horizon in which we live. Different horizons in the past have allowed different aspects of truth to be recognized and brought forward, depending on the "historical consciousness" prevailing at the time. I wish to stress here that what we understand, or try to discover and unearth, is whatever appears *significant to us* in the "historical consciousness" we possess. Yet, this proposition does not reduce "truth" to a subjectivist attitude; in the Gadamerian view truth also *exists* as long as it can be noticed and claimed.

Equipped with these considerations, we can now proceed to the point I just mentioned: the interplay between "us" and "truth" which appears important for the concept of truth I examine. We can firmly grasp, on the one hand, the impact (demand) of truth upon us and, on the other, the historical/linguistic boundaries of our questioning of truth delineated by our "historical consciousness." In addition, our questioning and search for truth is directed by what appears *significant* to us. These are the relationships that Gadamer reveals to exist between "us" and "truth." In effect, he imbues his conception of "truth" with a strong *dialecticity* holding between the two poles. Such an approach, which in many ways echoes his Hegelian heritage, brings the conception of "truth" beyond restricted paths that observe each pole separately: ourselves on one side and "truth" on the other.

Although I have examined certain similarities which might exist (in the Gadamerian view) between the truth of play and the truth of the text, and also attempted a further understanding which involves "truth" and ourselves, still Gadamer's conception cannot be easily exhausted and many aspects of it will continue to be both debatable and illuminating. I could understand his preoccupations of refusing to present a "clear-cut' definition of truth. Any such attempt, in a specific "language game," would immediately *restrict* the notion of truth he is alluding to and his definition would be in constant danger of being unable to include a variety of potential unforeseen examples. If it is this lack of clarity that one can attribute to Gadamer, yet he makes every possible effort not to restrict us, his audience, to a very limited view of truth.

With this in mind I accept the risk and the danger of being partial in giving a supplementary view to his conception; an attempt to name something that he does not wish to name. From the previous analysis, it seems to me that "truth" does not refer to any particular observation, thus being a subject of empirical verification. Instead, through his writings, we encounter "views," "statements," opinions, and so forth, that he declares to be true. For example, the ancient Greek division between *praxis* and *techne* he considers to be an important truth that could also illuminate today's character of technological civilization.[45] Truth, for Gadamer, is not something representing ontic qualities and relationships referring, for example, to particular objects or laws of nature. On the contrary, "truth" can bring to light any-"thing" in "the world." This "world" is not the customary objectified world of the sciences but the whole known universe that includes us, our cultures, our views, and our beliefs.

Therefore, I could conclude that Gadamer's "truth" shows basic features of "the world" that can be finally seen and recognized as *aspects of Being*. This Being, seen earlier as presented in language, is the Heideggerian Being stripped from the ontic preoccupations we ascribe to it and inherited from Descartes.[46] In a vocabulary similar to that which Gadamer uses referring to the *Die Sahe*,[47] I would also argue that "truth" discloses those essential and significant features of the "world" we are able to "see" and understand and which could also influence the ways in which we conduct our life.

Although I am aware that such a formulation risks an open invitation to criticism as a restricted view, it orients our reading of Gadamer along lines which do justice to him and his ontology as well as his Heideggerian heritage. We may reject the case that there are transhistorical truths—if such a conclusion could be attributed to Gadamer's intentions—we may even reject the strong connection between "truth" and "world." Nevertheless, there is the strong element of the *dialectic* relationship between truth and ourselves which remains and is important, not only to a philosophical approach but to the social/historical disciplines which foster hermeneutic positions in their practice and self-understanding. We search for "truth" but it also responds upon us. This is a situation in line with the notion of *Bildung* that Gadamer proposes.

Bildung

We translate *Bildung* as cultivation, education, or self-formation. The concept, with a long history in German literature,[48] is employed by Gadamer to indicate the idea or the desirable state of the self that has been put forward either by philosophy or literature. The education and the cultivation of the individual in this concept is more important than the (objectivist) notions of acquiring knowledge of "reality" in which the self is absent. The most recent notion of *bildung*, as Gadamer claims, is embedded in the humanist tradition of the last few centuries, and in this context we can understand the primacy of the self-formation of the individual in comparison to any other ideal of knowledge acquisition.

Richard Rorty, in his *Mirror of Nature*, paid particular attention to the philosophical hermeneutics of Gadamer and even proposed the term "edification"[49] to stand for *bildung*. He holds that Gadamer not only distances himself from the Cartesian dualism and the Kantian "transcendental constitution," but furthermore registers the claim of "rediscovering ourselves" in view of our "existential position" and that this is the most important thing to do.

> He [Gadamer] does this by substituting the notion of *Bildung* (education, self-formation) for that of "knowledge" as the goal of thinking.
>
> From the educational as opposed to the epistemological or the technological, point of view, the way things are said is more important than the possession of truths.[50]

When Rorty refers to "knowledge" it is a restricted conception bound up in the results of the methodical disciplines and in line with the Kantian critique of "Pure Reason." Rorty's comments amplify the importance of *bildung* which, if adopted as a desirable ideal of self-formation, implies the need for a reorientation of scientific activity and introduces the primacy of the education and cultivation of the individual instead of allowing, as its central aim, either the usual picture of "representation-domination" of nature, or the "problem-solving" activity of scientific theories. Knowledge oriented to self-formation stands in direct opposition to the ideal of knowledge as technologically exploitable. I must add here that the notion of *bildung legitimates* Gadamer's project especially when he questions the unreflective character of the methodical disciplines. A similar effect is also experienced when he directs our attention to areas such as the arts, literature, and history which, in the modern technological culture, are assigned to a position where no knowledge or "truth" is expected from them. This happens because they do not conform with the norms of knowledge reached in the scientific disciplines and therefore, their role in a technocratic society is minimized.

With the notion of *bildung* I have reached the end of the short presentation and evaluation of a number of Gadamer's positions ranging from questioning the notion of "understanding" and its linguisticality, to the ontological importance of language for philosophical hermeneutics. However, it would be advantageous in the next few chapters to refer to Gadamer's view that philosophical hermeneutics has a role to play as practical philosophy, rather than being restricted to the art of interpretation, or to a discourse treating cognitive problems. Referring to the special position of hermeneutics Gadamer points out that

> even Schleiermacher, . . . appeals emphatically to the idea that the art of understanding is required not only with respect to texts but also in one's intercourse with one's fellow human beings.
>
> Thus hermeneutics is more than just a method of the sciences or the distinctive feature of a certain group of sciences. Above all it refers to natural human capacity.[51]

In this remark one can appreciate the way in which Gadamer considers the hermeneutic experience extending beyond the text into the actual dialogue of the individual within a linguistic community. However, living out a life in a community or in a society involves a range of ethical and political judgments and decisions facing both the individual and society. The problems which such judgments introduce constitute the usual core of practical reasoning. Hermeneutics, therefore, in order to enter a similar discourse as practical philosophy, must prove able to inform us on moral issues, and provide possible knowledge and insight which allows ethical and political judgment.

We are familiar with the Kantian division of Reason which forces moral problems to be treated in a distinct sphere and argumentative grounds, as ethical (philosophical) discourse, separately from knowledge produced within the scientific disciplines. Gadamer's philosophical reasoning is tuned toward the overcoming of the Kantian paradigm, a process begun in German speculative philosophy by Hegel (as mentioned in the first chapter) and reaching Heidegger. Gadamer recognizes the present situation of practical reasoning, albeit negatively, repeating that "the unity of reason remains divided also in our eyes between theoretical objectivation and practical self-determination"; "the Kantian 'solution' represents no more than the insightful recognition of the split between science and the need of reason. Certainly, it is not obsolete, but it stands there like a challenge to us to go beyond."[52] Although the hermeneutic experience allows access to all problems (of life) faced by the individual in a community and, although one could claim that moral matters and judgments on what is ethically "right" or "wrong" could be approached by hermeneutical analysis, Gadamer introduces the Aristotelian conception of practical philosophy which he finds suitable for our own moral/theoretical awareness.

One could imagine oneself introducing a hermeneutic understanding on problems involving moral issues and moral decisions. One could then claim to be in a position from which to understand the issues at hand. However, it is not this employment of hermeneutics that Gadamer proposes. For him, philosophical hermeneutics is itself a practical philosophy. It is not only concerned with the interpretation of "texts" and their understanding, but it is also involved in the experiences unfolded in the text. In the end the understanding of these experiences provides the interpreter with knowledge and insight that is appropriate to the moral issues he faces. In Gadamer words:

> Hermeneutics has to do with a theoretical attitude towards the practice of interpretation, the interpretation of texts, but also in relation to the experiences interpreted in them and in our communicatively unfolded orientations in the world. This theoretic stance only makes us aware reflectively of what is performatively at play in the practical experience of understanding.[53]

This conception of hermeneutics is better emphasized with the Aristotelian notion of *praxis* that Gadamer invokes. *Praxis* is not to be defined in opposition to theory or to science, a situation that has evolved in philosophy in the last few centuries. In its classical definition *praxis* refers to "the actuation of life of anything alive" to a way of life "that is led in a certain way (*bios*)."[54] Animals in this respect display certain *praxis* and *bios*, but, as much as it concerns human *praxis*, it specifically refers to the kind of preference and choice (*prohairesis*) human beings exhibit in choosing their specific mode of life. Thus, human *praxis* is defined upon the *prohairesis of bios* (preference of a certain life), and Aristotle applies it mainly to the responsible life of a free citizen and the particular obligations he has to perform vis-à-vis the *polis*. Following this conception of practice then, hermeneutics, with its own particular vision of knowledge and truth which includes the interplay between interpreter and text, or citizen and moral judgment, can supply the means by which to decide upon the conduct of our life.

Gadamer locates the dangerous alterations of *praxis* within the advance of technological civilization which has imposed norms and patterns of life that the individual is almost unable to choose between or to question. We live in a contemporary "deformation of *praxis*" and he warns us that consequently, practical and political reason are in danger of becoming extinct. When Gadamer discusses practical reason or practical knowledge that guides *praxis* he emphasizes the difference between *praxis* and *techne*; the latter refers to acquired skills by the expert. This difference applies to his criticism of modern society where the expert, following the rules of his learned *techne*, has become the panacea for the solution of problems that instead require distinct practical knowledge.

However, the practical knowledge that philosophical hermeneutics can supply to the individual does not solve the problem of *praxis* in a straightforward manner. The community must secure those conditions in which the individual is able to decide and free to choose upon a variety of alternatives. Furthermore, concerning moral judgment, in Aristotelian philosophy the ability to judge is exemplified by the category of *phronesis* or practical wisdom. According to Aristotle the person who exhibits such ability to pass judgment and decide upon moral/political problems in the *polis* has acquired the virtue of *phronesis* (practical wisdom). In particular circumstances, this virtue can also be thought of as a form of reasoning that mediates between the universal and the particular. It enables one to solve specific moral problems by supplying insights from the knowledge of (universal) situations that *phronesis* masters. The virtue of *phronesis* is a state of awareness and ability acquired in the course of life. In this context, philosophical hermeneutics, with its ability for "self-reflection" and its continual elevation of interpretation and discovery of "truth" and insight, appears to provide the means for reaching the state of practical wisdom. Equally, the Aristotelian concept of *phronesis* (fused within the hermeneutic tradition), because of its increased attention to self-reflection and quality of moral judgment, provides a further credible dimension to philosophical hermeneutics as practical philosophy.

4

From Cognitive Interests
to Depth Hermeneutics

The evident endeavor of Habermas to provide a consistent idea of knowledge produced in the sphere of scientific disciplines, relies upon earlier similar attempts by Peirce and Dilthey. In this chapter I will examine Habermas's analysis of Peirce's understanding of the natural sciences and Dilthey's approach to the social/historical sciences. Both writers previously reflected upon the epistemological foundations of these two groups of sciences while Habermas extends their conclusions by claiming the existence of distinct cognitive interests that regulate the formation of knowledge in these disciplines. I will analyze such claims, as well as Habermas's attempts to consider the cognitive interests employing a materialist framework of reference. The existence of such cognitive interests will indicate that these two science groups are tied to specific methodical modes for the comprehension and interpretation of reality. For this reason, I will explore in more detail, Habermas's ideas concerning the "constitution" of reality through language. As already mentioned, the concept of "emancipation" goes hand in hand with Habermas's "critical theory." However, is there an additional interest in emancipation which can justify our theoretical quest for it? Habermas believes so. Furthermore, psychoanalysis provides him with an existing scientific model for "critique" and "emancipation." What, then, are the particular features and structure of psychoanalysis, as Habermas claims, that enable it to employ both a "scientific" hermeneutical analysis and a critical character? These issues are raised in this chapter which will conclude with the main Freudian conception of society from which Habermas draws support for his own "critical theory."

The Uncovering of the Technical Interest

Before his exploration of Dilthey's writings on the methodology of the social sciences, Habermas undertakes a reading of Peirce's understanding of the methodology of the natural sciences. He feels that the theories of Peirce and Dilthey represent methodological inquiries into the mode of *self-reflection* (in its epistemological sense) within the natural and the social sciences respectively. His interest in these inquiries accords with his attack on positivism which has "disavowed reflection," as presented in the first chapter.

It is necessary at this point to clarify Habermas's terminology concerning the notion of *self-reflection within a scientific discipline.* In the first chapter I discussed the double character of reflection. In the Hegelian tradition, self-reflection refers to the process of an individual consciousness (reflecting upon itself). In the Kantian tradition, reflection acquires meaning by speculating about the transcendental conditions which make knowledge possible. Habermas makes use of both notions. The Kantian notion is employed by Habermas in order to comprehend Peirce's and Dilthey's mode of reflection, and the Hegelian notion when he deals with Freud's psychoanalytic theory. Earlier I stressed the fact that Habermas indiscriminately utilized the notion of reflection in both of the senses just mentioned. In point of fact, during the writing of his *Knowledge and Human Interests* he conflated these two notions of reflection, later trying to correct this flow by employing, instead, the notions of "reconstructive" sciences and critical sciences correspondingly.[1] Using the term *self-reflection,* as a process taking place within a scientific discipline, Habermas indicates the questioning and awareness that the scientists or the scientific community develop in examining the validity of the methodological procedures and the ways in which knowledge is possible within that particular discipline. In order to avoid the confusion of this term with the (Hegelian) notion of *self-reflection,* which refers exclusively to the self of the individual (or individuals), I will refer to Habermas's concept of the reflective process promoted within specific disciplines simply by the term *reflection.*

Habermas pays particular attention to Peirce's logic of inquiry in order to recover the level of consciousness available in the domain of the natural sciences. His justification is that Peirce understands his task, which concerns questioning not the logical structure of scientific theories, "but the logic of the procedure with whose *aid* we *obtain* scientific theories."[2] This particular change of orientation allows Peirce to connect the processes of scientific inquiries with what we understand as reality. For Peirce what reality is, coincides with what we can *truly state* about it. Obviously, such a view demonstrates a realist hypostatization of what is presented in true statements; reality is constituted according to the model of language.

As a further consequence of adopting the previous position, Peirce, in Habermas's view, also succumbed to the problems arising out of the relationship between the universal and the particular. Do universals exist as they are stated in propositions? This is especially problematic for the notion of induction which constitutes common practice in the natural sciences. We can never prove that a number of particular individual cases that we encounter (e.g., by continually repeating an experiment), will ever give a truly universal statement (law). As Hume has clearly demonstrated, we cannot logically deduce universal statements (laws) from any number of particular individual cases.[3]   Nevertheless, according to Peirce, we infer the universal statement and consider it as true. Thus, induction, one form of "synthetic inference,"[4] appears to be possible. Additionally, Peirce needed to do justice to the existence of the universal, for example, to a law of nature, indicated by a universal statement. Although an antinominalist, he did not adopt a totally realist view, thereby implying the autonomous existence of universals or, similarly, that the particular cases we come across necessarily confirm the independent existence of universals. According to Habermas, Peirce reconciles realism with the principles of a transcendental (not empirical) philosophy, remaining satisfied with a limited notion of reality derived from the logic of language. From this perspective, reality is constituted through the grammatical form of universal propositions.

In order to understand Peirce's approach we need to examine it more closely. The reading and questioning Habermas directs toward Peirce demonstrates the latter's preference for a nonrealist concept of reality; indeed, a preference for a Kantian conception in which reality is constituted within certain transcendental (nonempirical) conditions. Peirce identified such conditions as the dominant features of the process of scientific inquiry. As such, they are modes of inference and, within their framework, reality is objectified[5] in such a way that we are able to understand the relationship between the universal and the particular. In simple terms, our logic of inquiry shapes the reality we come to know. As Habermas says, following Peirce

within the framework posited with the process of inquiry we constitute the objects of possible experience such that reality is disclosed in a definite constellation of the universal and the particular. This constellation can be demonstrated in the modes of inference on which the progress of inquiry logically depends.[6]

Thus, we are required to think of reality as constituted in a manner which accounts for all objects of possible experience. The consequent knowledge derived from our experience is thus based on the transcendental framework of inquiry. What we then accept as "particular" or "universal" depends upon the mode of inquiry and the specific relationship the inquiry has established between them.

We can now follow the steps that permit Habermas to discuss a knowledge-constitutive interest. According to him, Peirce, after demonstrating the logical rules of the process of inquiry (inferences), is unable to validate them. The logical patterns, followed during the inquiry, cannot be either demonstrated through formal logic or grounded empirically. Peirce can no longer appeal to a structure of reality which dictates the patterns of inference. Habermas stated that such a situation poses "a transcendental-logical question about the conditions of possible knowledge."[7]

Peirce resolved this difficulty by appealing to the "objective life context" within which the inquiry takes place. In such a context, the inquiry helps to strengthen (scientific) beliefs by removing uncertainty. The inquiry's conclusions become at best beliefs that are held to be true. His concept of truth then is not derived in a Kantian manner (by appealing to transcendental logical categories), but by turning toward the pragmatic life context itself. A belief orients one's behavior; "belief consists mainly in being deliberately prepared to adopt the formula believed in as the guide of action."[8] Habermas concluded that beliefs are behavioral rules and what Peirce presents is the behavioral system of purposive-rational action.

> Valid beliefs are universal propositions about reality that, under given initial conditions and on the basis of conditional predictions, can be transformed into technical control.[9]

Such an attitude, Habermas argued, is the actual content of Peirce's pragmatism. In scientific theories, concepts and judgments which are derived from "syllogistic reasoning" (deduction and abduction) fulfill their meaning in a context of possible "feedback-controlled action." Failures or successes in implementing the knowledge achieved remove behavioral uncertainty. This is, nevertheless, the framework of *instrumental action*, in which knowledge is employed as an instrument. Habermas can therefore conclude that "knowledge stabilises, purposive-rational, feedback-monitored action in an environment objectified from the point of view of possible technical control."[10] Therefore, knowledge in the natural sciences is not the outcome of an instinctual curiosity. Instead, the process of inquiry, based upon a transcendental framework, establishes the necessary conditions for the proliferation of technically exploitable knowledge.

However, remaining at this level of speculation, we do not arrive at an adequate conclusion concerning the reasons behind the development of such a process of inquiry aiming at the exclusive production of technically exploitable knowledge. Habermas quickly fills the gap by regarding knowledge of this kind as functioning as a substitute for "instinctive behavioral steering." This is a thought Peirce himself adopted. Peirce argued that both the methodology of inquiry and the corresponding behavioral patterns of action in the process of evolution, provide a substitute to lost animal mechanisms for direction and survival. Accepting that knowledge functions as an instrument for survival and technical control, Habermas concludes that the rationality of feedback-controlled action can be thought of in terms of a cognitive *interest* which continually tries to realize itself. At this point Habermas exhibits a strong naturalism by presenting the notion of a cognitive interest in close relation to the action of instinct. As the instinct drives the human activity to a gratification of a need, similarly the cognitive interest could fulfill the "need" for knowledge. However, unlike the gratification of an instinct, which leads to happiness, Habermas proposes that the fulfillment of the cognitive interest is bound up with success. Such success is evaluated with reference to "problem solutions that have both a life function and a cognitive function."[11] Already, the ambivalent position of a cognitive interest of this kind, which he calls : "technical interest," begins to emerge. It cannot be either entirely empirical because not reducible to the familiar idea of an instinct, nor an entirely a priori interest since it cannot be removed from the context of life processes. According to Habermas,

> in this at first negatively delimited sense we speak of a *knowledge-constitutive interest in possible technical control,* which defines the course of the objectification of reality necessary within the transcendental framework of processes of inquiry.[12] [Habermas's italics]

Concerning the dual quasi a priori character of the technical interest, Habermas contends that it suits both the "empirical character" of the species in their emergence, as well as the "intelligible character" of a community which, in its evolutionary process, from a transcendental point of view, constitutes the reality surrounding it.

At this stage, it is not necessary to examine the remarks Habermas directs against the limitations of Peirce and his underlying positivism inhibiting the completion of his reflection on the natural sciences. It is also worth mentioning that Peirce did not pay particular attention to the "community of investigators" who find themselves beyond the limits specified by the knowledge for technical control over objectified natural processes. These investigators, according to Habermas, communicate between themselves and enter "symbolic interaction" through language. They introduce actions aiming at communication and understanding, or what Habermas terms "communicative action." Such "communicative action" can neither be understood nor reduced to the framework of instrumental action that Peirce pursued. It is Dilthey who began an investigation into this aspect of knowledge and understanding.

Dilthey on the Hermeneutic Sciences

Habermas turns to Dilthey in order to pursue this reflection on the cultural sciences[13] which the latter achieved through his systematic studies. We saw earlier that Habermas pointed to the presuppositions accompanying any discipline in the natural sciences. On the one hand, there exist communication structures allowing communication between scientists; on the other, these structures indicate a common cultural background at the level of prescientific knowledge. Such knowledge is articulated through *ordinary* language constituting the horizon within which the community of scientists moves. This horizon is embedded in the cultural life context which in turn is based upon levels of intersubjectivity. Natural sciences cannot analyze or reflect upon the intersubjectivity and communication forming their background. Rather, it is the cultural sciences which consider the cultural life context as their object of study.

Within this formal separation of natural and cultural sciences Habermas asks whether the cultural sciences proceed in a different methodological framework and whether, finally, they are constituted by a different cognitive interest than that of the natural sciences. Dilthey undertook this line of investigation and Habermas follows his reasoning which involved the incorporation of hermeneutics into the cultural sciences. Dilthey's attempts also provide Habermas with the means by which to introduce a new cognitive interest, underlying the knowledge claims of the cultural sciences. In order to follow Habermas's argument, it is necessary to keep in mind certain central positions of Dilthey's theory which Habermas either accepts or occasionally rejects.

According to Dilthey the two different sets of sciences (the natural and the cultural sciences) have not been established upon some ontological difference of their object of study. The objects of their research, nature, and society respectively, cannot themselves impose a logical and legitimate separation of the two groups of sciences; rather, it is an *epistemological separation*. This happens because what we term *nature* and what is considered as "social objects," are *constituted* differently. For example, "nature" (its objects and phenomena) is accessible to us through language and further elaborate conceptions are processed through scientific theories. However, these available conceptions, and their function and corresponding scientific approaches to nature, must be referred to the orientations of the cognitive subject. The same applies to our knowledge of the social/cultural world: it has to be referred to the orientations (interests and aims) of the cognitive subject toward society. Dilthey's approach is Kantian in its perspective and comprehends both nature and society not as something given and existing on their own, but as constituted.

Although Dilthey's understanding of the natural sciences is not so advanced as Peirce's, following, as it does, the Kantian view on these sciences, Habermas contends that even such a limited view delineates the background from which Dilthey draws the distinctions concerning the methodological aspects of the social sciences. In the natural sciences we proceed with experimentation and close observation, the natural objects treated (objectified) according to categories of "number," "space," "time," and "mass." In the cultural sciences the "experience" that the subject receives is unrestricted. Unlike the processes in the natural sciences the subject's approach is not limited within categories for the experience of "social objects." Moreover, in the cultural sciences, the background of perceptual responses and knowledge accumulated at a prescientific level of experience (i.e., popular, commonsense knowledge about the social world) is recalled and plays a part in assessing new scientific experiences.

A further difference between the two groups of sciences is that, according to Dilthey, whereas the natural sciences aim at the formulation of theories and laws that can be controlled by experience, in the cultural sciences the theories or descriptions finally formulated help the "transposition" and "penetration" of understanding into alien expressions of life. In the cultural sciences it is the act of understanding that dominates the mode of inquiry. In Dilthey's view the cultural sciences achieve a "mental reconstruction" of what is available socially and historically. They attempt to recover what has already been objectivated.

The cultural sciences incorporate, primarily by taking the immeasurably expanding historical-social reality, as it is given only in its external manifestations or in effects, or as a mere product, the objectivated sediment of life, and translating it back into the living mental state in which it arose, ... we have here, the process of translating back into the fullness of life through a sort of transposition.[14]

For Dilthey, the historical life is an objectivation of mind. He proposed an "empathy theory" which views the understanding of "expressions of life"[15] via a model of knowing the psychic states of others. Concerning a critique of these ideas, I have already mentioned how Gadamer rejected Dilthey's claim that it is possible to re-create meaning intended by the author, or to re-create the psychic states of others. Keeping in mind these differences that Dilthey raises between the social and the natural sciences, I will now examine the introduction of hermeneutics in the social sciences by Habermas who, in his attempt, draws considerably upon the work of Dilthey.

Hermeneutics in the Social Sciences

Hermeneutic understanding, according to Habermas, is directed at the "traditional context of meanings." By this he means everyday experiences, dialogic situations, and all possible symbolic relations forming the life context in which we find ourselves immersed. Whenever hermeneutic understanding is directed toward deciphering "meaning" it becomes problematic, especially in its employment by the cultural sciences. The "meaning" that these sciences approach is supposedly "factual" or strongly connected to an empirical situation, such as when we deal with the "meaning" of a social activity, or the meaning of an institution. But how can such empirical situations be treated in a hermeneutics which resides in linguistic analysis? Additionally, there exists the problem of understanding hermeneutically individual life experiences and yet still remain able to express them in general terms (concepts) of language. How is this connection of the particular and the general possible?

Habermas observes that we do not possess rules of traditional meaning structures. If this were the case we would be able to reconstruct these rules and apply them for understanding symbolic relations, everyday dialogue, and so forth, as is the case in formalized languages. In such languages we can actually form any possible statement basing ourselves upon the explicit rules that determine their constitution. Unlike formalized languages, in the case of traditional meaning we find ourselves dealing with ordinary language; here a lack of such rules necessitates the introduction of the hermeneutic approach for understanding meaning. Moreover, Habermas believes that symbolic relations (e.g., a gesture, a ritual, or the utterance of a phrase), beyond their grammatical structure, must be apprehended as relations of fact. In this sense they retain their empirical facticity and thus allow scientific analysis. These positions indicate that, for Habermas, hermeneutics is both a grammatical analysis and a form of experience.

In dialogic situations of everyday language we share the experience of being understood and of being able to understand others. According to Habermas, there must be a specific feature in the structure of ordinary language that permits whatever is individual to be expressed in general terms and to be understood by others. Although this is an old and persevering philosophical problem, he approaches it via Dilthey's efforts. Dilthey employed hermeneutics in his attempt to solve the same problem arguing that, in dialogue, hermeneutic forms of understanding are at work and possess this ability of making individual cases communicable.

In Dilthey's exposition hermeneutic understanding is directed at three classes of life expressions he named "linguistic expressions," "actions," and "experiential expression" (i.e., bodily expressions, gestures, and other bodily responses that are connected to psychological phenomena). This classification offered by Dilthey is valuable; firstly, in that he argues that each life expression necessarily requires hermeneutic understanding and, secondly, in his expanded view that hermeneutics ventures into domains which lie beyond its initial employment in understanding texts. Meanings are always objectivated in these three categories of life expression and furthermore, there always appears to be a gap between the objectivated meaning and the real life context that it indicates. It is this gap which necessitates the employment of hermeneutic understanding. For example, in the case of the dialogic use of language, an attempt to understand the linguistic expression of another person in a straightforward manner always appears to leave a distance between the meaning understood by the receiver and what exactly is meant by the individual who uttered it in his own specific life relations. Hermeneutic understanding and interpretation, then, are called upon for minimizing this distance.

A similar distance between objectivated meaning and life context is also apparent in understanding actions. According to Dilthey, actions express the mental content and the intentions of the subject involved in them. It follows that there is always a relationship between actions and intended meaning. Each one of us bears in mind this picture of intended meaning, thus permitting interaction between people and reciprocal anticipation of behavior. But even here hermeneutic understanding is mandatory. No action can ever fully reveal the intended meaning of the individual, as such meaning has been structured around the individual's own life context. The receiver must employ hermeneutic procedures in order to give an interpretation of the other's action. Thus, the gap between the objectivated meaning in action and the original life conditions of the individual who performed the action is removed. Habermas, satisfied with this account of Dilthey concerning the justification of the employment of hermeneutics beyond the text, proceeds to describe the hermeneutic procedures with which Dilthey deals. These are more or less similar to those I examine in the second and third chapters and concern the involvement of preunderstandings, the reciprocal movement between parts and whole, and the admittance of the hermeneutic circle that appears within any hermeneutic activity.

It is very revealing at this point to recognize the ways in which Habermas "reads" hermeneutic expectations in the cultural sciences. The notion of the hermeneutic circle appears to him to be rather restrictive, possibly constituting a permanent dilemma for the social sciences. If the practice of interpretation, he argues, occurs entirely in linguistic form, or entirely in a form of empirical analysis, then it will be circular and unable to provide the expected results. Because of this double character of the objects of the cultural sciences, the circle appears only when they are approached singly: either as linguistic objects, or as empirical data. Nevertheless, he contends, there is a way out of the circle. This escape route would arise "if the objects of hermeneutic understanding could be viewed not as linguistic objects but as experiential data"[16] as well.

It seems to me that this claim by Habermas is rather unfounded, although it could be alternatively modified. To do this we can recall Gadamer's analysis of the linguisticality of all experience, and the fundamental position that there cannot be any (communicable) experience without the availability of a corresponding concept present in language. The objects of the cultural sciences to which Habermas refers, even if viewed in their empirical context and empirical relations, are communicated and understood in linguistic form. There always must exist a nonidentity of concept and reality; otherwise the two would collapse. Therefore, there is no escape from the linguistic interpretation of experiential data which Habermas seeks. He considers reference to the empirical (data) as having the ability to eliminate the circular movement that proceeds between parts and whole in the interpretive attempt. Perhaps, for Habermas, an empirical analysis could view the parts (the experiential data) as being captured and expressed in concrete and definite (unchangeable) statements. Thus, there would be no need for the circle to arise for a new evaluation of such data. Nevertheless, this is obviously wrong, because such certainty is not available; it could only arise in some "mirror theory of truth" which would force reality (the referent) and concept (received data) in a relationship of total correspondence. In such a naive approach what our observations and experiences state has an exact mirror-image in reality. However, this is not true; we always appreciate experience and data through (contingent) categories and theories usually altering in time. Our experiences in the cultural world are interpretations, not rigid, mirrorlike, relationships between statements (of experience) and their referent. The interpretive circle that Habermas fears, mainly occurs in textual interpretation where, apparently, grammatical analysis and understanding of the individual words and their connections continually takes place, upsetting previously achieved interpretations. What I believe Habermas wishes to elucidate—although unsuccessfully—is that, in the case of hermeneutic procedures in the cultural sciences, the circle cannot rely exclusively upon the initial linguistic expressions with which one approaches the objects of study. Fresh empirical evidence and empirical contents can supply and enrich the hermeneutic procedure. This can occur if the researcher/interpreter is not exclusively preoccupied with grammatical forms of meaning, but allows new empirical information—albeit in linguistic form—to enter the interpretation. However, the interpretive circle will always be present.

Later in this chapter, we will encounter a more persuasive attempt by Habermas to eliminate entirely the hermeneutic circle. He ventures this attempt by claiming validity for general interpretational theories (as in the cases of Freud and Marx) which substitute the "whole" in the interpretive circle. In this way, the "whole" (general theory) is valid and the need for apprehending it, beginning with the parts (individual cases) in repeated circular efforts, is removed. However, as I will argue, it will always be the case that any general interpretational theory, although referring to an empirical content, must be considered as an interpretation which cannot claim either absolute truth or transhistorical validity. It may fall prey to the hermeneutic circle at any time.

Alongside his concern for epistemological certainty Habermas wishes to claim that interpretation can be considered as linguistic analysis and, simultaneously, can assume the role of empirical analysis. Hermeneutic understanding is capable of bringing to light individual cases within their own life context and analyzing their grammatical structures for the deciphering of their meaning. Such a claim, which seems to me correct, legitimates the adoption of hermeneutics within the social/historical sciences and, furthermore, demonstrates "hermeneutics' immediately *practical relation to life*" (Habermas's italics).[17]

Interest and Cognition

The fundamental relationship of hermeneutics to practical life as the means of understanding and communication, is echoed in the words of Dilthey.

> Understanding first arises in the interests of practical life. Here people are *dependent* on intercourse with one another. They *must* make themselves understandable to one another. One must know what the other wants. (Italics mine.)[18]

In order to understand others we must approach their expressions (linguistic activity, actions, and experiential expressions). Such expressions, however, are immersed in the life context of the individual. Hermeneutic understanding is necessary in order to approach the horizon of this life context and thus more accurately interpret the life expressions of the other.[19] From such a position, it follows that there exists an *interest* in involving hermeneutics in practical life with an almost apparent aim of action-orientation. Practical life cannot be thought of without the element of activity; communication and mutual understanding between people shape the particular orientations for human activity. This is the model in which Habermas believes, although it attracts its critics who would avoid an immediate connection between understanding and action.[20]

As hermeneutic understanding is employed by the cultural sciences, Habermas argues that the same interest we just met, also underlies these sciences. Nevertheless, the understanding that accompanies the conduct of everyday life occurs within ordinary language and allows people to interact reciprocally. Thus, for Dilthey and Habermas, the hermeneutic sciences are similarly oriented toward interactions that take place within ordinary language. In contrast we have seen that the natural sciences were concerned with the behavioral system implied by instrumental action. Habermas, then, can conclude that

> both [groups of science] are governed by *cognitive interests* rooted in the life contexts of communicative and instrumental action. Whereas empirical-analytic methods aim at disclosing and comprehending reality under the transcendental viewpoint of possible technical control, hermeneutic meth-

ods aim at maintaining the intersubjectivity of mutual understanding in ordinary-language communication and in action according to common norms. In its very structure hermeneutic understanding is designed to guarantee, with cultural traditions, the possible action-orienting self-understanding of individuals and groups as well as reciprocal understanding between different individuals and groups.(Habermas's italics.)[21]

There are a number of things to be analyzed in this theoretical position adopted by Habermas. Firstly, how can we comprehend that the interest behind the cultural sciences, which Habermas calls *practical interest* due to its involvement in practical life, has a cognitive character? Secondly, what does Habermas mean when he ascribes to the cultural sciences the aim of "maintaining the intersubjectivity of human understanding?" Initially, these claims might sound quite strange in comparison to common beliefs about the practice of the social and political sciences.

Concentrating on my first question, there is a crucial reason which supports the cognitive nature of the practical interest. I previously mentioned that, in order to understand others via their life expressions, we must hermeneutically approach the life context in which such expressions are rooted. This involvement, necessary in social life, indicates our interest in communication and mutual understanding with others. However, the completion of this hermeneutic activity of understanding permits one to know, to a certain extent, the life context of the other person. Understanding someone's expressions (statements and bodily movements) in these circumstances results in knowledge because this effort encompasses, beyond the immediate grasp of the meaning of a statement or an activity, the understanding of further dimensions (social, historical, and rational) of the life context of another person. There is no doubt, nevertheless, that this notion of *knowledge* is quite different from the methodical knowledge of the natural sciences; it only makes sense in a broader conception of knowledge characteristic of the hermeneutic understanding as argued in the third chapter when talking about knowledge in the arts, in literature, or in history. Therefore, the interest in understanding others, which appears as an imperative in actual life, involves a *cognitive* process. The attribution then of a cognitive character to the practical interest is justifiable.

Arriving now at the second of my questions concerning the aim of the cultural sciences, that is, "to maintain intersubjectivity," we could observe the following: Habermas considers communication between people and mutual understanding as a *condition of survival*. We receive this image more convincingly if, as he suggests, we consider, if only for a moment, the consequences of a societal communication breakdown; as a result the survival of the species itself would immediately be threatened. The condition of maintaining communication and mutual understanding, then, is as important as the condition of survival dependant upon successful instrumental action. Here again, the naturalistic attitude of Habermas is evident when he accepts communication and intersubjective understanding as the basic natural conditions which accompany the species in their evolutionary process (consisting of learning and problem-solving activities). Such a view has a potent empirical stronghold but is also enclosed within a theoretical framework in which history is seen as an evolutionary process of the species aiming at self-formation (*bildung-prozess*) under certain empirical conditions of survival: that is, successful technical control over nature and freely attained intersubjectivity allowing "undisturbed communication" and "unconstrained consensus." According to Habermas, these two goals are the presuppositions of "practice" in a free (non repressive) society.[22]

The practical interest aims at the *preservation of communication* in ordinary language. Nevertheless, if we contemplate the popular image of the cultural sciences, could we claim for them the same aim? There appears to be quite a distance between a basic interest in communication and the practice of scientific disciplines, which would not necessarily claim such an aim. The significant point, however, in Habermas's view, is that the cultural sciences are based upon practical interest as the possible objects of experience within their area of study are constituted by this same interest. Therefore, they share the same aim together with this practical interest in the maintenance of communication and intersubjectivity which ultimately leads to the practical values of "unconstrained agreement" and "nonviolent recognition." Such an idea, I think, might appear strange and alien to a social scientist, mainly due to the positivist orientations of instrumental rationality (for control and domination) which are widespread in the social/historical sciences at present.

Notwithstanding my previous comments, there appears to be no reason why the cultural sciences, in the course of their practice and development, should not change direction while their basic founding principle is the practical interest in maintaining understanding and intersubjectivity with others. Naturally, in such a case we might have the *paradoxical* situation that the cultural sciences, on the one hand, are based upon hermeneutic structures and, as such, bound to the aim of communication and intersubjectivity; on the other, their results are used in an instrumental rationality resulting in the exercise of control, power, and domination upon groups or individuals in society.

If this is the case, the distance between the practice of the cultural sciences and their "normative foundations," with which Habermas provides them, can be met and explained. However, Habermas's aim is, firstly, to display the hidden rationality and *interest* that underlies the cultural sciences despite their positivist and "scientistic" facade and, secondly, to install the practical interest as a strong normative foundation within these sciences.

At this point, examining Habermas's attention to communication and our communicative actions, certain affinities but also differences begin to emerge in comparison to Gadamer. Certainly, the importance Habermas grants to the hermeneutic procedures involved in understanding each other and ourselves is on a par with the views of Gadamer. Habermas shares with Gadamer (and Heidegger) the idea of the human predicament in dialogue and understanding that reveal the structure of the hermeneutic approach. For Habermas, however, this is only one aspect of the human condition. *Interaction* between people, the category he uses to comprehend the notion of communication, is merely complementary to the category of *work* that the human species is subjected to for the reproduction of its life. In his own tradition, Gadamer is preoccupied with the structure of understanding in any possible situation that, finally, reveals the existential position of human beings; such an approach is treated in a philosophical context. Alternatively, Habermas's emphasis lies on "dialogue," considered as *communication*. He transforms it into a possible subject of a reconstructive scientific analysis in his "universal pragmatics."23 The orientation toward the scientific treatment of communicative patterns and competences, which leads him into the area of linguistics, illustrates both the distance he wishes to maintain from existential philosophical positions, and also his belief that certain philosophical problems can be transformed and analyzed at a scientific level. Although this indicates certain disagreements between Habermas and Gadamer, I will discuss the main corpus of differences and similarities between the two writers in the next two chapters.

Interpretation of Reality and the Species

Applying his Kantian transcendental approach, in order to explicate the epistemological presuppositions of the cultural sciences, Habermas concludes that the practical interest also establishes the *conditions of objectivity* of possible experience in the cultural world. How are we to understand such a philosophical view of reality? We saw earlier that the *technical* cognitive interest establishes the transcendental conditions (of what are the objects) of experience in nature. In a behavioral system of instrumental action it is action itself (for possible technical control) which determines what reality is. However, according to Habermas, in the context of communicative action that characterizes the cultural world, it is no longer "action" that provides the transcendental framework. Instead, such a framework is provided by the grammar of ordinary language. At this point his argument becomes complicated and therefore needs careful examination in order to perceive the picture of language and world he proposes in *Knowledge and Human Interests.*

Habermas, here, by following a Kantian epistemological approach faces the problem of the "constitution" of the world. In what terms can the *constitution* of the world be thought of? How is it possible that we have acquired *objective* experiences in such a world, that is, experiences shared by all members of the linguistic community? Although following a Kantian mode of questioning, Habermas does not imitate the Kantian solution. He does not introduce a priori categories in a Kantian fashion. Instead, he appeals to transcendental (not empirical) structures of grammatical rules which can be approached through the empirical study of language and of language games. His answers are woven around the notion of grammatical rules governing specific language games, a notion that he draws from the later Wittgenstein. Such rules link symbols (language), actions, and expressions. The form of life in which we find ourselves can be referred to these grammatical rules. These forms of life also *constitute* the reality in which we live in ways that ordinary language dictates. Habermas then reaches the conclusion that.

> reality is constituted in a framework that is the form of life of communicating groups and is organised through ordinary language. What is real is that which can be experienced according to the interpretations of a prevailing symbolic system.[24]

At any particular moment, people, groups, or communities have developed and live in life-forms in which reality has been already constituted and interpreted through their particular language.

Nonetheless, how does this happen? The argument of Habermas is rather sketchy and the total absence of examples, or of possible concrete empirical cases, makes it very suggestive. To begin with, he believes that community life is organized around ordinary language and that this language is governed by grammatical rules. Apart from this aspect of language, we can also conceive of the existence of language games that connect language with action. If we consider the well-known example of chess, where the rules of the game determine the action of the players (e.g., following the legitimate moves, or the best strategies for winning the game), then, similarly—but not explicitly—grammatical rules of ordinary language give rise to certain (*transcendental*) *structures* from which the linguistic community interprets reality for purposes of communication and action-orientation. The grammar of language games "establishes schemata of world interpretation and interaction."25 The grammatical rules of language involved in the process of life (here we must think of both grammar and syntax, e.g., tenses of verbs, transitive or intransitive verbs, and syntactical patterns determining the position of the subject in relation to the object) result in transcendental (not empirical) structures, which constitute, in part, the background of any life-form and determine the ways in which the members of the community "see" (interpret) reality. Any interpreter, as a member of the community and as a participant in such a form of life, "moves" at the level of such transcendental structures.

Therefore, what we "see" as reality is a *specific interpretation* based upon a system of grammatical rules which govern our symbolic system of interaction (language included). In this cycle of communication and interpretation of reality, ordinary language stands at the center around which life is organized. Ordinary language "constitutes" reality, that is, its conceptions and grammatical rules determine what can be experienced as real. We cannot experience beyond that which ordinary language "allows" or "constitutes." In other words, a life-form and the interpretations of it that its participants hold, revolve around the ordinary language in use and the structure of its grammatical rules.

All these happen at the prescientific level in the context of the "life-world." If we approach the region of sciences in order to examine the way in which they arrange their object-domains we encounter the logic which characterizes the natural and cultural sciences. Habermas's readings of Peirce and Dilthey aimed at recovering their achieved reflections upon the logical processes in both groups of sciences. Their logic, he states, reveals the "methodological rules for the organisation of the process of inquiry."26 We saw earlier that the framework guiding the natural sciences with the aim of possible technical control, "constitutes" nature in view of this particular goal and expectation. Habermas calls this framework transcendental, based upon the *technical* cognitive interest. However, he moves one step further in attempting to ground the frameworks of both the natural and the cultural sciences in a "materialist" idea describing the development of the species. He contends that it is not the rules of inquiry that are transcendental but only their function. Both methodological systems of rules have risen from *structures* of human life itself. The species is supposed to employ, for the reproduction of its life, learning processes amid socially organized labor. The species also finds itself in processes of dialogue, mutual understanding, and symbolic interactions. These are inescapable, empirical conditions of life, and according to Habermas, exhibit a fundamental "interest structure." Thus, we can follow Habermas's "reduction" of the transcendental character of the methods of inquiry, about which he speculated in an epistemological manner, to forms of life.

> The reduction of the framework of the monological and hermeneutic sciences to a *structure of human life* and the corresponding derivation of the meaning of the validity of statements from cognitive interests is necessary as soon as a transcendental subject is replaced by a *species* that reproduces itself under cultural conditions, that is, *that constitutes itself* in a self-formative process. (Habermas's italics.)[27]

The conception of a species that reproduces itself in a process that primarily characterizes the formation of the self (*bildungprozess*), permits the idea of history to be thought of as exclusively within the life context of the species. Habermas claims that he borrows this conception from Hegel and Marx.[28]

However, if the hermeneutic sciences can be reduced to the self-formation process of the species, further remarks concerning the approach of these sciences to their object-domain, must be made. Habermas argues that, unlike the natural sciences, the hermeneutic sciences do not establish a specific transcendental framework upon reality via their method of inquiry. I mentioned earlier that the transcendental condition of reality, in each specific community and form of life, has already been achieved through the structure of the specific grammatical rules of their ordinary language in use. The hermeneutic sciences direct their inquiries toward these transcendental structures. According to Habermas, their hermeneutic statements, although concerned with structures, finally "grasp interpretations of reality" with the aim of intersubjectivity and the orientation of action. Here, we encounter another instance in which Habermas incorporates the teachings of the hermeneutic tradition. If we recall Gadamer's position with regard to the understanding of a text, the conclusion was that one cannot simply comprehend its meaning at the first attempt. The horizon of the text, or the life context to which it belongs, must also be approached. Similarly, in Habermas's account, an interpretation of reality held within the life-form of a community cannot simply be approached by examining the symbolic interactions of such a community. The interpreter must approach the transcendental structures (systems of grammatical rules of ordinary language) that have shaped the particular interpretation. From this, we could conclude that hermeneutics have enabled Habermas to claim that interpretations of reality, embedded in specific forms of life, do not reveal their meaning unless first considered in the contextual background of the transcendental structures from which they originate.

The Interest of Reason

Although Habermas "reduced" the technical and practical cognitive interests to structures of the life of the species, so that they lose their transcendental nature, he is nevertheless in need of further support and argumentation for his idea of the universal condition of the species engaged in *work* and *interaction*. According to him, the "reproduction of life" is culturally determined by these two categories of "work" and "interaction" within the context of the species discovering itself in a process of self-formation. The cognitive interests mediate and shape the natural history of the species, although, as Habermas confesses, he cannot demonstrate such a claim but merely assert it.[29] We are evidently presented here with a *philosophical anthropology* to which his conception of "interest" and the species leads. Moreover, philosophical argumentation of this kind can never supply any "demonstration" (empirical or scientific) he would desire for his claims. Hence, Habermas needs to support his "philosophical anthropology" further and he does so by "locating" a third interest that appears to be embedded in Reason itself: an emancipatory cognitive interest.

Peirce and Dilthey, according to Habermas, did not sufficiently comprehend what they were dealing with in their reflection upon the formation of the sciences and in their processes of inquiry in relation to objective life structures. Otherwise, they would have maintained contact with the Hegelian notion of *reflection* as it is exemplified in the *Phenomenology*. Again, at this point, Habermas conflates the two notions of "reflection" and puts on a similar par the "self-reflection" that characterizes the ascending of the "subject" in the *Phenomenology*, with the transcendental (Kantian) reflection on the formation of scientific disciplines (raised in the first chapter).

However, in his discussion of "self-reflection," we could locate at least one reason for this conflation. In the Hegelian paradigm of self-reflection, consciousness (of the subject) reflecting upon itself transcends itself and moves, progressively, to a more complete notion of itself on its route to "total" or absolute knowledge. When Habermas examines the case of (Kantian) reflection on the processes of inquiry in the scientific disciplines—which Peirce and Dilthey began to accomplish—we may assume that he considers this reflective instance as a "moment" in this (Hegelian) category of "self-reflection." We can argue that, following Habermas's train of thought, the Kantian (transcendental) reflection can reveal developmental stages of consciousness in the history of the species. If the species has adopted two different processes of inquiry and two different attitudes in its self-formation (natural and cultural sciences), then a reflection upon such features and their comprehension can lead to the understanding of the phylogenetic aspects in the development of any individual. Such knowledge could be considered as an awareness of the formation of the self in the broad patterns of societal and historical processes. We know, however, that Habermas *collapses* this knowledge together with the awareness arrived at when an individual reflects upon his own actual self-history (the ontogenetic process). Although both cases of reflection contribute to an awareness of the *formation of the self*, in the specific ways just mentioned, the former indicates only the general background (linguistic rules, logical rules, and logical features of interpreting reality) the individual shares with everybody else in the community. Obviously, these two types of reflection, in opposition to Habermas's conflation, are two separate types of self-knowledge and awareness.[30]

Habermas characterizes the Hegelian notion of "reflection" as *emancipatory*. The "subject," through the experience of "self-reflection," becomes *transparent* to itself by knowing the process of its own genesis and formation; such a state of consciousness that disposes of obstacles and untrue beliefs about the self can be considered as an emancipation from previous states of consciousness and modes of life. The "master-slave" relationship in the *Phenomenology* is the primary example in which the process of self-reflection brings an emancipatory state to the consciousness and consequently to the activity of the "slave," enabling him to overcome his condition. Habermas then, following his usual tactics of providing firmer (if possible, empirical) foundations to the conceptions of speculative philosophy, is presented with the arduous question concerning the reasons which lead one to the activity of self-reflection. He conceives of the drive to "self-reflection" to be dominated by an interest that can only be attributed to Reason itself. He actually claims that such an attitude for Reason toward itself is well illustrated in the case of Reason pursuing "autonomy and responsibility." At this point, he is after an historical and philosophical justification for his claim, since "autonomy and responsibility" are the categories which Kant employs in order to describe the commitment of Enlightenment.[31]

> In self-reflection, knowledge for the sake of knowledge comes to coincide with the interest in autonomy and responsibility (*Mündigkeit*). For the pursuit of reflection knows itself as a movement of emancipation. Reason is at the same time subject to the interest in reason. We can say that it obeys an *emancipatory cognitive interest*, which aims at the pursuit of reflection.[32]

The notion of "self-reflection," as it appears in the German speculative tradition and later in Marxism,[33] is significant for Habermas because, as it will become apparent, it occupies the core of his views on what a "critical science" could be.

Therefore, one of the main problems Habermas must deal with is "the riddle" of "self-reflection." If the power of "self-reflection" can lead to emancipatory processes and to new attitudes toward life, where does it come from? Is there an emancipatory interest in Reason itself as he argues? Is this interest identical to the drive in Reason for "autonomy and responsibility" that initiates self-reflection? To answer these questions Habermas returns to the idea of a "permanent" interest of Reason toward itself, at the same time appealing to Kant and Fichte for a philosophical justification of such an emancipatory interest. The Hegelian notion of "reflection," although constituting the basis for later developments of the concept (in Marxism and Freudian theory), does not provide satisfactory "grounds" from which to explain the reasons for its employment. We can recall that, in Hegel's philosophy, "reflection" is entangled with the idealist notion of the *Idea* and begins, on a cognitive basis, from the lack of certainty in sense perception and in the contradictory nature of the latter. In the subsequent stages of Hegel's account, "reflection" is engaged in a phenomenological analysis of experience in order to overcome each stage of incomplete, false, or dogmatic consciousness.

In Kant's philosophy we encounter his notion of an interest in Reason when he examines "Practical Reason." What Habermas points to in Kant is the latter's admission that *pure reason* must have a relation with *practical reason* because "all interest is ultimately practical."[34] Nevertheless, it is Fichte who applies *primacy* to practical reason; in fact, this position forms a "principle" that characterizes Fichte's philosophy. For Fichte, the whole apparatus of reason springs from the intentions of the subject to "posit" itself. The practical concern of reason materializes in the form of an initial self-reflection that the ego performs. Such a process allows the ego to become *transparent* to itself in its own "self-production" and this process finally results in the ability of the ego to "free itself from dogmatism."[35]

The question which now arises is: why does Habermas follow Fichte? It seems that he is not so much concerned with the "principle" of the priority of practical reason over theoretical reason. Instead, his interest lies in the *act of self-reflection* Fichte evokes as the act of the ego in its attempts to become transparent to itself. Simultaneously, self-reflection becomes "intuition and emancipation, comprehension and liberation from dogmatic dependence."[36] The act of self-reflection in Fichte enables the identification of an interest within Reason for the independence of the ego. This is asserted in opposition to Kant's approach in which the interest of reason is dictated by practical reason since it only concerns the activity of the free will, that is, arising in relation to moral matters.

I can enumerate then the gains Habermas makes by appealing to philosophical tradition. Firstly, he can trace an interest in Reason which directs the subject to "self-reflection." Secondly, he can view this process as an emancipation that does not simply rid itself of dogmatic positions but also of "false consciousness." The context of his discussion indicates that "false consciousness" alludes to the corresponding Marxist conception of ideology, although it primarily refers to the idea of the Enlightenment promoting a consciousness beyond error and unfree existence.

After he borrows from the philosophical assertion of the interest in Reason, Habermas proceeds in combining this Fichtean view with his own notion of the "self-formative species" (mentioned earlier) by substituting the Fichtean ego with the species. The species, unlike the ego, does not constitute itself by the act of self-reflection, but depends on the conditions of "material exchange" that takes place between "communicatively acting persons." Reason, on the other hand, and its *interest in emancipation* is present, and it accompanies the species. According to Habermas, this interest has been "invested" in the self-formative process of the species which depends upon instrumental action and symbolic interaction.

> The concept of the interest in reason, introduced by idealism, needs to be re-interpreted *materialistically* : the emancipatory interest itself is dependent on the interests in possible intersubjective action-orientation and in possible technical control.[37] (Italics mine.)

Following Habermas, we perceive an idea of history where the notions of *work* and *interaction* are fundamental. (He later complements these two categories with the notion of power that institutions exercise in society.) The interest of Reason in emancipation performs two tasks. Firstly, in analogy to the Fichtean ego, it can lead the species to moments of self-reflection, although Habermas has to argue convincingly in order to present cases of "self-reflection" in societal forms. Secondly, the same emancipatory interest transforms itself into practical and technical cognitive interests that accompany the species in their self-formation. "At the human level," as he argues, these interests are the outcome for the "preservation of life." Thus, they are rooted in the life structure of the species which organizes its life around knowledge and action. The cognitive process seen earlier in Habermas's account is, then, rooted in life structures.

A number of remarks and criticisms can be made on what I have already written concerning Habermas's view of history, the species, and cognitive interests. I will restrict myself to only a few comments since the whole discourse suits debates that have revolved around *Historical Materialism*, Hegelianism, and the positions of the Frankfurt school. In my opinion, Habermas's account presents a restricted philosophical anthropology. With its help he can equip the species with the interests he claims he has unearthed via epistemological analysis. The view of history he held at the time (and which he follows even today with a few modifications) appears to be very narrow. One can easily discern in it aspects of Darwinism, Hegelianism, and Marxism. It is of no surprise, however, as all these three discourses share, in my view, common positions. The *teleology* of the *reproduction* of life toward possible *emancipation* appears to underlie his novel theory of history. His basic presuppositions concerning the "preservation of life" also rely upon a strong naturalistic approach. At the same time, the self-formation of the species follows an ascending route that repeats the conceptions of Hegelianism and Marxism. This trend will become more evident when I examine his attempts to argue for a critical theory of society that incorporates "self-reflection."

Psychoanalysis and "Self-reflection"

Having argued for the philosophical location of an emancipatory cognitive interest, Habermas turns his attention to Freudian psychoanalytic theory which combines, in his opinion, both areas of self-reflection and scientificity. For him, Freud's theory is of a new kind, a "critical theory" that also bases itself on a different process of inquiry than both the natural and the cultural sciences. "Psychoanalysis is relevant to us," as he says, "as the only tangible example of a science incorporating methodical self-reflection."[38] The members of the Frankfurt school, devoted to the construction of their "critical theory" of society, usually looked upon Freudianism as another discourse which brings to light areas that the Marxist theories were unable to approach. This is more true of Marcuse who also attempted an explicit combination of Marxism and Freudianism in his *Eros and Civilisation.*[39]

Habermas, however, does not explicitly incorporate any portion of Freud's positions concerning society into his view of "historical materialism," even if he borrows and transforms certain notions that are common within the analytic treatment, such as "therapy" and the "normal/deviant" distinction as well as the notion of "distorted" or "corrupt text" that the dream represents. His interest is mainly located within the view that Freud's theory constitutes a *critical scientific theory* which, by analogy, would enable Habermas to adopt a similar pattern for a "critical social theory" (with practical intent, as he always adds). Hence, his main preoccupation is to demonstrate the reasons for his assertions that Freud's analytic theory is both a science, involving a more elaborate hermeneutic understanding than usual literary hermeneutic and, at the same time, a critical theory. Consequently, his reading of Freud proceeds along such lines.

Although psychoanalysis might appear as a specific form of interpretation of "symbolic structures" providing rules and techniques, Habermas introduces the differences that exist between philological hermeneutics, as he calls Dilthey's hermeneutics, and Freud's analysis. Even Freud, Habermas contends, thought that the interpretation of dreams followed similar lines as philological hermeneutic analysis. What Habermas wants to point out is the restricted attitude of usual hermeneutic analysis toward disturbances and omissions in texts or in tradition, considering them as accidental (unlike their reception in psychoanalytic understanding). He actually refers to the Dilthean theory of biography which, although constituting an attempt at self-reflection for the reconstruction of the "life-history" of the individual, finally remains entrapped within the insufficient approach of Dilthey's hermeneutics. For Dilthey, the reconstruction of "life-history" could become the model for the interpretation of any symbolic structure. A problem accompanying the Dilthean attempt is that life-histories must be remembered through memory but personal memory is not always reliable. Notwithstanding these difficulties, understanding for Dilthey directs itself at symbolic forms and texts in which meanings have been *objectivated.* However, even at this level of the reconstruction of history, hermeneutic analysis encounters "corrupted memories" and "confused ideas" people hold for themselves. Dilthey then calls upon philology, which constitutes the basis for historical studies (because of its explicit aim of the study of languages and the traditions residing in them). In this way philological analysis can reveal the "intentional content" of *objectivations*. Nevertheless, according to Habermas, if such content has been disturbed, it is a result of external conditions and the limitations of transmission of memory or culture. The "omissions," the "distortions," and other flaws, which must be removed with hermeneutic criticism, are not seen playing a *systematic* role within the Dilthean perspective as their presence is accidental.

The opposite attitude is adopted in psychoanalytic hermeneutical efforts. The interpretations that psychoanalysis provides do not attempt to locate meaning that coincides with what is "consciously intended." It apprehends the "omissions," the "distortions," and the flaws that appear in a text (or in a dream), or a "life-history," as having a *systematic role,* and that they spring from "internal conditions." Therefore, the main importance when faced with a "corrupt text" is given to the understanding of the "corruption" itself which, finally, will permit the understanding of such a text.[40] Habermas draws our attention to this fundamental difference that initially distinguishes the hermeneutic understanding employed in psychoanalysis, from Dilthey's philological approach. The notion of the systematic role of "corruption" in a text brings us closer to the idea of internal structures which produce such systematic results, as well as the possibility of providing causal explanatory accounts for their understanding.

Another notion that the Habermasian reading of Freud finds significant is that of "self-deception." We saw earlier how Habermas, drawing from Dilthey, argued that the grammar of ordinary language dictates the rules not only of linguistic propositions but also of actions and expressions. In pathological cases, however, we reach the point where the subject *deviates* from grammatical rules or commits acts uncoordinated with linguistic expressions. The subject expresses and also misunderstands himself in this discrepancy, being unaware of the deviation. So, Habermas concludes: "Psychoanalytic interpretation is concerned with those connections of symbols in which a subject deceives itself about itself. The *depth hermeneutics* that Freud contrasts to Dilthey's philological hermeneutics deals with texts indicating *self-deceptions of the author*."[41] We can see a number of different cases in Freud's theory in which "self-deceptions" manifest themselves. In *parapraxes,*[42] or in neuroses, the mistakes and errors which occur (in language, actions, and bodily expressions) can be considered as sections of a text, which the author (patient) cannot comprehend. Such mistakes and errors are enlarged and given prominent position so that they are finally classified as pathological. Psychoanalysis, then, considers occurrences of this kind as *symptoms* which appear as incomprehensible to the "author" and indicate deviant cases. Freud began to penetrate into the structures that produce distortions in the text, from the nonpathological example of such a text, the dream.[43] He later transfered this experience of interpretations to everyday phenomena where distortions of its symbolism are similar to the distortions of the dream-text.

So far I have singled out the notions of the "systematic" role of distortion and the "self-deception" of the author because both underline the way Habermas constructs his view of psychoanalysis as science and as self-reflection and critique. A discussion of the dream theory and the psychoanalytic theory of Freud, as well as the way in which Habermas understands it, is beyond my immediate concern and would require a separate study. I am mainly interested in the notion of "self-reflection" which psychoanalysis is assumed to perform.

In Freud's words the task of psychoanalysis concerns the fact that "all representations must be undone" or "in making the unconscious accessible to consciousness, which is done by overcoming the resistances."[44] Resistances are the initial forces with which psychoanalysis is concerned. They do not allow the ego to have access to contents that inhabit the unconscious. Through the analytic dialogue (between the analyst and the patient) the aim is to bring into "public communication," as Habermas calls it, symbols that belong to a deformed private language. These symbols, which in Freud's terms are the symptoms of pathological behavior and can be language deformation, speech restriction, emotional unbalances, somatic functional disturbances, and so on, have always remained incomprehensible to the patient. Rendering such symbolic structures communicable by overcoming resistances makes parts of memory available to the patient and a reconstruction of his life-history possible.

Habermas feels that the analytic dialogue, in which the analyst instructs the patient with a hypothesis for the possible understanding of incomprehensible symbolic structures, cannot be described by the practice of translation. However, that the analytic dialogue leads into the reconstruction of the life-history of the patient, prompts Habermas to declare that psychoanalytic knowledge belongs to the category of "self-reflection" although unlike the usual hermeneutic understanding prevailing, for example, in a translation. The latter proceeds with the aim of establishing intersubjectivity between the two languages, since they belong to different social, cultural, or historical contexts. The analytic dialogue instead, through self-reflection, brings to consciousness what was unconscious.

The other pole that complements the self-reflection of analysis is the area of its therapeutic results. Analytic treatment manages to remove the mechanisms of repression and finally the compulsive repetition of the symptoms. For Habermas this process is a *critical* resolution of resistances. Psychoanalysis, besides being self-reflection, is also *critique* because it dissolves dogmatic attitudes. The abandonment of "dogmatic attitudes" happens after the patient himself accepts the reconstruction of his life-history reached in dialogue with the analyst. However, we should not forget at this point that the therapeutic results of analysis do not occur as the end product of a cognitive process. It is not only a question of a lack of information that the patient needs. "The pathological factor is not his ignorance in itself, but the root of this ignorance [lies] in his *inner resistances*."[45] The *critical* side of psychoanalysis, I believe, must always be considered in terms of overcoming resistances (through the successive steps of the treatment and the occurrence of transference) without being a purely cognitive process. However, any imitation of the psychoanalytic critical process, based on the reconstruction of life-histories, beyond the context of the patient-analyst relationship (and the process of transference), is in danger of missing the point made by psychoanalysis. This is exactly what the critics of Habermas level against him when he proposes a model of psychoanalytic critique for therapeutic results in society.

Metapsychology and Depth Hermeneutics

Psychoanalysis, as a "new" critical science, removed from the methodology of the natural and cultural sciences, employs a different logic of inquiry, according to Habermas. Earlier I provided a few indications of the different hermeneutic procedures it adopts. However, in the usual epistemological framework which Habermas employs, the questions that must be answered are: "What makes the knowledge of psychoanalysis possible?" or "What are the conditions for arriving at psychoanalytic knowledge?" Answers to such questions bring us to what Habermas calls *metapsychology* or *metahermeneutics*, that is, the area of basic assumptions that "explicate the conditions of the possibility of analytic knowledge." It is rewarding to observe, firstly, Habermas's beliefs concerning the structure of the critical science of psychoanalysis, and secondly, the kind of hermeneutics that such a science employs. His views on these topics, which appear rather demanding to the reader, facilitate the comprehension of certain basic positions that he adopts when answering Gadamer in their debate (presented in the next several chapters).

Following Habermas's thoughts on the epistemological status of psychoanalysis, we move far beyond Freud's conceptualizations. As with Peirce and Dilthey, Habermas charges Freud with a false understanding of his science since, many times, the latter thought of psychoanalysis and its scientificity as being at the same level of thoroughness and precision as the natural sciences. Abandoning this trend of thinking, which almost equates psychoanalysis with the natural sciences, Habermas concentrates on two main levels of theoretical propositions that are evident in Freud's work. Firstly, we encounter *general interpretations*. They are mostly theoretical propositions (theories) of interpretative character (assumptions) that, in general terms, approach and define childhood development (e.g., ego formation, child interaction with other persons, and childhood socialization and personality formation). These general interpretations are, however, not formed merely upon collections of clinical data. Their formation is guided by another set of propositions (assumptions) comprising the *metapsychological* or *metahermeneutical* area. Before we proceed further, let us look more closely at this *metapsychological* area. According to Habermas, the propositions composing the body of *metapsychology* deal with a fundamental connection: "the connection between language deformation and behavioural pathology."[46] The perspective of this connection establishes the general background to which all clinical observations and analytic practices refer.

There is, however, another aspect Habermas underlines. According to him, we should not assume that Freud constructed his *metatheory* based exclusively upon empirical data. The connection between language deformation and behavioral pathology was accomplished by Freud's study and reflection upon what makes psychoanalytic knowledge possible. He had to supply the theoretical connections and framework that allow interpretations of clinical symptoms at specific ages and phases of development. In this way the metapsychological domain provides the "transcendental" framework for the *possibility* of analytic knowledge. It is the answer to the (Kantian) question (concerning the conditions of the possibility of psychoanalytic knowledge) as just indicated. In his later writings Freud arrives at the general structure of *ego-id-superego*. Habermas believes that this model organizes the metatheoretical body in more detail. All its propositions are now set around the new categories. The *ego-id-superego* structure can be considered as a "general interpretation" (it has the character of an assumption) but belonging to the level of metatheory.

Based on this metatheory, Freud could then provide interpretations of the self-formative processes with empirical reference. These are the "general interpretations" of childhood development and, as just mentioned, they are *systematic* generalizations of clinical experiences. What must be understood here is that, without the presence of the body of metapsychological propositions concerning the link between "language deformation and behavioral pathology," it would have been impossible to arrive at "general interpretations"; there would be no general guiding background to systematically refer and structure the clinical experience.

The aforementioned demonstrate how general interpretations are possible. There is, however, another process that occurs during their formation and distinguishes them from usual hermeneutic procedures. Initially, general interpretations are developed from the results of clinical experiences following the usual procedure of the "hermeneutic circle" which permits further elaboration of their interpretive ability. This is achieved in the circular process between the preunderstandings and the clinical experiences that must be understood. The preunderstandings are mostly the body of the metapsychological propositions. However, when a "satisfactory" generalization of clinical data has been achieved in this way, the "new" general theory is no longer questioned or put under the scrutiny of the hermeneutic circle. The circle ends at this point. The "general interpretation" is used from there on to understand individual life histories and to close the gaps that appear in their recollection. The individual history, as a text, does not force the reopening of the hermeneutic circle or any further questioning of the preunderstandings involved in the "general interpretation." As Habermas insists,

in contrast to the hermeneutic anticipation of the philologist, general interpretation is "fixed" and, like a general theory, must prove itself through predictions deduced from it.[47]

This feature of a "general interpretation" to exhibit a "stable character" as theory and also to provide predictions (in order to fill gaps appearing in life-history recollections), in a fashion close to other scientific disciplines, is one of the major elements which count for the scientificity of psychoanalysis.

However, if this suggests that general interpretations share some common features with other (general) scientific theories, there are also fundamental differences. The testing of cultural scientific theories by applying the hypotheses of the theory to empirical observations, is performed by the scientist who is the subject of the inquiry. Conversely, in psychoanalysis, the results received in the general interpretation via the process of self-reflection, apply to the "object" of interpretation, the patient, who must then apply them to herself in the process of analytic dialogue. A further difference emerges when we consider the validity of scientific theories which extends to any investigator assuming the role of the inquiring subject. In contrast, general interpretations extend their validity only to those cases where the "object" of interpretation, the patient, agrees with the correctness of the individual interpretations of her life-history that are presented to her.

There are a number of other features which differentiate "general interpretations" from "scientific theories" and establish the former mainly within the domain of hermeneutic procedures.[48] Nevertheless, it is the claim that general interpretations provide both hermeneutic understanding and explanatory accounts that appears crucial. For Habermas this constitutes the case of "depth-hermeneutic" understanding which goes beyond the usual hermeneutic understanding of "translation." It is in this respect that Habermas's approach has frequently been referred to as "critical hermeneutics."[49] General interpretations, so far as they accomplish an explanation of the appearance of symptoms, appear to be very close to causal-analytic methodological procedures. Together with the empirical sciences, general interpretations rely upon universal propositions in order to introduce causal connections. There is, however, an important difference in the logical procedures of these two kinds of science. In the empirical sciences, when a theoretical proposition (e.g., a lawlike hypothesis) is applied to a particular case in reality, its content is not affected or changed by the context of the particular case. On the contrary, in the case of general interpretations, their theoretical propositions must be "translated" and "applied" to the particular life-history of the individual. The causal statements derived must make sense within the context of the life-history of the patient; they are context-dependent. In this case they are best conceived as instances of situational understanding, a basic feature of hermeneutic understanding.

Society and "Critical Theory"

The significance of the psychoanalytic paradigm for Habermas was not solely restricted to the location of knowledge based on self-reflection. The concepts and possibly the practice of psychoanalytic theory could be used, by analogy, for the whole of society and not exclusively for the individual. Freud had expressed such views on society and "civilisation,"[50] and Habermas draws from them certain fundamental ideas capable of justifying his search for a "critical social theory with practical intent."

According to Freud, extending the concept of the pathological state of the individual to society is difficult as there are no reference points of what is "normal" or "abnormal." If all members in a society live in similar disorder, an awareness of what is "normal" becomes impossible. Thus, Freud proposes the examination of communal neuroses against the background of "civilization" and thereby, through the process of "civilisation"[51] we can detect what deformations and pathological states have being imposed upon the members of society. For Freud, the motive of the human societies is an economic one. People, in order to live, must work and provide for themselves what is not freely available. In this respect, the members of society must restrict their energies from instinctual satisfaction (primarily sexual activity) and direct them into work. Under such pressures imposed by reality, "collective solutions" are found as "defenses," and they are similar to the neurotic solutions of the individual. To this end, society establishes *institutions* that guarantee compulsive results, especially the repetition and rigid behavioral patterns of its members, without the need of justification. Institutions thus correspond to the individual pathological forms of neuroses Freud analyzed, although operating from the "outside" as distinct from the individual neuroses that operate from "inside" the patient.

The social norms introduced by the institutions have a compulsory form and also play the role of providing "substitute-gratifications." Part of these gratifications can also be transformed to become legitimations of social norms. They can become widely shared beliefs and "collective fantasies" which compensate for the renunciations that have been imposed by civilization. They can also, as worldviews, be adopted for the rationalization of authority. They are what Freud calls "illusions," such as religious worldviews, value-systems, ideals, and products of art and, as such, are removed from criticism. "Illusions" are not pathological, since they are not *delusions* which contradict reality, basically coming from unfulfilled wishes. "Illusions" have a projective utopian character (fantasies) and we meet them in any culture.

Their transformation into fantasies can be seen as the work of social defensive mechanisms turned into ways of substitute-gratification. According to Freud, as long as technology advances and the control over nature accelerates, the institutional structure, regulating the distribution of wealth and keeping intact the suppression of instincts, can now be loosened. This process can go so far as to allow parts of the cultural tradition with projective character (the illusions) to be realized and institutionally gratified. The utopian content of illusions can actually be freed from ideological (delusory) elements and be transformed into a critique of the institutional structures that can now be seen as obsolete.

This is a brief and schematic description of Freud's theory of society and its pathology. Habermas retains a number of these Freudian theses which enable him to conclude his thoughts on the connection between knowledge as critique and the emancipatory interest in societal terms. The institutions and illusions Freud described, Habermas sees as "power" and "ideology." He accepts Freud's metapsychological theory of distorted "communicative action" which analyzes the origins of the institutions and the role of illusions. In addition, he retains Freud's concept of "communication free of domination," which Freud thought of as "the rational basis for the precepts of civilisation." Nevertheless, Habermas disassociates himself from Freud's concept of history. The latter has provided an objectivist construction of the history of the species by introducing "a model of instinctual dynamics." The process of civilization is seen as linked to the dynamics of the instincts. Nonetheless, Habermas believes that the reconstruction of the history of the species should be in the form of a critique, as in psychoanalysis, in which the life-history of the patient is constructed as critique for therapeutic employment.

According to Habermas, in psychoanalysis and in the act of self-reflection, we have observed the unity of reason (as insight) and emancipation (as freedom from dogmatic dependence guided by the interest of reason in itself). The same, he believes, occurs in society. As in clinical experiences, in society there is always an interest in abolishing pathological compulsions. However, at this point Habermas goes one step further than Freud. He argues that, if we look at the cognitive and critical capacity of reason displayed in the evolution of the species, we can conclude it "is reason that inheres in interest."[52] Even the interest in self-preservation according to him, could logically be deduced from Reason, since it cannot be seen naturalistically as in the animal kingdom. Habermas contends that this connection of human interests and Reason constitutes a materialist critique of Fichte's notion of "the interested employment of Reason" in self-reflection. Therefore, Habermas argues that the critical science of psychoanalysis depends upon an interest that is supplied by Reason. He can thus continue to say that if

knowledge and interest are one in the moment of self-reflection, then even the dependence of the transcendental conditions of the natural and cultural sciences on technical and practical cognitive interests does not imply the heteronomy of knowledge. What this means is that *the knowledge-constitutive interests* that determine the conditions of objectivity of the validity of statements *are rational themselves,* so that the meaning of knowledge and thus the criterion of its autonomy as well, cannot be accounted for without recourse to a connection with interest in general. (Italics mine.)[53]

In his remarks we encounter his aim to provide a more persuasive account of the basic theme that knowledge is constituted upon interests because these interests are now seen as Reason invested in by the species. I would claim, however, that in this case he displays a particular brand of *rationalism* stemming from Hegelian speculative thought. We observe here that Reason has been invested, or it has *expressed* itself, in the cognitive interests (technical, practical, and emancipatory) of the species. Although this account shifts away from Freud's view of history founded on instincts, it nevertheless provides us with an equally problematic view of history based on the unfolding of Reason in the history of the species. Habermas's view explicates the unfolding of the main interest of Reason in itself. In my opinion, this conviction of Habermas leads astonishingly close to the Hegelian perspective! It represents a rationalist and optimistic picture of history based on a *unified Reason* which stands above all humanity.[54]

5

Tradition and Authority versus
The Critique of Ideology

I have now examined a number of major issues which form the main
body of Gadamer's and Habermas's thought in *Truth and Method* and
in *Knowledge and Human Interests,* respectively. Mindful of their
positions, we can enter into the tone and context of their exchange
which began a few months before the publication of *Truth and
Method.* It is known as the Habermas-Gadamer debate, or the debate
between "critical theory and philosophical hermeneutics."

A Brief Review of the Debate

Knowledge and Human Interests, published in Germany in 1968, can
be considered to be an indirect challenge to the views of Gadamer,
although it primarily promotes a new approach to the notion of "critical theory." Here Habermas presents a meticulously structured argument in which he attempts to avoid the implications involved in an
adherence to philosophical hermeneutics which, according to him,
lacks both "scientificity" and "criticality." He does, however, accept
the notions of "hermeneutic understanding" and "reflection" for the
articulation of his "critical theory."[1] Nevertheless, it was Habermas's initial criticism of the Gadamerian philosophical positions in
the article, "A Review of Gadamer's *Truth and Method*,"[2] and later in
"The Hermeneutic Claim to Universality,"[3] that triggered not only
Gadamer's strenuous retorts, but a series of writings by other contributors who realized that important themes of philosophical, social,
and political origin were at stake.[4]

The central positions of disagreement between the two participants of the debate were discussed in their initial exchange and ref-

erences to the same theoretical problems reappear in later articles.[5] This is due to both the importance of the themes discussed, and to the relatively unchanged orientations of Habermas over the years, specifically toward the notion of "emancipation" and the possibility of "critical theory." It is not only the original context of the debate that has attracted theoretical attention, neither is such attention due to the reappropriation of the debate by advocates of either "critical theory" or philosophical hermeneutics; in the eighties we can observe reopenings and revisitings of the debate from new attitudes that emerge from intense discussions on what has been thematized as "modernity versus postmodernity."[6] Obviously, the plethora of questions raised in the debate are constantly present and reemerging in many current philosophical discourses. Moreover, the notion of *text*, with which philosophical hermeneutics deals, and its call for *intertextuality*, is also present; the *text* as a major paradigm for understanding meaning has not been replaced. On the contrary, it dominates the literary and artistic horizons as well as the social and historical sciences in which the object of study is best defined through linguistic approaches. These thoughts are well exemplified in the sayings of Umberto Eco; he states that we attempt to define or adjust our position toward the text, which perhaps shifts its meaning in relation to other texts but we are always in touch with it; we live in it.[7] Although this engagement with the text is reminiscent of discourses evoking the notion of "postmodernity," a subject beyond the immediate concerns of this work, it indicates that issues involved in the Habermas-Gadamer debate still preoccupy current thinking and are frequently under discussion in modified perspective.

The debate took place within a well-defined critical position, delineated by both participants, against the cultural environment and the consequences that the pursuit and spreading of "technological civilization" had begun to impose particularly during the sixties. Both Habermas and Gadamer recognized the dangers of technocratic rationality imposing its solutions upon the practical life of the individual and of communities. It is important to reiterate this point, already extensively canvassed in the first chapter, in relation to the intentions of "critical theory." Such orientations and critical positions adopted by both participants facilitate an understanding of their arguments, also showing their concern with actual life; both of them, envisaged their theoretical efforts as entangled with a particular way of life and critical stance.

Before embarking upon a detailed examination of the subjects in the debate, I will provisionally provide a brief indication of their content. The first criticism of Habermas was leveled against the role of tradition and authority that Gadamer ascribes to them in *Truth and Method*. While Gadamer appraises tradition and illuminates the role of "prejudices" we receive from it, Habermas finds tradition to be incompatible with the notion of "critical theory" which considers tradition as the main source of ideological beliefs and domination. Gadamer, nevertheless, is not short of answers and further insights on the need to understand tradition and an awareness of its importance for us, is necessary. I must also stress the fact that, in the whole range of the debate, although we encounter issues situating the two writers in opposing camps, we nevertheless find, in both Habermas and Gadamer, common underlying positions shaping their arguments. One of these concerns the notion of "self-reflection," raised in the fourth chapter; there, I demonstrated the reasons for the dependence of the "critique of ideology" upon the notion of "self-reflection." Similarly, "self-reflection" is an important concept for the attempts of philosophical hermeneutics at self-awareness and for the apprehension of our prejudices which form us. With regard to this issue I intend to show that Gadamer's position, despite Habermas's criticisms, displays a critical orientation which deserves attention.

A further theme within the debate is the concentration upon the notion of linguisticality of all experience and understanding, which Gadamer claims to be of universal character. For Habermas, such a claim leads us astray and conceals other forces in society that determine our intersubjectivity and the forms of life in which we live. A total acceptance of linguisticality of all experience, according to Habermas, also leads to an existential philosophy that has nothing to do with the premises of "critical theory" and the Marxist materialist heritage. Again, my intention when I examine this subject in the sixth chapter, will be to demonstrate firstly, the very restricted understanding Habermas shows in relation to Gadamer's thesis of linguisticality and secondly, the context in which Gadamer's approach appears legitimate. The object of the debate concerning the ontological character of Gadamer's hermeneutics and Habermas's attempts to specify the scientific character of his "critical theory," has introduced further discussion on epistemological issues. For example, we come upon the opposition and distance between "situational understanding" and its subsequent "relativism" on the one hand, and the credibility of scientific causal explanation that the "critical theory" adopts, on the other. (This theme will also be discussed in the next chapter.)

Referring to psychoanalysis as the model of "critical theory," Gadamer raised questions concerning the analogy between the psychoanalytic critique and the social critique that Habermas promoted.

Gadamer's serious doubts, also raised by other authors, contributed to the moderate change of course by Habermas regarding the notion of "reconstructive sciences" and the pursuit of normative grounds of an emancipatory interest within what he calls "universal pragmatics" (e.g., universal rules of our linguistic competence).

Ending this short preliminary review of the debate, I should add that a number of further issues appeared during the exchanges such as the notions of "dialogue" and "communication," or the thorny problem of the relation between theoretical insight and practical implementation. In the direction of shared themes, the attention of both writers to a profound humanism and the priorities of "a just and good life" serve as a strong example of the broader philosophical tradition they represent.

The topics of the debate I have already mentioned cover a wide range of philosophical problems spread between epistemological issues and social and political philosophy as well as what could be described as a discourse on ethical or moral issues. This is hardly surprising as both authors are engaged in proposing a critical theory or a critical stance toward the "life-world," viewing matters of cognitive theory as bound up with practical interests. Apart from the examination and reevaluation of the explicit issues of the debate, my aim is also to look for additional philosophical problems that latently underlie the debate. It is true that "the full implications of the Habermas-Gadamer debate have yet to be drawn,"[8] as J. Mendelson says. However, it does not appear to me that the horizon of implications of the debate have not yet been realized because of some inadequate analysis and study of it; rather, it is the changing perspectives from which the debate is read and reappropriated. With this in mind I could explain the fact that, as mentioned earlier, there are at least two different approaches devoted to the study of the issues involved. One trend revolves around the Marxist versus Heideggerian perspective and the main issue being the *status* of "critical theory," a predominant theme in the seventies. The other trend, present in recent articles referring to the debate, begins by incorporating the influence of "postmodernity" and of "radical hermeneutics"; here the main concern is whether the discussions about the debate can provide answers to the new intellectual climate of the eighties and nineties.[9]

Gadamer on Ourselves and Tradition

When (in the second chapter) I referred to Gadamer's rehabilitation of "prejudices" and the role they play for ourselves, I mentioned the notion of tradition as the basis of all "prejudices" and of everything

that is transmitted to us. In order to clarify and evaluate our prejudices it is essential that we comprehend the tradition we live in. Similarly, when interpreting a text, the interpreter must visit and understand the past; he must become aware of the influence of tradition
upon himself and the communality that exists between himself and
tradition. However, if these comments simply underline the cognitive importance of tradition in our efforts to understand ourselves
and the past, it must also be emphasized that, in Gadamer's view, tradition is part of us; we live in it. If we regard ourselves as historical
beings, our efforts should not be directed at distancing ourselves
from tradition which constitutes our historicality, but at elevating tradition back to its full value in order to appreciate the significance it
holds for us. Such demands illustrate the positive attitude Gadamer
maintains toward tradition and the space he allows for it in his
hermeneutical analysis. It would not be wrong, however, to say that
he produces a strong impression of conservativism with respect to
tradition and the authority that it exercises over us, a point Habermas
quickly raised against Gadamer. Is all tradition welcome? Is all tradition truthful and acceptable? These are questions that any reader
of Gadamer could raise legitimately but more so Habermas, who, in
line with (the tradition of) the Enlightenment, would see in tradition
the source of prejudice and ideological beliefs.

Firstly, I will consider Gadamer's attitude to this opposition which
the Enlightenment has constantly exhibited with regard to authority
and tradition. He writes: "It is the general tendency of the Enlightenment not to accept any authority and decide everything before the
judgment seat of reason." "It is not tradition but reason that constitutes the ultimate source of all authority."[10] Gadamer believes that
the absolute opposition Enlightenment creates between authority and
reason is misleading. For him, authority does not always entail the
unreasonable exercise of force and domination; "authority is not
always wrong."[11] He also believes that the key relationship to
authority depends on whether or not we accept it. If we recognize in
authority "superiority in knowledge" and insight (as the example of a
teacher or an expert can show), then we accept authority of our own
accord; otherwise, any other acceptance would be based on *force*
which must be distinguished from *free* acceptance and recognition.

Together with tradition, the Enlightenment discredited the notion
of "prejudice"; Gadamer undertook their rehabilitation in order to
re-instate most of the significance of "prejudice" which constantly
accompanies us. For Gadamer, the force which brought a correction
to the Enlightenment's attitude to tradition is Romanticism. The latter's appeal to tradition reallowed the recognition of the legitimate

establishment of authority by tradition. For example, the recognition of the validity of morals, brought forward with tradition, demonstrates the correctness of Romanticism at this point. Gadamer, however, disassociates himself from both Enlightenment and Romantic views on tradition. Romanticism accepted tradition as something given and natural before which "reason must remain silent." In opposition to both Romanticism and Enlightenment, he argues that there is no absolute, unconditional antithesis between tradition and Reason, concluding that "tradition is constantly an element of *freedom* and of history itself,"[12] a view counter to the beliefs of the Enlightenment. The act of preserving tradition, according to Gadamer, is an act of reason; something we freely choose. He argues, that even in times of revolution, the old is always preserved, combined with the new, resulting in the creation of new values. He concludes therefore, that both the Enlightenment's critique of tradition and the rehabilitation of tradition by Romanticism are incorrect.

The question we should ask is whether Gadamer's views are convincing enough and whether they can determine our stance with respect to tradition. Although we can recognize the need for the preservation of some parts of tradition, is there "space" for a critical position challenging what might appear unnecessary, false, or unacceptable within tradition? Before I get involved in seeking answers to these questions, it is worth mentioning a few further thoughts of Gadamer, which could help to understand his insistence on the recognition and rehabilitation of tradition. As I mentioned earlier, concerning the case of the interpreter, tradition is important not only for practical issues, but for cognitive matters as well. In *Truth and Method*, Gadamer challenged firstly the attitude of the human sciences assuming that their historicality lies in the prejudices derived from tradition; secondly their belief that, by getting rid of these prejudices they can become "unprejudiced sciences," or at least more scientific. "Only a naive and unreflective historicism, in hermeneutics," he says, "would see the historical-hermeneutical sciences as something absolutely new that would do away with the power of 'tradition'."[13]

Another important conclusion of Gadamer's position is that we cannot think of ourselves living beyond tradition; instead, we must accept the fact that we have been formed by tradition and, through it, everything from the past is transmitted to us. I have argued that our strong interest in tradition, which Gadamer reveals, is justified because tradition can teach us: it includes and transmits *truths*. (Such a concept of truth, coming from tradition, I have developed in the third chapter.) It is not a simple historical dependence which keeps us in contact with tradition, but the valuable insights from the past that we find in it which we can always interpret and utilize. "Our historical consciousness is always filled with a variety of voices in which the echo of the past is heard. It is present only in the multifariousness of such voices: this constitutes the nature of the tradition in which we want to share and have a part."[14] Although this quotation presents itself as a metaphoric expression, it nevertheless conveys a strong picture of that which tradition incorporates and the way we are intertwined with it. This relationship between ourselves and tradition that Gadamer reveals, constitutes one of his strongest claims. A similar point, showing the importance of tradition for us and our connection with it, is suggested by Ricoeur, who believes that values are not created *ex nihilo* but are always *transvaluations* of previous values which tradition transmits to us.[15] Ricoeur, therefore, recognizes the role of tradition in the values we share (I will mention his comments on this subject later).

Tradition as a Source of Domination

In examining Habermas's criticisms of Gadamer, I will concentrate on the reasons he provides for the need to criticize tradition, as well as his explanation of Gadamer's failure to establish a critical position toward tradition and authority. These criticisms emanating from Habermas's basic views on tradition, can facilitate the understanding of his whole program for the specific critique of tradition he proposes. Habermas charges Gadamer with the inability to arrive at the consequences of *hermeneutic reflection* which, if employed as a vantage point from which to view our prejudices, liberates us from dogmatic forces residing within tradition. Concerning the constitution and transfer of tradition, Habermas understands it on the level of a model of educational process, suggested by Gadamer. According to this model the acceptance of authority during processes of learning, as in education, allows the "internalisation of norms and sedimentation of prejudices." These prejudices, in turn, become conditions of possible knowledge. By reflecting upon such knowledge, Habermas concludes:

> Hermeneutics makes us conscious of that which is already historically pre-structured by inculcated tradition in the very act of understanding.[16]

However, when reflection is employed, what is pregiven no longer remains the same. A preconception that has become *transparent* through reflection can no longer be considered as a prejudice. But, Habermas argues, if this is what Gadamer suggests, the employment of reflection has not brought any considerable change. The prejudices are legitimated and held as valid. The mature individual will first assure herself of the prejudgments (prejudices) she holds and simply transfer the "unfree" recognition of authority from the teacher or guardian (in the example of the educational process) to "an objective authority of a traditional framework" which legitimates such prejudices. Reflection would not have removed her from the authority of current tradition; she would still have to move within the available limits of tradition. Habermas ascribes such power to authority especially when it is combined with knowledge, as in the example of educational and learning processes. The tradition, then, that stands at the back of the educator, or the teacher, can easily legitimate and reassure any reflected upon prejudice.

Habermas, I think, oversimplifies the views of Gadamer; we cannot attribute to the latter a position, in which reflection finally legitimates *any* prejudice. The transparency and the recognition of a prejudice has been worked upon by reason and its *acceptance* or *rejection* is also based upon rational choice. The individual retains the choice of *rejecting* an unjustified (unproductive) prejudice and this is clear in Gadamer's view of prejudices, thus disproving Habermas's accusation that hermeneutic reflection legitimates all prejudices. Therefore, *reflection*, in Gadamer's employment of the term, can result in a more radical outcome than Habermas suggests. His accusation that "Gadamer's prejudice for the right of prejudices certified by tradition denies the power of reflection" cannot be justified. Even if we could only recall the expectations of Gadamer, that the individual can reach the stage of *phronesis* through reflection, this demonstrates the extent to which he invests in the power of reflection. Nevertheless, Habermas could be justified in questioning Gadamer for the *effectivity* of the latter's employment of reflection for *the critique of tradition*, a basic underlying issue of the debate. Is the critical acceptance or rejection of single prejudices, which Gadamer proposes, enough to criticize larger aspects of tradition and oppressive institutional forces that might be at work? I will supply an answer to this question when more arguments on both sides have been examined.

It is time now to turn to the other arguments Habermas provides in order to support his position in which tradition must be regarded with "suspicion" and critique must be extended to encompass it. He accepts the point that knowledge is rooted in tradition, bound at the same time to contingent conditions and norms. However, reflection, when employed, encounters these norms and questions their validity.

Habermas accepts the fact that we receive these internalized norms from tradition (as shown by Gadamer), although we have learned "to follow them blindly" under the pressure of external forces. He contends, then, that reflection can trace back along the path of authority and discover "the grammars of language games" imposed dogmatically upon us as rules for interpreting the world and engaging in action. It is obvious here what Habermas's presumption suggests: tradition, and the authority it exercises upon us, include norms and judgments of repressive or dogmatic nature which stand in opposition to today's appeal to Reason and consensual agreement. Although his views on tradition might to a great extent be correct, he nevertheless does not consider Gadamer's claim; that tradition is also inhabited by "truths" which can teach us and be of great benefit in the construction of our lives. The absolute gap between reason and tradition Gadamer ascribes to the Enlightenment, is again apparent in Habermas's position.

There are further thoughts expressed by Habermas which shed light on his reasoning. He considers the continuity of tradition and its preservation to be *translation*, which is achieved "through a large-scale philology proceeding in a nature-like manner."[17] The end result of this translation is the preservation of the intersubjectivity of communication in everyday language whenever it is broken. If "translation" and the subsequent understanding of the meaning of each other's utterances is the large-scale picture of communication which Habermas proposes, this is exactly the view of language and its ontological character that Gadamer maintains (examined in the third chapter). Habermas's particular attention to language allows him to agree with Gadamer that tradition is finally "transmitted language in which we live." Gadamer wrote in *Truth and Method* that "the mode of being of tradition is language"[18] and elsewhere that "language is the reservoir of tradition and the medium in and through which we exist and perceive our world."[19] However, Habermas, considering tradition as language, establishes further relationships between language and society. He argues that we can think of language as a "meta-institution" upon which all other social institutions depend. But such a "meta-institution" itself depends upon social processes; it is shaped by them. Thus, language as a social "meta-institution" proves to be another medium of domination and exercise of social power because it is used to legitimate relations of organized force.[20] A view of language in these terms permits Habermas to draw the conclusion that language is also ideological. On the one hand it institutionalizes power relations, while on the other it conceals the true nature of these relations; that is, it never explicitly articulates them.

Therefore, we are finally driven to the conclusion that *deception* occurs *in* language and *in* tradition which, after all, is language. It is for this reason, according to Habermas, that we should treat tradition with "suspicion."

Following this analysis of tradition as language, it becomes the basic reason for which Habermas considers the critique of tradition paramount and opposes the Gadamerian welcoming of "the voices from the past." Not stopping at this point, Habermas picks Gadamer up on another "weak" position which, he feels contributes to Gadamer's failure to respond to tradition critically. The disputed position occurs when Gadamer argues that "the linguistic communication between the present and tradition is the happening that extends its trajectory to all understanding."[21] Or, the same dispute appears, when Gadamer claims that the hermeneutic experience cannot enjoy an absolute freedom toward what it is presented with, in the act of understanding; "it cannot undo the happening that it [itself] is."[22] Gadamer repeatedly states that tradition lives within language and texts. In order to understand its truths we must relate tradition to our own linguistic attitude. This is the linguistic communication between present and past that Gadamer describes as a "happening," which extends to all understanding. Moreover, hermeneutic experience must understand what is given to it; it cannot disregard what has been understood. In this respect, hermeneutic experience is unable to enjoy "absolute freedom" by disregarding or rejecting truths that come from the past. To summarize: hermeneutic reflection is bound to language and to what language brings to it. This is actually the "happening" that Gadamer claims: an act of the things (said in tradition) upon us. In the eyes of Habermas such a position *absolutizes* the hermeneutic experience, while the "transcending power of reflection" is unconsidered, although part of the hermeneutic experience. This charge continues even further, in the claim in which Gadamer is seen as exhibiting idealistic tendencies by insisting on a "happening of tradition" composed entirely of symbolic meaning (language), without incorporating real objective forces. This, Habermas argues, is the heritage of the Hegelian concept of reflection which brings us into an awareness of belonging to a happening in which "the conditions of rationality change irrationally according to time and place, epoch and culture."[23] A similar sort of irrationalism is then attributed to philosophical hermeneutics. Although this criticism alludes to Hegel's idealism, in my opinion Habermas specifically implies that Hegel never provided us with a consistent theory showing how history moves in actual "objective" terms; or, how, and what kind of, rationality is reached and employed in each particular historical time. Instead, we are looking with embarrassment and uncertainty at the succession of concepts in Hegel's *Phenomenology* and in his *Philosophy of History*.[24]

Gadamer is similarly charged with falling victim to tradition itself; in the hands of philosophical hermeneutics cultural traditions have been absolutized. This inability to describe the actual conditions and reasons of the rationality prevailing in a tradition, or the empirical ways of its change, results in viewing tradition as an unending inertia. This is characterized by Habermas as idealism. "Hermeneutics comes up against walls of the traditional framework from the inside, as it were."[25] But is it possible that Habermas can criticize tradition "from outside" such walls? The issue at hand concentrates on the question: How can we criticize tradition? Is there a vantage point beyond it?

Habermas attempts to deliver the general guidelines of a reference system which can move "beyond the framework of tradition," as he says, but is aware, that finally, such a system must be legitimated "by the appropriation of tradition." I will examine and evaluate his claim that he moves beyond tradition, and the presuppositions it is based on, in the next chapter. I will now concentrate on the way in which Habermas's strategy unfolds when presenting one further criticism against Gadamer.

Habermas opposes the notion of interpretative sociology (which seems to him to be the outcome if one accepts Gadamer's approach) as reaching a rather idealist result. Such a sociology concludes that a "consciousness," which is linguistically articulated in its entirety, determines material processes of life. That is, all the social processes can be accounted by "consciousness" or cultural tradition. This view, according to Habermas, overlooks predominant constraints such as nature (labor) and the relations of social power which determine the course of social life. Habermas refers to the categories of "work" and "domination" (mentioned in the previous chapter), constraints, which "affect the very grammatical rules according to which we interpret the world." In order to comprehend social action we require a system of reference which includes "language" but moves beyond it, employing in addition the categories of "labor" and "domination." Habermas argues that in the "happening of tradition" (just quoted) Gadamer must appreciate (interactive) mediation proceeding between "linguistic structures" and "the empirical conditions" under which these structures change historically. This amounts to a detailed analysis of how traditions, and hence their world-interpretations, alter in relation to empirical constraints and conditions.[26]

In summary, then, Habermas proposes a framework of the categories "language," "work," and "domination" that determine the course of life. From within such a reference system, tradition (as language) is viewed with suspicion (as being ideological) and then criticised. In other words, the specific system of reference ("language," "work," and "domination") which allows us to comprehend how tradition is reproduced and how it changes, provides us with the means of its criticism. If language is ideological and a means of domination, we can understand why hermeneutic experience considering tradition as language should, in Habermas's system of reference, transform itself into a "critique of ideology." I must acknowledge at this point that, following Habermas's suggestions we move to a sociological level of discourse which, he claims, offers us a better view of what constitutes tradition. As I will argue later, we can observe in the debate a constant oscillation between a philosophical reasoning, offered by Gadamer, and a sociological-scientific one adopted by Habermas. Although Habermas's argumentation is not lacking in offering dimensions of philosophical criticism, it is designed more in accordance with his intention to present "a critical social theory with practical intent."

Is All Tradition Ideological?

There are a number of answers, questions, and refutations that Gadamer delivered in response to the charges leveled against him by Habermas. I will only mention those of his views which, in my opinion, are central to the debate concerning tradition and the critique of ideology. Gadamer argues that "the universality of the hermeneutical dimension is *narrowed down*" when Habermas separates the notion of "cultural tradition" from certain elements of social reality such as "work," "power," and "domination" which, for Habermas, are the basic determinates of social life. While "cultural tradition" is open to hermeneutic understanding for the comprehension of its meaning, the triad of basic categories of social life are kept beyond hermeneutic understanding, for Habermas, although they represent "real" (undisputed) determinates of social life. Gadamer insists that this is not correct. The categories of "work," "power," and (political) "domination" do not really fall outside the area of hermeneutic understanding. It is true that these categories are approached by Habermas from a Marxist theoretical background and therefore they stand as basic categories in viewing, explaining, and understanding social reality. The fact that these notions are key elements in Marxist thought, does not exempt them from questioning and from an hermeneutic appropriation. After all, Marxism, through Gadamer's approach, can be seen as an interpretation of history that belongs to our present historical consciousness, and as such its categories have to be seen as limited and historically bound. Gadamer, therefore, is correct in challenging Habermas's basic presuppositions; the system of reference the latter proposed for criticizing tradition rests upon presuppositions that should always be open to hermeneutic understanding (either for their acceptance or their refutation). Gadamer adds, however, that hermeneutics is also interested in "work" and "politics" since they might be the main sources for a number of prejudices that hermeneutics uncovers. Nevertheless, in his work, he never furnished a proper framework for the comprehension of such social categories in a critical mode, like those developed by Marxism and "critical theory." Therefore, although Gadamer is correct when charging Habermas with the narrowing of the hermeneutic dimension, he cannot himself effectively encounter the critical position of Habermas and utilize the benefits from a critical discourse on society. Nevertheless, my comments are not intended to erase the critical elements in Gadamer's approach.

Gadamer denies the charge that he absolutizes tradition. To point to the world and tradition as the medium of human understanding, he believes, does not lead to the conclusion that tradition is absolute. Instead, his position is that "we should try to understand everything that can be understood."[27] Again, I think, Gadamer avoids the main problem previously indicated, that is, whether tradition needs to be criticized at all and by what means. There is a third issue, here, on which Gadamer seems to hold a strong view. He disagrees emphatically with Habermas's position concerning the *role of reflection* for penetrating ideology and dissolving its dogmatic assertions. On this point Gadamer argues:

> But does this mean that we "understand" only when we see through pretexts or unmask false pretensions? Habermas's Marxist critique of ideology appears to presuppose this meaning.[28]

It is as if the power of reflection presents itself only when it has this effect of disclosure. Nevertheless, reflection, Gadamer insists, does not always lead to the termination of prior convictions.

I would argue that there is a significant difference between the two positions that must be taken into account. Habermas's argument about the power of reflection is strengthened only when we accept the fact that the convictions which reflection reveals are always ideological and false. The employment of reason when dealing with ideology, or, in the case of psychoanalytic reflection, the employment of a much more complicated process (involving as well psychological stages of overcoming resistances), "guarantee" the overcoming and erasure of what is found to be false or illegitimate. In Gadamer's approach, the convictions and prejudices that reflection is able to disclose are not necessarily false or unjustified. On the contrary, they might reveal themselves as "productive" prejudices and thus are retained and trusted. From his position on what constitutes prejudices, Gadamer's criticism of Habermas's narrow concept of reflection appears justifiable. Reflection is employed by the latter in a specific manner which follows the presuppositions of the Marxist view of ideology (attributing to it concealing and deception). Gadamer calls this attitude a prejudice which Habermas inherits from Marxist discourse. It is true that Gadamer refers here to the prejudice of "suspicion" that applies both to Marxism and Freudianism. (Ricoeur has actually called the two theories "hermeneutics of suspicion."[29]) However, I would not dismiss this prejudice of "suspicion" as unjustified, as Gadamer implies, but rather (using his terminology) see it as a significant stage in our "historical consciousness." The acceptance of the prejudice of "suspicion" has at least enabled the development of critical positions during this century, either as Marxism or Freudianism.

If we return to Gadamer, I would argue that, in fairness to him, his philosophical concept of reflection is much broader than Habermas's and it can actually cover situations of what is valid in language, in tradition, and in culture that Habermas's approach was never designed to deal with. Gadamer feels that the issue at stake is whether reflection brings something to awareness which one can either retain or reject, or whether (as Habermas implies) bringing something to awareness always dissolves previously accepted convictions. This formulation is rather misleading. It does not appear to me that we can dismiss one approach in favor of the other, since in either case valid positions are included. Rather, I would suggest that both *instances of reflection* retain their validity and should be explored in the particular circumstances and theoretical framework in which they are employed.

Habermas's notion is applicable only when we can show, with strong argumentation, that aspects of tradition are ideological or illegitimate. It can apply to such aspects and beliefs but obviously cannot claim universality, since not all tradition is ideological. Gadamer's notion of reflection appeals to larger areas of hermeneutic experience and is in a position to claim universal application. Its merit lies in the fact that it permits the recognition of something valid from the past. Nevertheless, his writings lack a "coherent" view of society which restricts the development of a sufficient critique of tradition. For such a purpose, he relies upon the evaluation of prejudices. However, the judgment for the retention or the dismissal of prejudices cannot deal with the whole context of society, its structure, its reproduction, and its available forces. (Even if we are aware of the fact that these concepts only represent certain current ideas of what society is, this picture does not change.)

The exchange of views and criticisms on the topic of tradition, authority, and the critique of ideology continually presents itself from two antithetical sides. One side is occupied by Gadamer's voice, speaking of tradition containing "truths" that always teach us, as well as our inescapable position within tradition and the lack of any external vantage point from which to view it. The other side consists of Habermas's positions and critical remarks; he considers tradition (as language) to be ideological and a medium of domination and legitimation of force. He then demands its critique and our emancipation from its dogmatic or false teachings. One initial approach would be to consider this debate on tradition as represented by a radical view opposing a conservative one. I have tried, however, to show that both writers introduce valuable views on what tradition is and what our stance toward it could be. What kind of mediation could one expect then between these two antithetical views? There is room for approaching the subject in a different way. In my opinion, these two opposing views on tradition express possible characteristics of the content of tradition itself. They express opposing features which can be found in our tradition; this means that we live together with such contrary elements, *with* them and *within* them.

Holding such a view is quite legitimate. Values, truths, and insights we follow today exist with their origins located in the past; even Marxism and Freud's theory have become part of our tradition. Similarly, we can admit that we share beliefs of an ideological (false or distorted) nature that are part of tradition and are based upon certain interpretations and initial viewpoints. I cannot accept tradition to be a homogeneous sphere composed entirely either of distorted and dogmatic (false) views, or of truths and insights.

The difficulty with Gadamer's approach is that, although he would admit the existence of unjustified prejudices or of wrong beliefs, he would not think of a (linguistic or sociological) theory of ideology as necessary. In his view the reflection upon our hermeneutic experience, the ensuing critical judgment, as well as consensual agreement make us capable of finally deciding upon what is worth keeping or rejecting. But is it enough? Our "historical consciousness" in this century has been exposed to Marxism and Freudianism. The notion of ideology belongs to our exceptionally strong paradigm of understanding "society." In this paradigm one needs to be informed of the "material" processes that generate or contribute to the ideological aspects of tradition. Such an approach, of course, we cannot find in Gadamer. I would argue that there is a lack of critical stance toward tradition in his views, which, however, retain other critical elements as regards society discussed later in this chapter. It is evident that Gadamer does not want to reduce his hermeneutic reflective experience to a sociological critical theory. After all, Marxism for him is "an interpretative standpoint that our century has developed as ways of going behind what is meant in subjective consciousness."[30]

If we turn now to the other side of these two competing views, it is apparent that Habermas also uses traditional notions of critique, although it is hard to accept because they are in use and well assimilated in current critical projects; he makes use of Marxist and Freudian theory (e.g., the categories of "ideology" and "distorted communication") in order to criticize tradition. Habermas does not wish to pay attention to the fact that he also acts within tradition, with traditional theoretical tools, even when he considers them to lie beyond tradition. Additionally, he must locate and (reflectively) bring to light the presuppositions of his "critical theory." Gadamer's theory of understanding is capable of assisting in this direction. "Critical theory" must "meet" tradition and its own dependency on tradition, as already indicated. Neither are all beliefs *ideological* (in a Marxist use of the term) nor is all tradition rejectable. The logical conclusion of such observations is to acknowledge Gadamer's conception of tradition as quite true, although in need of incorporating "a critical view of tradition." Philosophical hermeneutics may not require the adoption of a sociological view of society; however, it is in need of assimilating further "critical views" that can play this role. It is in need of locating already existing "critical prejudices" or "critical prejudgments" and of accepting them in case they can be judged as productive.

Ricoeur on Tradition and "Critique"

Another writer whose conclusions on the subject of "tradition" and "critique" in the debate stand very close to the conclusions I have just reached, is Paul Ricoeur. He is a philosopher who has developed his position along a *hermeneutical* variation of Husserlian *phenomenolo-*

gy that he describes as *reflexive* philosophy.[31] In my opinion, Ricoeur is one of the few commentators of the Gadamer-Habermas debate to understand both the explicit and latent issues involved, and is able to probe deeply into the debate. In an article reflecting upon the opposing views of the two participants he concluded that we need a critical stance toward civilization in which interests are reduced almost to mere instrumentality and where we witness daily the industrialization and manipulation of all dimensions in our cultural life. This critical stance would enable us to preserve the difference, between the idea of the "good life" introduced and discussed by philosophers, and the growth of material goods that appears to be the law of the industrial system.

> Only the conjunction between the critique of ideologies, animated by our interests in emancipation, and the reinterpretation of the heritages of the past, animated by our interest in communication, may yet give a concrete content to this effort.[32]

To arrive at such a position Ricoeur studied both Gadamer's and Habermas's approaches appraising the shortcomings in either direction. Although Ricoeur's interest lies in the study of the origin and the emergence of (moral) values in history, the debate seems to him to be exemplary to provide access to his questions. At this point it would be helpful to refer in brief to Ricoeur's extension of Gadamer's notion of "temporal distance" and the consequent strengthening of philosophical hermeneutics; as well as to the picture Ricoeur presents about the transmission of values in history and their reinterpretation or *transvaluation*.

According to Ricoeur, philosophical hermeneutics brings to light the "scandal" of modern consciousness, the "alienating distanciation" that is the basic foundation and "presupposition of every human science." Ricoeur recalls here two concepts that Gadamer uses for the articulation of our experience both in the areas of art and history and the human sciences. The first is the concept of "temporal distance," the gap that separates us from the past, which we met in the second chapter, together with our effort to overcome it by the fusion of horizons. The second concept refers to "our belonging to tradition" which Ricoeur calls "participation."

In the domain of the sciences, Gadamer describes the *distance* they preserve from their object of study in order to examine it under methodological procedures, as "methodical alienation." This is exactly the attitude of "objectivism" in the sciences referred to it in the first chapter. Ricoeur, nevertheless, thinks that the diametrical opposite to this "distanciation" Gadamer describes lies is the concept of "participation." Hermeneutics demonstrates our sitedness in tradition and shows that all our initial prejudgments have been transmitted to us by tradition. We never become totally free from tradition and our situation in history and, therefore, we need to become aware of our ontological predicament. This situation or predicament describes the notion of "participation," our belongingness in history and tradition. Thus, finally, hermeneutics is trapped in this massive opposition between "alienating distanciation" and "participation," according to Ricoeur. To him this particular conflict appears as a renewal of the arguments between Enlightenment and Romanticism which, in our time, he considers sterile. While the Enlightenment would admit reason and tradition to be totally opposing and antinomous, Romanticism could not find a way to attack the presuppositions and prejudices of the former according to which reason and judgment based on reason are universal and correct, or that free will can be established beyond historical boundaries.

Ricoeur, therefore, attempts to go one step further by calling for a *critical distance* that has developed within philosophical hermeneutics. He considers Gadamer's concept of "historical effective consciousness," analyzed in the second chapter, to be the answer to this direction. This concept takes into consideration the state of consciousness "exposed to the results of history" and the historical distance involved is brought to light. Approaching something in the past, for example, an "object" or a "value," is accomplished through their "effective history," and, according to Ricoeur the fusion of horizons that takes place occurs in an open and distant horizon. We do not live within an hermetically closed horizon, he argues, nor in a unique one. The communication and fusion of two horizons is accomplished at a distance; the tension represented between our horizon and the other alien one is resolved in an open distant horizon.

If we now recall the linguisticality of all human experience as I considered in the third chapter, stemming from Gadamer's positions, our belonging to a tradition is exercised through the *interpretation* of symbols, signs, and texts, which carry traditions, customs, rituals, practices, and everything from the past that, in Ricoeur's terminology, can be characterized as "cultural heritage." Ricoeur regards "writing" as one section of this experience of interpretation (involving both historical distance and participation). A written text from the past enjoys a triple *autonomy*. Firstly, it is independent from its present reader and his intentions. Secondly, it appears to be independent from its initial position: the discourse and sociocultural conditions affecting its position at that time. Thirdly, it enjoys independence from the initial audience. But why is such independence and distance created through history so important? It is this distance that Ricoeur calls "productive distanciation" and is characteristic of civilizations that possess *writing*; it is "productive because it allows the *transmission* of every past heritage." Ricoeur, I think, provides us with a very strong case of cultural transmission through writing, though one would not deny that other means of transmission could be possible. What is important, though, in his exposition is the *autonomy* of the text through history and that the textual model of transmission through history is applicable to all parts of our cultural heritage. A transmission of this kind is exampled by the case of values. He demonstrates how the value of "nobility" is finally inscribed as part of our own "cultural patrimony" but at the same time it has become independent of the conditions of its genesis. Ricoeur can then say that "a value becomes valuable beyond the historical-cultural circumstances of its birth."[33]

Such an *autonomy* from the past and the initial audience invites us to a series of reinterpretations (and "applications" in Gadamer's terms) of each new situation that arises. In my view, the notion of "critical distance" that Ricoeur had in mind, makes itself felt here, in our freedom and possibility to *reinterpret* values from the past, to transvaluate, and to receive other parts of our cultural heritage. Nevertheless, it must be emphasized that a reinterpretation of past heritages, in order to be critical, requires additional guidance or presupposition. Such a thought forces Ricoeur to suggest that philosophical hermeneutics needs to adopt "a regulative idea of emancipation," otherwise, it would be in danger of remaining a "hermeneutics of tradition" similar to the nostalgia of Romanticism.

What Ricoeur introduces is a widely accepted view: a consistent critical stance in reinterpretation and reevaluation is further guaranteed when it is based upon a regulative idea of emancipation. This is what he attributes to the "critical social sciences": they have the ability to incorporate a *projection* of our future autonomy as the basic meaning of any critical enterprise. But again, normative emancipatory ideas may originate in different discourses. One possibility is that they can be provided by humanism and by the Enlightenment itself (as in the case of Gadamer and Habermas). Such ideas could represent ambivalent positions incorporating universal (utopian) plans for saving humanity; they could be criticized as belonging to the arena of metaphysics (a subject that I will refer to in the last chapter). However, as another future possibility, "less ambitious" normative ideas are also available and are supplied by the Enlightenment, as those of *autonomy* and *justice*[34] detached from universal plans of emancipation (associated with Marxism).

In the "critique of ideologies," Ricoeur discovers invaluable gains since such a critique serves to realize what has been imposed upon the human agent. He argues, however, that a simple critique of "distortions" (as Habermas defines ideology) cannot restore communicative action to its full capacity. A "critical theory" must look back at tradition and establish its normative content in mediation with it. Ricoeur justifies this position by arguing that we do not *create* values from nothing, rather it is always a matter of *discovering* values in our heritage and transvaluating them to the present situation. He considers the continuous efforts to transvaluation to be connected to our interest in emancipation. "It is only under the aegis of our interest in emancipation that we are stirred to transvaluate what already has been evaluated."[35] Any evidence of lack of projecting new values and course of life would be indicative of lacking in emancipatory interest in freedom. "Freedom only posits itself by transvaluating what already has been evaluated."[36]

It is not only the suggestion that "critical theory" needs to look back at tradition and reinterpret it that constitutes one of Ricoeur's charges against Habermas; there is another valuable point he makes against the latter's normative idea of emancipation. In the previous chapter we encountered Habermas's attempt to ground the emancipatory interest philosophically; drawing from Kantian ideas he concluded that the emancipatory interest is but Reason's interest to itself. The normative idea, which exists in the background of emancipation, points to a society in which "free communication" can be exercized without constraints and repression. This normative idea, proposed by Habermas, opposes the situation of present societies in which ideological mechanisms reign in the form of distorted communication. The concept is codified as "ideal speech situation" and can become the norm for any critical project within the perspective of "critical theory." Ricoeur, nevertheless, terms it "an eschatology of nonviolence" with a utopian character which undermines the theory's critical position as "critique of ideologies." Instead, he argues, the content of the emancipatory interest must be supported by our practical interest in communication.

I understand Ricoeur's position in the following way: the possibility of emancipation relies largely upon dialogue and communication. Critical projects of freedom and autonomy, their insights into what is valuable and worth achieving, cannot be imposed upon societies by any dogmatic unmediated theory or concept. Alternatively, dialogue, the exchange of views, and the ability to understand each other, seem to be some of the basic presuppositions for critical projects. Pursuing this line of thought, the interest in emancipation must be traced in our practical interest in communication. We are interested in the successful restoration of communication, whenever it is broken or distorted, as the "critique of ideologies" implies. We can therefore conclude that we are not in need of a utopian normative idea of "an ideal speech situation." Instead, Ricoeur argues, we already have the experience of an "effective communication" even though this experience is derived from the restricted sphere of interpersonal relations in everyday communication. To me, Ricoeur's suggestion is very powerful and it is no accident that Habermas's later shift toward a theory of communication and a theoretical reconstruction of our linguistic competences, coincides with it. Still, even in this later shift in the rules that dictate our ability to understand each other, Habermas continues his attempts to locate normative foundations for the existence of an emancipatory interest.

"Reflection" and "Criticality" in Gadamer

In view of Habermas's criticisms against Gadamer's "uncritical" position with regard to tradition, it is worthwhile indicating whether philosophical hermeneutics possesses any critical positions or critical stance, or whether any notion of critique can be detected amid its premises. I will begin with the notion of "reflection," mentioned earlier in this chapter, which attracted many exchanges between the two participants. We witnessed Habermas's accusation that Gadamer denied the power of reflection, but in the latter's view Habermas had narrowed the concept of reflection only to the point of dissolving all previous (false or ideological) convictions; a misinterpretation of reflection according to Gadamer. My position at that exchange was that each side preserved legitimacy within their respective discourses.

I will now consider more fully the concept of reflection which can support claims of a critical position available to philosophical hermeneutics. We learn that "to reflect" can mean to "call to mind," to think on, or to hit upon,[37] in the form used by Heidegger. These are possible translations and illustrate initial directions of how to understand "reflection." However, in phenomenology and hermeneutics, it acquires a more extensive specialized use. Heidegger wrote that reflection is more than reaching a simple awareness of something.

> To venture after sense or meaning [Sinn] is the essence of reflecting [Besinnen]. This means more than a mere making conscious of something. We do not yet have reflection when we have only consciousness. Reflection is more. It is calm, self-possessed surrender to that which is worthy of questioning. (Italics mine.)[38]

Although his language might reach poetic dimensions, it neverthe-less presents a lively understanding of reflection as a phenomeno-logical category. It is important to observe that, for reflection, it is necessary to enter a dialogue and questioning that can render some-thing more "visible" and within our grasp. If the object of reflection is the self we then talk of *self-reflection*. This point is stressed by Ricoeur who says that for *reflexive* philosophy (which he follows) the most radical philosophical problems orbit around the possibility of *self-understanding*. "Reflexion is the act of turning back upon itself" and the notion of reflexion carries with it "the desire for absolute transparence, a perfect coincidence of the self with the self."[39] Ricoeur's notion suits, as he argues, the dominant phenomenological view on reflection as well as the mainstream view of hermeneutics which is on the same path (since it employs phenomenological analysis). In Ricoeur's approach, however, we can observe that "reflection" still appears to retain within it the Hegelian echo of absolute knowledge;[40] it also differs from Heidegger's notion which has no directionality.[41]

If we return to philosophical hermeneutics we discover that reflection is part of the hermeneutic experience itself. The structure of understanding, according to Gadamer, includes a reflective dimension. When we are engaged in understanding we also attempt to bring to light that which is involved in the act of understanding. This is especially evident when we confront an alien tradition. Reflection coincides with the emergence of the hermeneutical prob-lem we encounter when we need to understand others and the world. We have already seen how reflection was able to trace back those prejudices (preunderstandings) that exist within each one of us and make possible any understanding. But let us follow the conse-quences of this theoretical position on "reflection."

I examined earlier that some prejudgments might be correct and some incorrect or unproductive, so one has to abandon them. Therefore, the act of reflection enables us to project before us our prejudgments and convictions and thereby judge them. I would claim that such a possibility within our hermeneutic understanding constitutes a *critical* position toward our prejudices and our own self-constitution. Gadamer never stopped repeating the idea of making our prejudices transparent; passing judgment upon them is a critical position and accompanies the act of reflection. A similar situation can be observed in the social-historical sciences; a possi-ble shaking of their presuppositions (prejudices) that the act of reflection can bring about is but a critical intervention. Gadamer thinks that reflection, which can undermine the fixed presuppositions in these disciplines, makes new questions possible and helps their further progress. From this involvement of reflection either as self-reflection or reflection upon the foundations of a discipline, a further consequence is inevitable; *our presuppositions and prejudgments*, under reflective questioning and scrutiny, *are always at stake*. Although, initially, this conclusion, might appear to suggest a source of instability, I believe that it should be met positively, because it challenges dogmatic reasoning and unchallenged dogmatic prejudices that we may hold. Concurrently, aside from the fact that our presuppositions are always at stake, we never cease to form new preunderstandings in view of further reflection and of our dialogical participation in society.[42]

Gadamer's point is that the contribution of hermeneutic reflection in the sciences cannot be restricted to making them aware of incorrect presuppositions or initial standpoints that would contribute to an epistemological correction. Reflection, especially in the case of the social sciences, exposes "a deeply rooted alienation," which they also transport upon the "natural consciousness" (our everyday consciousness). Gadamer has in mind the *methodical alienation*, the price the social sciences have paid for their progress. In his view "these sciences increasingly see themselves as marked out for the purpose of scientific ordering and control of society." They impose their "scientific" and "methodical" views for the development, planning, and organization of a society which encompasses the whole of our life. The social scientist or "social engineer" who undertakes the task of looking at society in order to introduce "scientific" solutions, is "methodically alienated" and separated from the same society in which he is a member. "It is the function of hermeneutical reflection, in this connection, to preserve us from naive surrender to the experts of social technology."[43] I must add here that, even though Gadamer's views are more than twenty years old, the situation within the social sciences is largely as he describes it. Nevertheless, one cannot dismiss the existence of certain schools in the social sciences, which, with the help of critical discourses, have developed self-critical views concerning their own position in society. In this respect Gadamer's claim is not universally applicable, but proves to be correct when it concerns the majority of popular beliefs; for an example, I could mention the attitude which the modern state and its institutions show toward the adoption of social engineering. The employment, then, of hermeneutic reflection in the social sciences, can point to the adoption of *critical* questioning of, and *critical* opposition to, those practices which impose or introduce "methodically alienated" orientations and nondialogical rationality.

Concluding these comments on the subject of reflection I would like to mention that Habermas attributes to reflection major liberating powers (directed toward the self) of which Gadamer would be sceptical; this applies especially to the case of dissolving dogmatic or false convictions and beliefs. Of course, Habermas's conception of self-reflection is almost identical to the Freudian concept; the latter, dissolving dogmatic states of consciousness (demonstrated in individual clinical cases), seems to me to be derived from the more familiar aspect of the Hegelian notion of reflection and the subsequent Aufhebung (sublimation) that consciousness achieves. Gadamer, although remaining within the Hegelian notion of reflection (as a phenomenological category), is less eager to accept its ability to disperse previous stages of convictions and judgments. Instead, his attention is focused upon the *transparency of consciousness,* as Ricoeur just suggested. The Heideggerian influence on Gadamer's notion of reflection is also apparent; in no way is reflection employed with the single aim of dissolving false consciousness. After reflection, the arrival at a judgment for the acceptance or rejection of a prejudice does not have the strong resonances of a total "overcoming" of previous convictions as the Hegelian notion suggests. Such conclusions might sound somewhat strange, because Gadamer himself accepts the fact that after entering a dialogue we never exit as the same person. It is not so much the change and the *Aufhebung* which occur after reflection that Gadamer is stressing, since he agrees that we always reach at a new stage of awareness and that hermeneutic reflection frees us toward ourselves.[44] Rather, he emphasizes the point that hermeneutical reflection leads to *self-understanding* and also gives us *the choice to retain* something that we judge to be correct, justified, or true.[45]

If reflection can reveal its critical implications for our self-understanding and for our dealing with our prejudices, I would claim that the hermeneutic theory of Gadamer, as a whole, can be considered as *retaining aspects of a critical enterprise*; it cannot be simply doomed to an uncritical "theory of understanding," as Habermas tends to suggest. Nonetheless, there is a further critical side to philosophical hermeneutics. In order to make us aware of what happens in any situation of understanding in which we find ourselves, Gadamer reveals two cases of *alienation*: the aesthetic and historical alienation of consciousness present both in our aesthetic judgment and in our historical understanding (especially in the historical sciences). According to Gadamer, (mentioned in the second chapter), before a work of art, whenever it becomes an object of aesthetic judgment, we judge it purely on its aesthetic qualities; something in it, however, which might be more important and familiar is inaccessible because it has been rejected and alienated by our initial approach. This is particularly the case, he argues, when we withdraw ourselves and are not "open to the immediate claim of that which grasps us."[46] The same occurs, as we have already witnessed, in the historical sciences which cannot retrieve from the past what is essential to us, because they transform history to an object of study by detaching ourselves from it; this results in historical alienation. Gadamer also recovers the "hermeneutic consciousness" restricted in the case of avoiding misunderstanding between "I" and "thou"; which in his view "betrays an enormous alienation." For Gadamer there can never be two isolated realities, "I" and "thou;" this account simply represents a partial description of what is the real "life world" where "we all are." Therefore, we should attend to his conclusion, that our task is to overcome the alienations present in the aesthetic, the historical, and the hermeneutical consciousness,[47] and consider this engagement of philosophical hermeneutics as a *critical* enterprise. It is critical in the sense that it informs us of alienated forms of experience and the ways in which we conduct our relations with tradition and the past. In fact, these aspects of alienation residing in our consciousness and revealed by philosophical hermeneutics, can play an invaluable role in a critical position with regard to society and those forms of life that give rise to such alienations. This conclusion reduces further the negative image of philosophical hermeneutics as incapable to provide a critical stance toward society and tradition. In addition to these critical abilities of philosophical hermeneutics, Gadamer's theory leads to "truths" from the past that can be of use today; otherwise, such "truths" can easily be lost as we are unable to retrieve them from within our alienated forms of experience and awareness. Although the past is so close, as "effective-history," it also appears distant and irrecoverable through the attitudes of modern sciences (with their "methodical alienation") and of modern thinking which ascribe to us the role of observers rather than that of participants. Gadamer has shown us the way in which we can become aware of this situation by reflecting upon our hermeneutical experience.

During the years that followed the publication of *Truth and Method*, this critical stance that I have ascribed to Gadamer was unable to make itself felt, because of the weight he placed upon approaching tradition, by coming to "agreement" with it and rehabilitating the concept of "tradition" and "authority." His message was mainly heard as an uncritical welcoming of tradition. His critical views on technology and the deterioration of language to technical codes and monologues, instead of the pursuit of dialogue, does not erase the main image of his *Truth and Method*. In the Foreword of the second edition of *Truth and Method* he himself accepted that, in this work, the universality of hermeneutic understanding resulted in a one-sided picture because it lacked a "critical principle" vis-à-vis tradition. The reason for this was that the emphasis was laid on "the element of the assimilation of what is past and handed down."[48] He also admitted that his exposition had not shown "the projective character of understanding" Heidegger described as the futural character of there-being. This point coincides with what Ricoeur was indicating earlier when he suggested that philosophical hermeneutics is in need of a regulative norm, or a project of emancipation, according to which it can strengthen its critical positions. Although this appears as a shortcoming of Gadamer's positions, he nevertheless contends that his hermeneutics "has the truth of a corrective": firstly, it can enlighten the current attitude of our participation in life and secondly, it can enable us to draw the distinctions between that which is feasible and welcome (e.g., self-understanding, dialogue, and critique of alienated forms of life) and that which should not be within the range of our interests since it belongs to an eschatological consciousness (e.g., universal plans of emancipation, such as Marxism, "ideal speech situation," and "total liberation").

6

The Universality of the
Hermeneutic Problem

I now enter another issue of the debate which concentrates upon the acceptance or rejection of what Habermas has termed the "hermeneutic claim to universality." To achieve this I will firstly reiterate Gadamer's position on the universality of hermeneutic understanding as well as his ontological claim. Secondly, I will follow Habermas's introduction of depth-hermeneutical analysis in everyday "normal" speech which presents nonpathological cases of "distorted communication." Thirdly, I will examine the claim that depth-hermeneutics, an alternative mode of understanding, can refute the universality of hermeneutic understanding, and fourthly, I will study Habermas's questioning of the "consensus" that underlies any dialogue which is his second attempt to refute the hermeneutic claim. Following these main issues my attention will focus on the criticisms and reservations Gadamer levels against the psychoanalytic model upon which Habermas bases his "critical theory." Finally, I will introduce the controversy between "situational understanding" and its "relativism" versus scientific approaches and their "objectivity." This last issue elaborates on the implications of the debate in hand and has been intensively discussed by many philosophers in the Anglo-Saxon tradition.

The Hermeneutic Claim

I have examined the theses of Gadamer concerning understanding and that language in the third chapter. Briefly, Gadamer supported the idea that "all understanding *is* interpretation"; this claim constitutes *the universal claim of hermeneutics* in the sense that any understanding we can achieve exhibits its hermeneutical dimensions as a linguistic interpretation. In a further claim Gadamer asserted that all our experience is of linguistic nature. At this point I indicated a plausible way of understanding the linguisticality of all possible experience as language is involved in each step of perception and cognition. There is always an interpreted world that we find ourselves in. Because of its linguistic nature, we (inescapably) receive and understand any experience in linguistic terms, as interpretation. Such a conclusion leads to the position that the experience of the world is hermeneutical and this situation is universal.

A further consequence drawn by philosophical hermeneutics is that, because of the *universality* of the "hermeneutic problem" (our inescapable position to be always engaged in interpretive understanding), or the universality of the hermeneutical experience, *we are interpretative beings*. Our basic mode of existence in the world is within language (although we are not captives), and through constant understanding of each other in dialogue or in any sort of experience coming from both the familiar and the alien. This claim, which represents the ontological aspect of hermeneutics, has also been referred to as the "hermeneutic claim to universality." Gadamer however, following this theme, was faced with the "anonymous authority of the sciences" and their pronouncements: how do we legitimate the ontological position of our being, or the "hermeneutical conditionedness" of our being in the world, before the modern sciences which proclaim unbiased and nonprejudiced statements? Gadamer's answer was that we should detach our "hermeneutic conditionedness" from the prejudices of science. However, in order to justify Gadamer's suggestion we must follow the debate itself.

The discussion on the hermeneutic claim to universality concentrates upon the use of language or the ways in which we move within it. Martin Jay points out that both Gadamer and Habermas share common assumptions about language.[1] First, they disassociate themselves from the traditional view of philosophy in which language is considered to be an underrated medium in which to describe the "real world." Instead, they believe that language is an intersubjective activity that brings speakers together. Another shared position is that they both discuss language at the level of *parole* instead of the level of *la langue*[2] (which is the ground of Saussurian semiology and of French structuralist philosophers). However, Gadamer uses the term *dialogue*, while Habermas prefers the term *communication*, stressing the pragmatic and rhetorical dimensions of language. It is also the dimension of *parole* that permits them to introduce the historical moment (or historicality) in their theories that would have been impossible within any semiological theory of language.

These remarks on the hermeneutic claim, on our hermeneutic predicament, and on our "dialogic" engagement, establish Gadamer's main premise that Habermas proceeds with, even though he disagrees with the former. Habermas introduces an essential difference between hermeneutics and philosophical hermeneutics. The first is the art of understanding "linguistically communicable meaning." It helps us to restore communication whenever it has been broken and is an ability everybody acquires when mastering a natural language. Philosophical hermeneutics, on the other hand, is not an act but a *critique*; the fact that it always moves within language and the range of its "reflexive engagement" brings to our awareness experiences gained from within the use of language. This demonstrates a new appreciation of philosophical hermeneutics as a critical discipline that Habermas introduces in distinction to his treatment of it as a philological translation (in his *Knowledge and Human Interests*). Here I take the notion of *critique* as meaning the ability of self-reflection involved in philosophical hermeneutics, to raising and consciously judging the prejudices that accompany any understanding. It is further capable of passing judgment upon the success or failure of communication that appears in everyday life.

Therefore, philosophical hermeneutics defines its critical nature thorough its ability to engage in self-reflection. For Habermas it represents "the philosophical consideration of the structures of everyday communication."[3] By using the term *communication* instead of *dialogue,* he is able to draw further distinctions between *distorted* and *undistorted communication*, of which the notion of *dialogue* is incapable.

Such a description of philosophical hermeneutics, though, falls short of what Gadamer contemplated and altogether fails to address the basic ontological positions of his approach. What is Habermas's purpose then? By employing this difference between philosophical hermeneutics and hermeneutics, Habermas wishes to demonstrate that philosophical hermeneutics remains encircled within natural language (everyday language), yet standing in a reflective relationship toward it. In this way philosophical hermeneutics is unable to understand distorted communication because it cannot base itself on a meta-language (outside natural language) which could permit an explanation of the distortions. *Distorted communication*, or ideology, appears to Habermas to be *objectivations*[4] in everyday language in which the subject cannot understand the intentions guiding her expressive activity. This definition of distorted communication is borrowed from the Freudian theory of pathologically distorted communication.

Finally Habermas counterproposes, to the notions of hermeneutic consciousness and reflective awareness, the idea of *reconstruction*. Self-reflection brings to the awareness of the individual the nature of her understanding and her specific ways of "belonging" to language, which is both dependence and freedom of movement since fusion with other linguistic horizons is possible. Nevertheless, this reflective awareness, according to Habermas, cannot explain to the individual her linguistic competence. Instead, such an explanation becomes only possible through "the rational *reconstruction* of a system of linguistic rules." Obviously, Habermas's intentions are to show the "limited" character of philosophical hermeneutics to sustain any scientificity and its inability to examine distorted communication in a systematic and methodical way. However, we must remember that such an aim was not the intention of Gadamer's philosophical inquiry into the interpretative nature of understanding.

Habermas continues by questioning the relevance of philosophical hermeneutics to the sciences and the interpretation of their results. He does this by locating issues crucial to the sciences' understanding of themselves, in particular, the refutation of the objectivist self-understanding of the "traditional *Geisteswissenschaften*," the "scientistic" self-understanding of the natural sciences, and the problems involved in the social sciences during the symbolic (linguistic) pre-structuring of their object of study.[5] For all these issues the reflective capability of philosophical hermeneutics can be crucial. Nevertheless, Habermas's main task remains; whether there is a *different way of understanding meaning* methodologically, especially the meaning of distorted communication, which can avoid and "transcend" the hermeneutic understanding. He suggests that there are two possibilities for such a project. Firstly, he considers the psychoanalytic model, with its depth-hermeneutics, capable of serving as a guide by transferring its methodological experience to the critique of ideology which refers to collective social phenomena. Secondly, a rational reconstruction of a theory of linguistic competence could fulfill the same aim. If this reconstruction can be achieved, then any particular element of the natural language could be described by, or correspond to, a statement in a theoretical language; thus, such a theoretical meta-language could entirely replace the hermeneutic understanding of meaning. However, he admits that such an ambitious theory was not available at the time of his investigation.

Habermas then proceeds to examine whether psychoanalysis can by-pass the usual way of hermeneutical understanding of meaning by deploying, instead, a "theoretical semantic analysis." He believes that if such a *different mode of understanding* meaning can be validated, the hermeneutic claim to universality can no longer stand (as its universality would cease to be true). I would argue that his aim, through the examination of the critical science of psychoanalysis, is twofold. Firstly, as I just indicated, he attempts to show that a different kind of understanding is possible apart from the familiar hermeneutic one. Secondly, psychoanalysis opens the way for the introduction of the psychoanalytic concept of language distortion or distorted communication into nonpathological cases: actually within everyday, "normal" speech. The case of depth-hermeneutics that I examined in the fourth chapter can consequently be legitimately used beyond psychoanalysis, in other areas of distorted communication which, according to Habermas, characterizes our everyday dialogue in present societies. Philosophical hermeneutics informs us about the way we understand based upon our linguistic competence. It promotes a hermeneutic consciousness that Habermas considers incomplete, because it cannot see its own limitations. Hermeneutic understanding, he claims, cannot understand "incomprehensible expressions." Although it is adequate to approach meaning that lies at "cultural" or "temporal distance," it is entirely inadequate when approaching cases of "systematically distorted communication." He admits that if the systematic distortions of language occur in pathological cases, then hermeneutics justifiably considers such cases irrelevant to its approach of meaning. Nevertheless, he believes that cases of systematically distorted communication do happen in "normal" speech situations, but hermeneutics cannot detect them as it approaches all "normal" speech as dialogue the meaning of which must be understood. The result of such situations, Habermas argues, is "pseudocommunication."

In "pseudocommunication" the speech is "pathologically unobtrusive" and the participants cannot see any failure in their communication. However, in Habermas's view, a whole system of *misunderstandings* occur which remain undetected, hidden beneath the consensus which prevails between the participants in communication. In these circumstances the consensus is a *false* one. Habermas believes that if we want to detect and examine a pseudocommunication we must call upon the perspective of a possible *external* observer who would be able to view and assess the ways in which the participants misunderstand one another. However, is such a possibility available? Can one step outside language and be able to identify the case of a pseudocommunication? Habermas openly admits that when we move within the natural language we become participants in it and, as philosophical hermeneutics teaches, we cannot put ourselves outside and beyond it. So, he accepts the fact that there is no "general criterion" available, which, when employed, could inform us of our presence within a pseudocommunication and the development of misunderstandings of which we are unaware. Systematically distorted communication cannot be approached by hermeneutics in the usual way within natural language; it requires the engagement of "systematic explanation." Habermas employs a different approach which suggests an acceptance of philosophical hermeneutics predicated on an understanding of its limited nature.

> The experience of *the limit of hermeneutics* consists of *the recognition of systematically generated misunderstanding* as such—*without, at first, being able to "grasp" it*. (Italics mine.)[6]

What then is Habermas suggesting? I could look at his effort in a hermeneutic way. He puts forward a new *presupposition*: we must assume that speech in present societies is distorted, although not pathologically; rather, a distortion arising from "systematically generated misunderstanding" which usual hermeneutic procedures cannot render comprehensible since it requires a systematic explanation. Habermas wants us to look upon any communication we can participate in, with this new prejudgment. Such a setting and view leads us to see the distorted (misunderstood) meaning, which now appears in a systematic (repeated) way, coming from certain mechanisms and structures in society; they generate distorted meaning and are responsible for its systematic form (i.e., similar initial conditions generate the same repeated symptoms).

Is such a view or presupposition justified? There are empirical cases in speech situations where we can detect difficulties in understanding their meaning, or even cases where we could observe repeated cases of censorship, although such incidents could be referred back to the Freudian model of distorted speech. We can also suppose that, many times in everyday dialogue (or if we put ourselves in the position of the audience in our mass media societies), we *use* (or hear) a language that in the end is passive toward, and uncritical of, a number of institutions. Our speech ultimately legitimates their presence, despite the fact that we frequently have strong convictions that such institutions are repressive in nature. We could perhaps enumerate many examples with similar discrepancies between speech content and empirical experiences, or examples where hermeneutic understanding could not reveal the repetitive character of an "unobtrusive" symptom in language. All these possible examples, however, could at most, only support *convictions* of suspicion and encourage dissatisfaction with hermeneutics which, in certain circumstances, might be unable to confront "meaning" critically.

A Critical View of "Distorted Communication"

Let us observe how we could comprehend Habermas's plan to reinforce our critical position. The question which I would pose is: How can we accept something even if we cannot "grasp" it? How can we accept the presence of distorted communication if we are unable to locate it? Habermas's program, as an answer to these questions, can be described in three steps. Firstly, out of strong convictions and of similarities with the Freudian theory when it refers to pathological language deformation, we *suspect* that there is distorted communication notwithstanding our inability to detect it. The notion of distorted communication is initially structured in terms similar to the Freudian concepts of deformed language. Secondly, we have to form a theory of what constitutes a normal speech situation, thus enabling ourselves to judge what is distorted. The construction of such a theory can be achieved by borrowing corresponding concepts from the psychoanalytic experience. To this end Habermas supplies us with the theoretical assumptions that the psychoanalyst has in mind concerning "the structure of undistorted everyday communication." Alternatively, this task could best be accomplished by a reconstruction of the rules that govern our linguistic competence (a project he followed later). Here, the theory must be supplemented with the connective link between systematic speech distortions and societal mechanisms, conditions, or structures that produce such distortions. This theoretical link could then provide the explanatory account for systematic explanation. Thirdly, the new theory would then be able to consider any "speech act" critically and, following the theory's criteria and norms, to judge what is a systematic misunderstanding, a systematic distortion or (it amounts to the same thing) an ideological case. It would also be able to elucidate the mechanisms that have produced the distortion. The end result then, as Habermas believes, is that the comprehension of meaning in such pseudocommunication has not employed hermeneutic understanding. But is this the case? Can he claim that the construction of such a critical project for questioning distorted communication is beyond the realm of hermeneutical experience? I will answer this question after I have considered the example of depth-hermeneutics or critical hermeneutics that Habermas locates in psychoanalysis and which seem to be transferable to the area of communication.

I mentioned earlier that one of the basic aims of Habermas was to demonstrate the existence of another way of understanding in order to refute Gadamer's hermeneutic claim to universality. This he initially undertakes to accomplish, not with his theoretical projections on understanding and explaining pseudocommunication that I just examined, but with the case of depth-hermeneutics that the well-tried practice of psychoanalysis has employed. The level of analysis and understanding that depth hermeneutics employs is, for Habermas, removed from the range of hermeneutic understanding that takes place within natural language. We considered these notions at the end of the fourth chapter and I explained the formation of the "general interpretations" and their role in explaining systematic pathological disturbances. However, in the essay I presently follow,[7] which Habermas wrote after *Knowledge and Human Interests* as a reply to Gadamer, he attempts a closer "linguistic" approximation of the Freudian theory in order that the transposition of the Freudian conceptualizations to his theory of "distorted communication" can be achieved with ease.

To follow Habermas's analysis of the Freudian theory at this point is unnecessary. I am mainly interested in the notion of "scenic understanding"[8] that accompanies depth hermeneutics. Habermas provides a description of how, in neurotic cases, the "inner exile" that Freud talked of is formed as an excommunicated content from public usage.[9] It is the case with neurotically distorted forms of expression that, finally, the excommunicated part becomes incomprehensible, privatized and inaccessible to the author himself. In the patient one can observe a discrepancy between the "I" which participates in everyday communication, and the "inner exile" which has been privatized. Depth hermeneutics then is employed in order to decode the meaning of incomprehensible objectivations appearing as symptomatic expressions or scenes. Thus we are dealing with an understanding and clarification of such scenes. The analyst attempts to interpret the meaning of the symptomatic scene which the patient enacts (in the case of neuroses they are deformed language-games). Scenic understanding aims at the reconstruction of the *original scene* that the patient can validate with his self-reflection. In this way a "resymbolization" and reintroduction into public use of the excommunicated content (that had been desymbolized previously) is attempted. Scenic understanding therefore, aims at the explanation of the emergence of the symptomatic scenes by referring them to the initial conditions of the distortion.

Habermas stresses the fact that it is the explanatory ability of the scenic understanding which differs from the practice of hermeneutical understanding. What also distinguishes scenic understanding from hermeneutical understanding is that it does not rely exclusively upon the skilled application of communicative competence as is the case with hermeneutical understanding; instead, it follows theoretical assumptions and presuppositions[10] that allow it to furnish explanatory accounts for the distorted cases. Let us examine, then, whether these opinions of Habermas are beyond dispute. I will first recall the ability of the analyst to be in dialogue with the patient. The analyst and the patient have to use both natural language and their linguistic competence in order to find themselves in dialogue. Habermas argues that this is a specific form of hermeneutic experimentation and that conditions are established for free association on the part of the patient and for reflective participation by the analyst, so that a "transference," which is vital in the analytic process, can occur. However, even if this situation has the character of an experiment (it might fail; it might not lead to the expected transference), it does not detract from the fact that a hermeneutical understanding is employed in the initial stages of the dialogic relationship of analyst and patient.

Nonetheless, let us continue and consider the case at the point at which the reflective participation of the analyst is required as well as her understanding of the meaning of the patient's recollections. It is obvious, as Habermas argues, that the analyst does not trace the meaning in the usual way of understanding, for example, a text; she relies upon her theoretical assumptions. I would claim that although the analyst's understanding does not follow the path of textual interpretation, it is still an *ordered*, or *controlled interpretation*, a part of which is carried on in natural language. We can observe the presence of natural language in the analytic interpretations in the following instances. Firstly, the reconstructed original scene and the explanatory comments referring it to its initial conditions have to be articulated in everyday, natural language. Secondly, we should not forget that the patient is part of the whole analytic situation; he does not rely upon theoretical presuppositions in order to understand what the analyst says but instead he relies upon his natural language and his competence in it, as well as upon his self-reflection which may help him to validate the original scene. We see here that, in the analytic experience, certain understandings occur in natural language, within the dialogue that develops between the analyst and the patient. Yet, as I said, I would not at all doubt the specificity of the "new" way of interpretation and especially its ability to provide "causal"[11] explanatory statements. But these claims invite closer scrutiny. I just mentioned the term *controlled interpretation*. The analyst uses theoretical hypotheses, assumptions, and presuppositions which, while they can provide explanatory potential, they can, on the other hand, be thought of as parts of the overall cycle of a hermeneutical interpretation. Instead of moving between the parts and the whole, as in the hermeneutic circle, the whole here is understood in accordance with a fixed theory; it is preunderstood in specific guidelines which the psychoanalytic theory in use dictates. Also, the way in which the parts belong to the whole is also supplied by the theory. The symptomatic expressions are relayed to specific structures that generate them. The distortions can be traced upon explicit confusions between the prelinguistic and linguistic organization of symbols (as the theory informs us). It is in this sense that I have used the term *controlled interpretation*. The whole process is a reshaping and breaking of the hermeneutic circle in such a way that enables the analyst to avoid an entirely accidental and "situational understanding" that might erupt. Instead, the new "controlled or methodical" interpretation permits the "reading" (explanation) of what has been identified as symptomatic (repeated symptoms point to a constant source for their emergence).

Habermas contends that depth-hermeneutics differs from "translation" which is the norm of traditional hermeneutics. The difference is located at the point that, whereas hermeneutical understanding proceeds from preunderstandings (prejudices) that are formed within tradition, depth-hermeneutics instead proceeds from "a systematic preunderstanding that extends to language in general."[12] The difference for him indicates that "translation" is based upon the structure of an everyday communication susceptible to deformations and distortions, while depth-hermeneutics begins with a specific perspective of what these distortions are, so it is free of them. The claim made by Habermas that depth-hermeneutics can rely upon a theory of linguistic competences which gives a total, all-inclusive, and correct view of what is normal or distorted, is far from true.[13]

Moreover, as I have tried to show, depth-hermeneutical understanding is itself based on assumptions and prejudgments, but it attempts to relate the "whole" and the "part" causally, in patterns which can be generalized, thus covering individual cases. In this way it can provide explanatory statements that ultimately depend on the hypotheses of the supporting theory. Pursuing this to its end, depth-hermeneutical understanding cannot avoid the *interpretative* character of its results, that is, its statements or the knowledge that it produces. This, in my opinion, coincides with a further consequence of the hermeneutic claim to universality; as all *understanding* is interpretation, it means that all of our *knowledge* has this character as well. From what I have mentioned up to this point, I can still consider the fact that the depth-hermeneutics of psychoanalysis retains a basic hermeneutic character and complies with a broad view of the hermeneutic experience. I have endeavored to demonstrate that the structure of analytic understanding is ultimately interpretative even if it does not coincide with the norms of textual understanding nor follows the "open" character that the hermeneutic circle provides. This leads me to argue that the hermeneutic claim to universality is left intact, if one tries to refute it in Habermas's way.

Although Habermas believes that the universality of hermeneutic understanding is at stake, I would argue that his notion of "distorted communication" is also threatened. In order to evaluate what is "distorted" in communication, but not pathological (unobservable), one needs to establish what is normal, or undistorted. I mentioned earlier that Habermas assumes a theory of linguistic competence that can provide the norms of the normal speech situation. Even so, such a theory would, at best, form another particular theoretical framework of language and communication. It can never, in my view, exhaust the richness of natural language; in this century we are already witnesses to different linguistic paradigms for the theoretical apprehension of language and communication. Such a theory of linguistic competence—even if Habermas believes that it is a rational reconstruction of the rules of our communication—will still include presuppositions and prejudgments, so that it cannot become the *absolute ground* or *absolute foundation*. In cases of pathologically distorted communication we come across symptoms where rules of syntax or other discrepancies are accountable. In cases of nonpathological ("nonobstructive") distortions that Habermas believes litter our everyday communication, natural language, despite their presence, is used in excellent competent ways. What criteria of "normality" can one employ in order to detect such distortions? Also, in view of his insistence that undistorted communication is to be found only in societies which are free of force and constraints, we have to presume that in present societies the majority (or perhaps all) of instances of everyday communication are distorted; this is a consequence of the position that the ideals of "free communication" are not met at present. Extremely efficient criteria would then be required to clarify what is distorted or ideological.

The next point yielding problems in Habermas's theory is the *equation* of the distorted with the ideological. The transfer of a critique of ideology in linguistic terms presents a series of disadvantages. The whole spectrum of ideological beliefs and "false consciousness" has to be studied in linguistic form. The problem, here, appears to be whether "classical" Marxist examples of ideological discourse can be studied within the notion of distorted communication. As an example we can consider the concept of "wages" as "paid work" that Marxist theory identifies as an ideological category. In what terms can one see a discussion on "wages" as distorted communication, or a collective bargaining about "wages," perhaps, as a distorted demand? Would one need to see the emergence and the linguistic use of the concept (its objectivation) on some "deeper" repressive societal mechanism, or some other deformation, at an earlier stage of its linguistic articulation as Habermas suggests? On what terms can we decide that the concept of "wages" is a "misunderstanding" that gives rise to distorted communication? Will we still need the Marxist (scientific) analysis to inform us about the "falsehood" or the ideological concealment of the concept? Such thoughts point to one particular difficulty (in relation to Marxist theory) of the Habermasian project and the questions it leaves unanswered. On the other hand the restricted character of the classical Marxist explanation of ideology is well-known, as it is based upon the "false appearances" that we perceive and which conceal the "true" nature of the underlying processes. This "true" nature can be revealed by a "correct" scientific (Marxist) explanation, for an awareness of them. Such an approach, besides the major theoretical problems it accumulates, cannot bring the phenomenon of ideology to the level of language.

We should not, therefore, overlook the gains that Habermas can make from his theoretical project of distorted communication. The notion of the "distorted" allows him to introduce a "critical theory" in terms of the psychoanalytic paradigm. He is also able to study objectivations in linguistic form which are empirically accessible thus avoiding the classical phenomenological (Hegelian) approach of Marxism, trapped in the terminology of "phenomenal appearances" and "false ideas." Moreover, he can presume the existence of repressive forces and powers as the cause of the deformations and distortions of meaning in communication. The old theories on ideology were based on the "opaqueness" of "reality." Now the distortions, as misunderstandings, are responsible for the ideologically loaded consciousness.

False Consensus and the Ontological Claim

While this expresses my critical remarks of the concept of distorted communication, I will refer to another aim of Habermas's vigorous attempt to refute the hermeneutic claim to universality. I explained in both the second and third chapters how Heidegger conceived the ontological character of *Dasein* to be interpretation and how Gadamer, following the same idea, showed how the linguistic investigation of understanding (as parole) leads to the same conclusion. According to Gadamer we live within language. All our experience is primarily of a linguistic character and all our understanding based on this experience of a hermeneutical (interpretative) nature. This leads Gadamer to pronounce the universality of the "hermeneutic problem" and consequently the ontological situation that we find ourselves in: always within language and dialogue as interpretative beings. If Habermas could refute the hermeneutic claim to universality, I assume he could reduce the *ontological* significance of understanding and of the hermeneutic experience.

As if he could sense the difficulty of such an enterprise, especially talking from an epistemological/linguistic perspective (by promoting the possibility of an explanatory, depth-hermeneutical understanding), he strives to reach the same result, this time by *undermining* the dialogic situation in which we encounter ourselves, "the dialogue we are," as Gadamer describes it. Many times Gadamer has insisted that the description of understanding, aiming at removing misunderstanding, never adequately defines the former. Such an aim brings us back to the position of Schleiermacher we met in the second chapter. Gadamer has moved beyond this initial step, by revealing what underlies either dialogue, or our relation to tradition before attempting to understand it. In the case of dialogue any understanding that might occur is preceded by a consensus which unites speakers and is formed and provided by tradition. Being initiated and introduced within tradition, we share basic beliefs and a consensus which makes the dialogue possible. Habermas accepts this situation as correct, but draws the conclusion that one cannot criticize such a consensus that has been formed in misunderstanding, from outside; one must *enter* into dialogue with the other members of the community. That, it would entail that one, at least initially, *accepts* the dominating consensus in order to participate in the dialogue. He continues, stating that it is senseless to suspect this "agreement" as being false, since we cannot transcend the "dialogue we are." It is for this reason, this predicament, Gadamer concludes with "the ontological priority of linguistic tradition over all possible critique," at the same time conceding that tradition is possible "only on the basis that we are part of the comprehensive context of the tradition of language."[14] The fear that Habermas expresses is that a consensus, held valid in tradition, might have been arrived at in pseudocommunication. In this respect it can be a false or distorted consensus; a consensus that has been imposed by force or a consensus promoting a context of domination.

Although Habermas relies for his approach on the presuppositions of what might be pseudocommunication or distorted communication, his views can also provide a critical insight and a critical stance toward tradition and the accepted consensus.

However, my aim is to clarify whether his undermining of the validity of consensus bears any relation to the refutation of the ontological conclusions of Gadamer. I think that Habermas, as I just quoted him, conflates two things: our inevitable position in dialogue and the possibility of criticizing it. It is not the inability to suspect the "dialogue" and its underlying consensus that leads Gadamer to his ontological conclusions. Our position in the "dialogue we are" and our *predicament* within language as well as the inevitable existence of a consensus—either "true" or false—is a *different* issue than the way one can criticize a consensus or tradition. I have previously attempted to reveal the logical arguments through which Gadamer arrives at the inevitability of our *predicament* within language. His ontological conclusion is unaffected by Habermas's argument. The latter's contention can only question whether Gadamer's position allow us, from within a consensus, to criticize the consensus itself; it appears to be the same problem, although in different terms, which I examined in the previous chapter concerning the critique of tradition (when Habermas accused hermeneutics of "banging the wall of tradition from inside"). I would accept, though, Gadamer's weak position concerning a systematic "critique" of consensus. However, the approach of philosophical hermeneutics could be strengthened, if at the same time, it incorporates the view that tradition, although carrying truth and agreement, could also be "the *locus* of factual untruth and continued force";[15] this is feasible without the danger of any logical inconsistency.

I would argue that the strategy of Habermas was not only to propose his critical approach regarding any consensus—which should always be a welcome addition for a critical stance to our belonging in a community—but he simultaneously desires to attack the ontological existentialist position that penetrates Gadamer's and Heidegger's philosophies. There is no need to mention the hostile attitude of Marxism against non-"materialist" philosophies, or in particular the Frankfurt school's hostile attitude (especially Adorno's) against Heidegger's existentialist philosophy. It is predominantly the fear that such (existentialist) philosophies start from premises that cannot either reveal the "material" basis of life or come to terms with the course of history where the most important "real" features of the human condition are to be met. History has to be understood from the materialist thesis that "men have to produce in order to reproduce themselves" (Marx's "historical materialism"); also, in Habermas's eyes, history must be considered as a process of self-formation carried on by the species themselves (see the first chapter). The Heideggerian quest of "Being" then, or the Gadamerian "the dialogue we are" are usually viewed with suspicion from within the Marxist camp or the Frankfurt school followers. Heidegger's and Gadamer's philosophies have also been accused of the concealment of the actual social/historical condition of the species which has resulted in class-relations. Therefore, such philosophies are supposed to lack any critical position toward society.

This well-known argument has been discussed for decades and leads to a range of problems and questions that are beyond the limited space of this work. Nevertheless, it would be worthwhile to mention the following. If Heidegger and Gadamer enrich our awareness of certain basic features of human life, and of the human agent, should they be ignored? Would Heidegger's critique of metaphysics (including both "humanism" and technology, that I will refer to in the last chapter) put him in an "uncritical" position as regards society? The question which always persists at the end of such debates is whether philosophical reasoning, as that of Heidegger and Gadamer, can offer significant insights on issues related to the ontology of human beings, which cannot be addressed at all by historicized scientific endeavors, and vice versa. Questions of this kind always remain open, without canceling either of the two modes of reflective inquiry.

With Gadamer we get the opportunity to observe the complex picture arising in our efforts to understand history. In addition, he brings to light our historicality and our position within language, which, I argue, we should accept. If we then come to the conclusion that any criticism of society has to be carried from within language and tradition, in the sense that we cannot escape our linguistic and historical horizon, this is a theme that any critical theory has to listen to and take account of. I would also argue that our ontological predicament within language and the hermeneutic experience does not prevent an understanding of society on Marxist terms or on the modified terms supplied by the critical theorists of the Frankfurt school. On the contrary, Gadamer's conclusions play the role of "a corrective" (as he himself has argued) and also put at risk the premises of any critical theory, showing their limited character. Thus I find the opposition to Gadamer, when guided from such (materialist) "prejudices," to be unjustified; rather, we need to learn from Gadamer's conclusions something that Habermas, I believe, has also been forced to appreciate: to give priority to dialogue. He does so when he attempts to extract from it the counterfactual agreement for "free-speech" situations that unites us all in dialogue (as I will explain in the following two paragraphs). This said, I should not give the impression of holding a one-sided view. Gadamer has not provided us with exact ways of criticizing tradition and society. He has only emphasized our reflective capability to become aware of our prejudices and the alienations we carry within us, and our ability to adopt a critical position toward them. His "range of vision" is at a philosophical level that cannot obviously meet the methodical needs of a sociological critical view of society.

But let us look at what Habermas proposes instead of following the philosophical hermeneutics of Gadamer. He says that

> a critically enlightened hermeneutic that differentiates between insight and delusion incorporates the meta-hermeneutic awareness of the conditions for the possibility of systematically distorted communication. It connects the process of understanding to the principle of rational discourse, according to which truth would only be guaranteed by *that* kind of consensus which was achieved under the idealised conditions of unlimited communication free from domination and could be maintained over time.[16]

For Habermas, since in principle all present consensus established within the conditions of pseudocommunication is suspected as false, the only logical possibility to avoid distortion would be in a society free from coercion and domination. It is here where the "ideal speech situation" (that I mentioned in the fifth chapter) can freely arise. However, as Ricoeur has pointed out, to the "dialogue we are" of Gadamer, Habermas proposes "the dialogue we ought to be"[17] which proves to be a rather weak position that cannot oppose Gadamer's claim.

Following this orientation of an "ideal speech situation," which presents not only idealized but idealistic overtones, Habermas enters a discussion which, in my opinion, shows further prejudices carried over from a long tradition. He states that the "idealized dialogue" he has reached theoretically is something that we all anticipate will happen in the future. Furthermore, this anticipation "guarantees the ultimate supporting and contra-factual agreement *that already unites us*; in relation to it we can criticize every factual agreement, should it be a false one, as false consciousness."[18] (Italics mine.) Gadamer had pointed to the conditions of the dialogue in order to uncover the underlying consensus that makes understanding between speakers possible. Habermas goes beyond the linguistic limits of the dialogue into beliefs that are supposed to underlie our everyday consciousness uniting us. Such beliefs, however, could be seen from two perspectives. Firstly, they could be regarded and justified as an ideal under the guiding principle of "absolute freedom." This view of freedom has been raised potently within the Enlightenment tradition by the German speculative philosophy (Kant, Hegel, Fichte, and Seller). Secondly, this future uncorrupted, not-distorted dialogue, which we all are supposed to share as *anticipation* and as a welcome, *rational,* state of affairs, does not seem to me to be far from the Christian-Judaic message of heavenly life and redemption, in which "freedom" can be enjoyed. It is Hegel who has been charged with such implications but the same theme has definitely spread through his epigones. On the other hand, these two perspectives are not necessarily disconnected; whether the notion of freedom in the Enlightenment, although strongly attached to Reason as a rational choice and value, bears a connection to the strong roots of Western thought within Christianity, is an ongoing matter for discussion. Nevertheless, nothing can restrict such beliefs from revealing themselves even in a critical writer like Habermas. This argument bears close affinity with Ricoeur's claim that Habermas's view is *eschatological.*[19]

From a position similar to his disagreement with "consensus," Habermas unfolds his suspicion of the idea that we could receive "truth-claims" from tradition, as Gadamer has always maintained. The knowledge which these "truth-claims" can yield can be trusted, Habermas argues, only when conditions of "freedom from force" and of "unconstrained agreement" have been secured in a society. But is it not the case that we always live in societies that Habermas sees to be immersed in distorted communication? His state of "free communication" is an ideal situation and if accepted, can *only* work as a normative model, as he himself has affirmed. Could the fear of distortion prevent us from thinking and debating upon "truths," their reevaluation and reinterpretation, even if this takes place in the restricted historical horizon available to us? At the time of the debate, Habermas did not differentiate possible conditions which could distinguish between the validity of some "truth-claims" and the falsehood of others.[20] In the debate, I take his argument to imply that *all* of our truth-claims are suspect because of the underlying false consensus upon which they have been produced. All knowledge available from these claims seem to him to have the same fate, although such a conclusion would put in serious doubt his earlier notion of interest and knowledge that I have already examined.

Gadamer's concept of truth as insight, produced in the particular historical horizon we live in, or Ricoeur's notion of "transvaluation," are both strong arguments indicating the legitimacy of our convictions in arriving at "truths"; not all our consensual agreement, necessary for a dialogue and the production of "true" statements, seems to be corrupt. Nevertheless, Habermas's critical view of consensus (although suggestive rather than explicit) can serve as a regulative idea for questioning anything that, at first hand, appears as "true"; we can demand the exploration and explicit awareness of the supporting consensus. The limitations of the "critical theory" that Habermas proposes are also obvious to him. I have earlier stressed the presuppositions (hypotheses) that form the starting-point of his theory; he further accepts the fact that "the hypothetical status of general interpretations" limits the ways in which critical understanding can be applied. As in the psychoanalytic dialogue, the validation of depth-hermeneutical conclusions can only be achieved by the self-reflection of all those who participate in dialogue. This view represents an ambivalent and ideal situation which cannot be realized. In this respect, Habermas accepts that such limits prevent any claim to universality by "critical theory" itself.

I would conclude then by saying that Habermas offers us an articulation of the type of theoretical framework we can apply when considering "communication" so that the presence of "power" and "domination" is related to ideological discourse. This model provides us with a critical knowledge of society in which "language," "domination," and "work" are basic elements; its critical position is enhanced by trying to show how "domination" distorts our speech situation. Habermas's theory of "distorted communication" could also be seen as forming the *nucleus* of a critical sociological theory in which power, repression, and other dominating features of society can be located and studied at the level of communication and communicative action,[21] in which ideology also (as distorted communication) resides.

Criticisms on the Psychoanalytic Model

Before leaving the subject of depth-hermeneutical explication on the model of psychoanalysis it is worthy to encounter some acute comments by Gadamer. We have seen that Habermas, after comprehending the psychoanalytic discourse and practice into the theoretical framework of depth-hermeneutical analysis, transported it to the case of (distorted) communication, in order to derive a depth-hermeneutical analysis of speech. At the same time this theoretical analysis can play the role of a critical social theory with therapeutic results, following closely the therapeutic practice of psychoanalysis. But we must bear in mind that therapeutic results in the analytic treatment are achieved in combination with the power of self-reflection which the patient conducts and which allows him to validate the reconstructions arrived at in dialogue with the analyst.

To discuss this more fully I will now follow the charges Gadamer levels against Habermas. Firstly, Gadamer argues, the psychoanalytic approach is not universalizable, despite Freud's claim that he introduced natural-scientific hypotheses, in order that the resulting knowledge could claim the validity of "acknowledged laws." Even if the results of psychoanalysis are authenticated in its therapeutic successes, Gadamer claims that the knowledge which the analytic practice provides cannot be reduced to a "pragmatic validation" (i.e., by reference only to its results). The whole of the psychoanalytic exercise and the knowledge it arrives at, Gadamer states, has to be questioned aided by a hermeneutic reflection upon the initial conditions and especially upon the position of the analyst. Such reflection will reveal the "methodical alienation" that is present in psychoanalysis, an outcome of its methodological structure, and the hypotheses that represent "general laws." The presence of "methodical alienation" is the second charge of Gadamer and, if taken seriously, one can examine the ways in which each particular case or life history of a patient can be affected and fall prey to the anonymity of the method and the "distance" that the scientific "law" introduces.

The third disputation directed at Habermas's view of psychoanalysis concerns the involvement and position of the analyst. Gadamer argues that the analyst cannot escape the fact that she is a member of society and relies upon the consensus which forms the dialogic situation of her community. If true, this reveals the limitations of the psychoanalytic reflection, as a special case of reflection, the boundaries of which must be traced "through the societal context and consciousness, within which the analyst and also his patient are on even terms with everybody else."[22]

Having questioned Habermas's attempt to separate psychoanalysis from a broader context of hermeneutical experience, Gadamer presents his last question about the validity of transferring the psychoanalytic model of analyst-patient to some societal form. He asks:

> Where does the patient-analyst relationship end and the social partnership in its unprofessional right begin? Most fundamentally: Over against what self-interpretation of the social consciousness (and all morality is such) is it in place to inquire *behind* that consciousness—and when is it not? (Gadamer's italics.)[23]

Such questions Gadamer thinks cannot be left unanswered, and he is led to the conclusion that the emancipatory reflection is but an "anarchist utopia"; anarchist since it is oriented to overthrow and dissolve the power of authority. These remarks by Gadamer seem unjustified, considering how the overall attitude of the critical theory toward authority (that I have examined in the previous chapter) has been shaped. However, I consider Gadamer to be correct concerning the difficulties of imposing the psychoanalytic model upon society and the impossibility of achieving therapeutic results in such a mode which presupposes the analogy of "social pathology."

Answering to these charges Habermas accepts the fact that he cannot refute the hermeneutical engagement in the dialogic relationship between analyst and patient. Neither can he dispute the particular hermeneutical position of the analyst, nor can he dismiss the presence of the larger framework of consensus that binds together, in a community and in dialogue, the analyst and the patient. Instead Habermas turns to the problem that any consensus poses: we are unable to trust it because it might be a forced consensus, that is, a product of pseudocommunication. Therefore, he argues, any hermeneutical understanding which has been extended to critique (as in the psychoanalytic process) must abandon the consensus and move beyond Gadamer's "existing convictions" of tradition. A different direction must be taken, relying upon a depth-hermeneutics that can still reveal cases of distorted communication within basic agreements and legitimations that form our social condition. However, Habermas does not recognize the problem that his proposals introduce. A depth-hermeneutical methodical understanding, as I have tried to show, is still based on new presuppositions and *new* "radical" convictions. The same questions can now be asked of them: how far can we trust the presuppositions and the convictions of depth-hermeneutic analysis? Especially when such new convictions form part of the tradition (as has happened with Marxist and Freudian ideas). Finally, Habermas, handling Gadamer's criticism on the analogy between the psychoanalytic model and society, appears to have shifted his position on the therapeutic results of depth-hermeneutics in communication. He now maintains that "the enlightenment, which results from radical understanding, is always political."[24] However, in "true" dependence upon the psychoanalytic example, as before, he suggests that such political enlightenment needs to be validated by the self-reflection of all participants (achieved in dialogue); again, a rather overoptimistic and idealized situation. This view confirms Gadamer's criticism that the psychoanalytic reflection is not universalizable by simple analogy.

On Science and the "Situational Understanding"

Although I have already discussed the main themes of the debate between Habermas and Gadamer, it is obvious that (because of the broadness of the debate) there exist a number of other issues which were promoted by the literature following the debate itself. The appropriation of hermeneutics by the social sciences and its combination within methodical approaches—different from those of Habermas—or the hermeneutic involvement in the overall perspective of the natural sciences (a highly debatable issue in the philosophy of sciences) are but two examples. Nevertheless, I am compelled to refer to an issue which is central to Gadamer's and Habermas's approaches. This will give me the opportunity to shape more accurately Gadamer's position in regard to the sciences. Richard Bernstein discusses the subject of "relativism *versus* objectivism" as a central issue arising from Gadamer's and Habermas's philosophical commitments.[25]

He feels that a relativist's "essential claim is that there can be no higher appeal than to a given conceptual scheme, language game, set of social practices, or historical epoch."[26] The opposite position is to be found in "objectivism" which he defines as a deep conviction that there is some permanent framework or "a-historical matrix" from which knowledge, truth, rationality, or even rightness can be determined. This definition of "objectivism" is very close to the concept of "foundationalism"; that is, the belief in ultimate grounds or foundations upon which knowledge, truth, or ethics can be secured. It seems that, according to these definitions, Gadamer could be placed in the group of the relativists. We have already seen that hermeneutical understanding does not follow methodical rules but, instead, approaches the meaning of the text (or any other meaningful "object") individually and brings to light the uniqueness of each meaning understood in the specific historical relationship that binds together the text and the interpreter. This kind of understanding has been codified as "situational understanding"[27] in contrast to the methodical understanding that the sciences utilize. Habermas on the other hand, is close to the group of the "objectivists," notwithstanding his pursuit of foundations for his theory of knowledge or of the emancipatory interest as *normative* foundations rather than as absolute ones.

The danger from relativist positions in Bernstein's view is that one can be led to extreme (or absolute) relativism where there would be no criteria to validate knowledge claims; in this case, knowledge could be considered "true" or valid by appealing to the particular circumstances of its production. Gadamer, however, cannot be placed in such a position as he has always tried to show that we can arrive at "objective" knowledge and "truth" through dialogue and agreement, whether the partner in discussion is another person or the text. Nevertheless, he also emphasizes that such knowledge or "truth" is valid in our own historical time and "hermeneutical situation" and cannot be extended as transhistorical knowledge; in this sense it is "relative" in time. If this is Gadamer's position (in brief), I must mention here two further points that could aid us in understanding Bernstein's treatment of these subjects. His concern for the outcome of the "struggle" between objectivism and relativism, which he considers to be one of the most urgent topics for discussion, stems from the Anglo-Saxon tradition of the philosophy of science. He considers these opposing epistemological tendencies to be an expression of "an uneasiness that has spread throughout intellectual and cultural life."[28] I would not share Bernstein's view on this matter concerning cultural and intellectual life, but I believe he has vividly expressed the concerns of the philosophy of science, which depict the ideals of scientific research in overcoming the "uncertainties" of relativism. Thus, Bernstein has turned to Gadamer and Habermas in the hope of finding indications for a move "beyond objectivism and relativism." Nevertheless, this epistemological opposition has not preoccupied either Habermas or Gadamer to any significant extent.

My second point is that we need to look at Gadamer's position in relation to science, to avoid misunderstanding his views which stand at a philosophical level and at a philosophical critique of science, rather than contributing a direction of an alternative "scientific method." Gadamer himself emphasises this point in a letter to Bernstein, having read the latter's book, *Beyond Objectivism and Relativism*. He writes that he never offered a "discipline that guarantees truth" as a type of scientific method. "Here I mean 'discipline' in the moral sense of the word, and by 'guarantee' definitely not methodic achievement."[29] Evidently, Gadamer's critique on the sciences concentrates most of all upon one subject: their inability to reflect upon their presuppositions and to admit the *methodical alienation*, that is, the price they pay for their methodical achievements. He is also aware of the fact that it would be absurd for someone to propose an "antiscience" or to attempt to change the course of the sciences as it goes on today.[30] Instead he has always called for the introduction of hermeneutic reflection within the social/historical disciplines.

Finally, it is worth mentioning the presence of another reason determining Gadamer's position toward the sciences. He argues that the hermeneutic phenomenon has been accepted by both the social sciences and philosophical reflection,[31] even though there is a "tension" between the two. In his view, the tension appears because the philosophical approach insists on paying attention to the position of the interpreter, that is, his "membership in society." This, we know, affects the epistemological foundations of the disciplines. Conversely, the scientific disciplines have as their primary underlying theme the "sovereignty of investigation" which runs contrary to this philosophical approach. The social sciences have recognized their involvement with subjects that are bound to speech, thus a major shift toward the investigation of communication is justified. We can recall for example, that for Habermas, the social sciences aim at communicative understanding and at possible action orientation. Gadamer fears, however, that the ideal of scientifically organized and controlled society cannot come to terms with the basic unity and agreement forming the basis of every communication; rather, he supports the idea that there is a "fundamental solidarity at the basis of any form of social life."[32] Therefore, he seeks an orientation for both scientific and critical effort which shares the methical ideal without losing sight of the "solidarity" that permeates practical life. The tension I just mentioned does not stop him from granting the social sciences his "full recognition" and accepting their premise to go beyond hermeneutics; however, he cannot see how this claim could mean going beyond philosophy.[33] In contrast to rhetoric (met in political or technical institutions or in the mass media) and the transmission of scientific knowledge that are both happening in monologic form, Gadamer reminds us of the "corrective role" of hermeneutical philosophy which forces us into an awareness of the dialogue necessary in any community. This "corrective" and fruitful involvement of hermeneutical philosophy applies, he writes, to the sphere of practical and political reason. With these thoughts in mind we can follow him in his conclusion that

> the chief task of philosophy is to justify this way of reason and to defend practical and political reason against the domination of technology based on science. That is the point of philosophical hermeneutic. It corrects the peculiar falsehood of modern consciousness: the idolatry of scientific method and of the anonymous authority of the sciences and it vindicates again the noblest task of the citizen—decision-making according to one's own responsibility—instead of conceding the task to the expert.[34]

These remarks potently present the views of Gadamer on his hermeneutical philosophy as practical philosophy and his comprehension of the technological-scientific domination as the major threat to social life. At this point, we can also recall the concept of *phronesis* which complements this statement and remains in line with the responsibility of the individual in defending practical and political reason based on dialogue.

7

Critical Theory or
Recollection of Tradition?

It seems to me appropriate to begin the final chapter with a recapitulation of the most important issues I have examined and the conclusions I have drawn. At the same time, I would like to add to these conclusions, as I am now in a position to consider the work as a whole. Initially, I will concentrate on the themes that I have presented in the first four chapters which shape the philosophical positions of each participant. Next, the focus will shift to the particular issues which were raised in the debate. At this point, however, there are at least two options open to me: the first would involve staying close to the actual exchange as it unfolded in the fifth and the sixth chapters and reexamining the conclusions reached at that stage. The second option would call for a further evaluation of the exchange which would possibly trace deeper reasons and latent themes. However, it appears that both routes have to be covered in order to attain a clearer understanding of the outlooks and aims of the two participants. With this in mind I propose to reflect upon the debate at three levels. Firstly, there is the task of reviewing and clarifying the immediate theses in dispute and the way in which they are connected with the philosophical background of each author. This is the goal which commentaries on the debate usually project and then stop short. At a second level, I wish to show that there are general underlying aims present in the philosophical standpoints of the two contributors which also penetrate the debate itself; such aims exemplify targets and philosophical convictions that each particular exchange in the debate relies upon. These positions must be clear, since, to a great extent, they justify the sayings of both Habermas and Gadamer. But is it possible that these preconceptions, convictions, or beliefs could also be questioned? Could the "underlying aims" and the "solutions" each one presents be seen differently? This is the third level of reflection I propose, and my intention is to accomplish it in a short and provisional manner by referring to other philosophical standpoints critical of, and running in opposite directions to, those evident in the writings of Habermas and Gadamer.

A Review of the Themes Discussed

I start then with the issues discussed and examined up to this point. In the first chapter my purpose was to trace the strategy and views of Habermas offering a critique of "scientistic" ideology he considered to prevail in matters which extend from the formation of knowledge up to the solution of practical (ethical) problems in life. I traced the origins of Habermas's thought and his critical intentions in the critical theory of the Frankfurt school and especially in the notion of "instrumental reason." The school's critical and emancipatory attitude was found to be based upon the contrast between that which could be accepted as rational, as against that which appeared to be rationally or morally unacceptable in present societies. The same perspective of the school applied equally to the concept of "instrumental reason." I have argued, however, that Habermas's critique of "scientism" can be viewed as an extension and elaboration of the "instrumentality of reason." In order to accomplish his critical standpoint, it was necessary for Habermas to reintroduce the concept of the Kantian "epistemological reflection" upon the necessary conditions for the production of knowledge positivism has managed to erase in its domination as the only paradigm of scientific rationality. Habermas saw the abandoning of "epistemological reflection," or the "dissolution of epistemology," as stemming from the radical critique of Hegel upon Kant and Marx's metacritique of Hegel's philosophy. Marx, conflating his critique with the natural sciences, did not sense the need for (epistemological) reflection, so the dissolution of classical epistemology was accomplished. Although such an account of the dissolution of classical theories of knowledge might not be convincing, as it does not trace all reasons and events that have led in such a direction, it nevertheless allows Habermas to reflect upon positivism as "scientism" and to disassociate himself from the belief that "science" is the only category of possible knowledge. In addition, such reflection and questioning enables Habermas to trace human interests that establish the possible conditions for the acquisition of knowledge. These theoretical positions will actually constitute Habermas's early approach to the location of foundations for his critical theory, especially for the purpose of delineating an emancipatory interest that can ground knowledge as critique.

Habermas's strategy was also to reflect upon the influence "scientism" has exercised within the social/historical sciences, which results either in their illusion of "pure theory" or the attitude of "historicism" in relation to their object of study. It is the significant differences that the social/historical sciences exhibit in relation to the natural sciences in which Habermas is interested. He thus presents the hermeneutic dimension that accompanies any social/historical discipline, a dimension concealed by the "scientistic" beliefs and the equation they prescribe between the social and natural sciences. Habermas's critical attitude toward the social/historical disciplines does not go so far as to include all aspects of the methodical alienation that Gadamer introduces. He, instead, draws the line between naive methodological approaches resulting in "historicism," and those which are aware of their presuppositions. As we have seen, his "critical theory" depends upon methodological procedures in order not to "discredit" the methodological enterprise, which, for him, is necessary so as to provide explanatory statements. Although in *Knowledge and Human Interests* he used two notions of *reflection* indiscriminately, one as an "epistemological reflection" and the other as "self-reflection," this conflation does not appear to endanger his approach inasmuch as the reader keeps these two notions of reflection separate.

Finally, we saw how critical theory, as distinct from positivism, denounces the illusion of "pure theory" and states that problems of practical life cannot be referred to technocratic solutions "scientism" imposes. On the contrary, the question of the relations between knowledge (theory) and practical life needs to be asked again. Habermas points out that scientific claims do not aim at the cultural cultivation of the individual and that, in their monological attitude, they do not promote dialogical processes for the solution of practical problems. Instead, they objectify such problems leaving them at the mercy of technological solutions and scientific rationality. Hence, the first chapter is a key to Habermas's early epistemological orientations concerning his critical theory and the way in which he accepts the hermeneutic background within the social/historical disciplines.

The second and third chapters I devoted to the study of philosophical hermeneutics developed by Gadamer. The lengthy material and the large number of issues discussed do not permit any detailed review. Rather I will briefly recapitulate the most important points and conclusions that were drawn. My presentation started with the early stages of textual understanding from the Reformation period up to Schleiermacher and Dilthey. My aim at the time was twofold. Firstly, I wished to show the engagement of hermeneutics in the understanding of history and the shift of ideas which indicated that history could be treated as text. This engagement, together with the awareness of the "hermeneutic circle," proved to be important events in the development of hermeneutics. Secondly, I intended to show how Gadamer benefited from the early tradition of hermeneutics, particularly the weak or mistaken positions with which he charged Romantic hermeneutics and Dilthey. Thirdly, I examined Heidegger's hermeneutics of *Dasein*, considering it important to trace the way in which Gadamer's work has been influenced by Heideggerian positions, especially the premise of our ontological predicament as hermeneutic beings. I unfolded Gadamer's philosophical hermeneutics beginning with his notions of "prejudice" and "historicality." His major conclusion was that any understanding involves "prejudices" or preconceptions. Gadamer had undertaken the task of the "rehabilitation" of the notion of "prejudice" Enlightenment discredited. However, our prejudices, or preconceptions, can be examined during the course of interpretation or in our actual daily involvement in the "life-world": the interpreter (and also the speaker) must become aware of her own prejudices in order to overcome the misinterpretations and the limited horizon false prejudices force onto her.

The "historicality" of understanding appeared vividly in the notion of "temporal distance" which I considered to be a productive aspect in hermeneutic experience. "Temporal distance" assumes the role of a critical-methodical concept which permits the filtration of productive and unproductive prejudices. In fact, these are the first signs of a critical consciousness that can be achieved with the capacity of philosophical hermeneutics for self-reflection. The picture was completed with the notion of "effective-history," that is, the effects an historical object "releases" in history forming our preunderstanding of it. Another conclusion was reached at that point; to ignore our prejudices and the "effective-history" of an historical object, or a text when we try to understand it, is a gross mistake. To understand a text we must reconstruct its "horizon"; but this would be inadequate if we were to ignore our own horizon. The interpreter needs to *fuse* his horizon with the horizon of the text. As far as tradition is concerned, we have to know it in order to understand ourselves; our present horizon cannot be imagined without tradition. Furthermore, any act of understanding, accepting its own "historicality," must appreciate the role of tradition (as a transporter of "prejudices" and "effective-history," and as an indicator of "temporal distance"). I concluded that the fusion of our horizon with the past takes place continually and is part of our hermeneutical experience in the world. Finally, the notion of "application" is accomplished by an awareness of what is involved in interpretation. Understanding a text or understanding the "other" in dialogue involves the fusion of horizons and the application of the text's horizon to our own. The awareness of "application" in interpretation (and in understanding) is significant because it overcomes the forgetfulness of the historical immersion of (our) "consciousness."

In both the second and third chapters I strived to make sense of Gadamer's claims and to evaluate particular ones, especially when they were found to run counter to other philosophical convictions. One of the main proposals in Gadamer's philosophy was that all understanding is interpretation. It seemed to be justified, although problems appeared when the case of explanatory understanding was juxtaposed. A further claim was made: that all interpretation complies with the linguistic form of understanding. This claim presented problems for its comprehension. I concluded that we can make sense of it only if we realize that language is always involved in the background of any understanding, even if this is not immediately apparent. The claim that all understanding is linguistic in nature could then follow, supplemented by the linguisticality of all experience. All these claims, however, needed some philosophical theory of language (at the level of *parole*), capable of transferring language to the center of the discourse also showing its affinity to reality. Gadamer, drawing from Humboldt's insights, claimed that the world is linguistic in nature. This statement too proved difficult to accept. I opposed the view that the world *is* only language, or that language *creates* the world. Instead, I suggested that the world is *constituted* by language. What we come to know as "world" is available to us through language; through language we *have world*."

Gadamer's expression "we have world," stressed the active and reflective attitude human beings exhibit toward their habitat due to language. "Having world" indicated our ontological situation within language but also freedom from habitat. However, Gadamer had a further claim, that the world comes into language and is represented in it. Such a claim displayed acute problems difficult to justify as it now touched upon fundamental philosophical positions concerning the relationship of "word" and "object." The best suggestion for the representation of the "world" in language (in accordance with Heidegger's philosophy), is that Being is *extended* within language; "language is the house of being where man dwells." In this way language acquires an ontological significance and becomes the space in which the "I" meets the "world."

The fact that we are immersed in language results in the powerful conclusion that there is no exclusive perspective for "seeing" the world. Although I found the connection of "word" and "object" in Gadamer's philosophy to exhibit serious weaknesses, it successfully runs against "objectivist" conceptions met in science which project an "absolute world" or a "world-in-itself." This led me to suggest that the ontological conclusion "Being that can be understood is language" has repercussions for current beliefs about truth. With this in mind I argued that we have to follow a different conception of truth, a conception never fully detailed by Gadamer. Following the notion of truth as "disclosure" (Heidegger) and as insight (Gadamer), as well as the example of the "play" which includes truth that affects its audience, I indicated, firstly, the strong interaction between truth and us: I argued truth, when discovered, cannot be ignored. Secondly, I showed how truth, as insight, can be seen to be connected with Being (when Being is stripped of our ontic preoccupations). The most important aspect, however, was the strong dialecticity prevailing between truth and us, which potentially can be incorporated in the concept of self-formation (*Bildung*), a concept strongly attached to the humanist tradition. Finally, I encountered Gadamer's proposal of the Aristotelian conception of *praxis* and *phronesis* (practical wisdom) that augments the status of philosophical hermeneutics as practical philosophy.

In the fourth chapter I examined the claim made by Habermas concerning the construction of a "critical social theory" employing the psychoanalytic model. Habermas was in need of foundations upon which to ground an interest in critique and emancipation. I presented and evaluated his borrowing of the epistemological inquiries of Peirce and Dilthey into the natural and the cultural sciences respectively. Habermas suggested that, in Peirce, we are able to locate the rationality of feedback controlled action and to conceptualize it in terms of *technical* cognitive interest. I detected a strong naturalistic claim in the attitude of Habermas in his efforts to ground such an interest close to an instinct. After the technical interest my next point concerned Dilthey's employment of hermeneutics in the social sciences and the legitimacy of such an attempt. Habermas endeavored to avoid the "hermeneutic circle" that appears with the introduction of hermeneutics. He suggests that we should treat the objects of hermeneutic understanding not as linguistic objects but as experiential data. I opposed such suggestions since there is no escape from the linguistic interpretation of any experiential data. The substitution of linguistic objects by experiential data was Habermas's first attempt to overcome the "hermeneutic circle" which dictates that the results of any interpretation are always "open" and "at risk" to new interpretations; a claim which obviously annoys the "objectivist" demands of science for epistemological certainty. I did however agree with the indispensability of hermeneutic understanding within the social sciences for deciphering meaning (by analyzing grammatical structures) and for empirical analysis (by bringing to light individual cases in their life-context).

Dilthey said that "understanding first arises in the interests of practical life." There is an interest in action-orientation; Habermas has called this interest *practical*. I agreed that this practical interest has also a cognitive character because, as I explained, it strives in the direction of communication and mutual understanding. This attempt proves successful in arriving at knowledge of the life-context of the other person. According to Habermas these two interests establish the conditions for the "objectivity" of all possible experience. Although this idea is of Kantian origin, instead of a priori categories, he introduces structures of grammatical rules upon which reality is constituted.

I provided a possible analysis of what, in Habermas, appears patchy and not well-supported. Reality is a specific interpretation based upon the grammatical rules that govern our symbolic system of interaction. Although this is the situation in the prescientific world of ordinary language (our "life-world"), the hermeneutic sciences grasp and study such interpretations of reality with the aim of intersubjectivity and action-orientation. Habermas reduced the two cognitive interests to "work" and "interaction" for which I charged him with the promotion of a "philosophical anthropology." However, apart from the natural and social sciences, he still needed to ground the "critical sciences." For this purpose he strived to locate an interest in self-reflection with emancipatory character by appealing to Kant and Fichte. I demonstrated the way in which he *reduced* this interest in the life of the species, and criticized his views of history as restricted and exhibiting Hegelian-Darwinian overtones (transmitted through Marxism), especially in the notion of the ascending self-formation of the species.

Next I followed Habermas's claim that, in a way analogous to that of psychoanalysis, he is able to constitute a "critical social theory." In order to do this I analyzed the ways in which critical knowledge of psychoanalysis is constructed on the model of *depth-hermeneutics* suggested by Habermas. He feels that depth-hermeneutics constitutes a new scientific approach capable of overcoming the hermeneutic circle in the deciphering of meaning and thus able to move beyond usual hermeneutics. I argued that his last claim cannot be accepted (notwithstanding the ability of depth-hermeneutics to provide explanatory results). Its statements must make sense of the life-history of the patient. For this reason the statements of depth-hermeneutics are context-dependent, displaying the dimensions of "situational understanding," a basic feature of hermeneutic understanding. Finally, I presented the analogies with Freud's comments on society which Habermas adopted for the construction of his "critical social theory."

A Review of the Conclusions in the Debate

In the last two chapters I treated a number of issues that appeared to be the points of dispute between Habermas and Gadamer. I will only refer to selected topics, repeating certain conclusions that seemed to me the most important. I will also refer to Ricoeur's ideas on similar topics which I found helpful either in confirming my own conclusions or in entering further dimensions that he contributed in relation to the debate.

The first subject of opposition between Habermas and Gadamer was their attitude toward tradition and its authority. For Habermas tradition is always the place of prejudice and repression, where political domination is also transmitted and imposed. Gadamer aimed at rehabilitating the notion of "prejudice" as the preunderstanding that we receive from, and share in, tradition. In doing so he was able to detect "truths" that are within tradition and which are indispensable to us, thus viewing tradition positively. However, it appeared that almost all of the other disputes which developed during their debate could, almost entirely, relate to the subject of tradition and our attitude to it. This is not accidental as notions of tradition come only to be defined by a wide range of other conceptions that refer to society: language, beliefs, our historicality, transmitted values, and so on. Habermas considered tradition and its linguistic form to be the source of deception in language. Therefore, language proves to be the basis of ideology allowing domination and legitimation of force. Hence, a critique of tradition, crucial for Habermas, becomes a critique of ideology.

My first reaction to these two antithetical positions referring to tradition was that both contain valid assertions, to which I could do justice by concluding that tradition cannot be seen as a homogeneous place either of truth or deception. Instead, it incorporates "truths" and values in reinterpretation and, at the same time, is the locus of ideological beliefs. I then posed the question: How can we criticize tradition particularly when there is no privileged point outside it? Despite Habermas's claims, Gadamer showed indisputably that we live within language and tradition unable to move beyond it, but he never provided a specific stance from which we may be critical of tradition. For this purpose, Habermas's critique of ideology opened up more promising avenues. It became evident, and that was my intention, that Habermas's analysis was based on a number of *presuppositions* that made his critique possible. He criticized Gadamer by saying that his employment of "linguisticality" in every aspect of life had prevented the latter from looking at other constraints of life such as "labor," "power," or "domination"; also that Gadamer was unable to see language as part of the whole structure of the exercise of power and domination. Habermas could make such claims only by adopting a reference system which included categories of "language," "labor," and "power." With the help of these categories (from Marxist and Freudian discourses) he could rely on a theoretical account which claimed to be "beyond" the natural language of hermeneutic analysis and was thus able to criticize tradition and language as ideology. In this first exchange I asked whether Gadamer's approach could offer any critical position at all. My answer was that, through the "hermeneutic reflection," the attitude of philosophical hermeneutics could be regarded as a *critical enterprise*, although of a restricted type. I stressed its critical attitude with regard to our prejudgments and convictions, which reflection puts constantly at stake in its attempt to make them transparent.

A similar attitude of philosophical hermeneutics has also been extended within the social sciences contributing to their "self-reflection" upon their presuppositions. However, a major critical category of Gadamer's hermeneutics proved to be the concept of "methodical alienation" which is deeply rooted within the practice of the social sciences and orients their aims into a "scientific ordering" of the whole spectrum of life. A hermeneutical reflection upon this alienation appeared to be a critical task taken against a total "surrender to the experts of social technology." Nevertheless, Gadamer's critical categories were inadequate in raising a serious challenge to tradition in other dimensions of repression and forced authority to which Habermas pointed. I then drew conclusions concerning Habermas and Gadamer: critical theory must become aware of its presuppositions, not only of epistemological presuppositions but also of the categorial framework of distorted communication upon which the critique of ideology is possible. This framework was drawn from the theoretical perspectives of Marxism and Freudianism which form part of tradition. Thus critical theory must "meet" tradition; the first step being to realise that tradition already exists amid its own presuppositions.

As far as philosophical hermeneutics is concerned, I suggested that it must develop a critical stance toward tradition greater than anything the judgment of productive or unproductive prejudices can offer. Although I reached such conclusions in considering the impact that each participant could exercise upon the other's views in the debate, I also stated (as Gadamer himself believes) that philosophical hermeneutics is not in need of a sociological view of society. Therefore, previous suggestions concerning critical theory and philosophical hermeneutics do not point to any merging of the two, which, in any case, seems to be impossible. Similarly, Ricoeur expresses the need of bringing the two "discourses" into dialogue. However, since he is aware of the fact that they speak from different positions, he does not attempt a fusion of the two "views" in a "supersystem."[1] Rather, he believes that each should recognize in the other a legitimate claim. He then reflects upon possible areas where hermeneutics can develop a critical position regarding ideology and also upon the reasons that the critique of ideology should scrutinize tradition.

I will only refer to two suggestions proposed by Ricoeur which are important and which strengthen the previous conclusion that each "discourse" can benefit from the other's intentions. Beside the critical possibilities of hermeneutics that I examined in the fifth chapter, Ricoeur discusses another one quite convincingly. He suggests that there is a critical attitude in hermeneutics which can be developed upon the *referential* moment of the text, that is, its ability to refer to "a world." I have analyzed, in the third chapter, the connection between "word" and "object," and how the "world" is represented in language. Ricoeur observes that this is a decisive break with the Romantic era, as hermeneutics does not search for an intention (of the author) hidden behind the text. On the contrary, we have "a world" unfolded in front of us. The new world, or the new dimensions of the world that the text "opens up" in front of us, according to Ricoeur "implies in principle a recourse against any given reality and thereby the possibility of a critique of the real."[2] He employs the example of the poetic discourse whose subversive power can be seen in this possibility of critique. He even goes further by suggesting that the world which is opened up by the text can be seen as belonging to the range of our possibilities (as Heidegger suggests with the projection of our own possibilities). So Ricoeur therefore is able to call upon the power and subversive force of the imaginary to reside in such projected possibilities. What the text shows corresponds to a mode of being as "power-to-be." Therefore, Ricoeur concludes, hermeneutics, by projection and recourse to other possibilities and "worlds" which the text opens up, develops a critical attitude toward ideology.

Although such an opening of another "world" seems to provide a resource for a critical stance within hermeneutics and can also be subversive, it depends upon philosophical reflection to decide what might or might not be ideological. Even if the critical ability of hermeneutics increases, by using the projected world as a new basis, the criteria of what might be ideological remain blurred and unclear. Poetic discourse, nevertheless, can be justified as "critical." Therefore, I will grant this critical possibility to be significant in its own terms, and to increase the critical ability of hermeneutics, even though it is too unspecified and restricted for its employment as a critique of ideology. The second suggestion of Ricoeur concerns "critical theory." He argues that it must consider cultural heritage in order to provide new forms of communicative action which, at the moment, have fallen victim to patterns of instrumental action and instrumental rationality. Only then can the idea of emancipation be something more than pious thinking. This remark is similar to the "transvaluation of values" (mentioned in the fifth chapter) and constitutes an advance on Gadamer's turn to tradition for discovering "truth." According to Ricoeur, the return to cultural heritage is essential for the "critique of ideology," particularly its claim of promoting interest in emancipation.

Continuing with the second part of the debate on the "hermeneutic claim to universality," I concluded that this claim proved too strong to be refuted by Habermas. All understanding, according to Gadamer, is of an interpretive nature. Habermas employed the notion of "scenic understanding" as part of the depth-hermeneutical approach that is employed in psychoanalytic discourse in order to show that it lies beyond the hermeneutic process of understanding embedded in natural language. Instead, I tried to show that "scenic understanding" does retain the basic character of hermeneutic understanding, although it does not coincide with the model of textual understanding upon which hermeneutics depends.[3] However, I suggested that the introduction of depth-hermeneutical analysis for the understanding of distorted communication or of ideology provided significant advances. Firstly, the "critical theory" can offer an immediate critical position (even based, as it is, on certain presuppositions), which "sees" the forces permeating society as exerting distortions upon the level of intersubjective communication. Secondly, with this presumption, it can closely (empirically) examine objectivations or distortions of a systematic appearance, and offer causal explanatory statements for their formation. This represents an advance upon earlier conceptions of ideology that could not study the phenomenon of ideology at the level of language and thus had the difficult task of drawing correlations between "false ideas" and the corresponding social formations, or social conditions which are responsible for the emergence of such "ideas," or beliefs.

Another focus of Habermas's refutation of the hermeneutic claim were the ontological consequences of Heidegger's and Gadamer's approach: that we are constantly engaged in dialogue and that we are interpretative beings. Habermas tried to accomplish his critique of the hermeneutic claim by undermining "the dialogue we are"; instead he suggested the notion of "pseudocommunication" a strong possibility amid conditions of ideological beliefs we share in present societies. I reached the conclusion that Habermas's assault on dialogue was directed at the consensus, or "agreement," underlying any dialogic situation. An assault of this kind could provide us with a critical stance when dealing with or arriving at such consensus. However, Gadamer's ontological claim, resulting from our interpretive predicament, was unaffected by Habermas's criticism. At stake, of course, were the existentialist philosophical positions of either Heidegger or Gadamer which the Marxist camp had always regarded with suspicion. My reply was that neither our "materiality" nor our (projected or anticipated) "freedom" becomes threatened if we support the ontological thesis of Heidegger. What actually happens is that the emphasis is *transferred*; we begin with an "ontology of dialogue" rather than with a "materialist" ontology of production. The two are not logically conflicting and are not mutually exclusive. It appears to me that the opposition lies mostly in considering the priorities and philosophies developed by each premise. These priorities are seen to be in conflict, especially when the philosophical considerations of Gadamer cannot be articulated from within the categories of class, power, and domination introduced by the language of "historical materialism."

The Underlying Aims and Issues

At this stage, although I have discussed all major exchanges that took place in the debate, we can still ask whether there are other angles from which to approach it, or ask as Ricoeur does: what is it all about? He, at first, questions whether we have to deal with a conflict between a hermeneutic consciousness versus a critical consciousness. Instead, he argues that the debate has presented this opposition as an antinomy. It is obvious that the arguments of each side were enforcing the idea that either the critical theory's approach is beyond the hermeneutic understanding of Gadamer, or that the philosophical hermeneutics and the consciousness it achieves cannot be attained from the restricted notion of "critical hermeneutics." However, we saw that, in all cases, a mediation seemed to be possible between the two positions and none of them could claim superiority over the other. I claimed that there cannot be a strong and defensible critical consciousness without having absorbed the lessons provided by hermeneutics. Similarly, philosophical hermeneutics, in order to gather the fruits of its own reflective capability, needs to further extend its own critical possibilities, in particular, developing a critical relation to tradition.

We can, however, put ourselves beyond the range of these questions by locating other interests or aims that underlie the philosophical position of each participant and therefore the debate itself. This is the second level of questioning that I proposed to follow earlier. Ricoeur asks again whether we have to deal with an opposition between "an ontology of prior understanding" and "an eschatology of freedom." Ricoeur ascribes this last project to Habermas, concerning his views on the "ideal speech situation" (as mentioned in the previous chapter) and finds this opposition to be another false antinomy that has to be overcome. Matters could become clearer if we look at these subjects by recalling the whole context surrounding the aspirations of the two projects.

In this direction, I wish to stress two themes which both Gadamer and Habermas appear to share to a certain extent (though from different angles) and which indicate the existence of common ground behind their opposition. Gadamer has always insisted upon the task of philosophical hermeneutics, as practical philosophy, for the critique of "technological civilisation" and of the "instrumentality of knowledge."[4] This task becomes essential especially in the face of the "deformation of *praxis*" we experience in present societies. Habermas shares a similar attitude toward the technocratic rationality that, as science and technology, has become the main ideology guaranteeing the present reproduction of the industrialist system and legitimating the necessary conditions of force, domination, and inequality.[5] We saw aspects of this rationality in the critique of "scientism" in the first chapter. This asserts that both of them share the need for a critique of technocracy and the rationality that accompanies it.

Such critical demands, however, do not stand alone. They are connected with ideas of "emancipation" and "humanity" which are central to the philosophical traditions both writers follow. Habermas's project appeals to "Reason" for the promotion of the emancipatory interest; later, when developing his project, he appealed to a "rational discourse" in free idealized conditions of unlimited communication, whereas Gadamer, appeals directly to the idea of humanity—a "truth" that we already know from within our tradition. These ideas I take to constitute the second theme that is explicit in their philosophical approach and which they share with the whole Enlightenment tradition. They also share the view that, for the realization of emancipatory and humanistic ideas, there must be the reconnection of knowledge and practical life which can undo the "deformed *praxis*" of the present. On this topic, each one retains his own particular approach. As we saw, Gadamer proposed the Aristotelian conception of *phronesis*, which represents a state of consciousness, where unity between knowledge and practical life can be achieved. Habermas, however, thought of such a possibility in the therapeutic results of a critical theory adopted by all members of society and in the promotion of critical knowledge based on (self)-reflection. The point I wish to make here is that Gadamer's project is as preoccupied with the aim of liberation and humanism as Habermas's, although he would not appeal for a version of Reason as "critical scientific rationality" that Habermas proposes. Instead, he sees Reason in a wider context involved in dialogue and in the virtue of *phronesis*.

It is worth looking at the underlying aims of the two writers from as many angles as possible. Ricoeur argues that the tradition to which Gadamer relates, because of the latter's attention to history and the past, is one of *recollection*; that is, recollecting the "truths" that are available in tradition. This makes Ricoeur claim that Gadamer belongs to the tradition of Romanticism, which would be debatable.[6] As far as Habermas is concerned it is mainly his emphasis on *critique* which leads Ricoeur to judge him as belonging to the tradition of *Aufklärung*, or Enlightenment. However, there is no doubt that both traditions share the humanistic ideas that we recall today as the ideas of the Enlightenment. In addition, Ricoeur points to the fact that the notion of "critique" constitutes a tradition; his wish is to see this tradition extended "into the most impressive tradition, that of the liberating acts of the Exodus and the Resurrection."[7] His position is that the present interest in emancipation and "anticipation of freedom" would vanish if these acts of liberation "were effaced from the memory of mankind."[8] It may be so, especially among the conditions of "social amnesia"[9] that the modern world imposes as a norm. This argument, from the perspective which sees the interest in emancipatory ideas to be supported by certain liberating aspects of tradition (Exodus and Resurrection), can offer a plausible alternative way of considering claims for an interest in "anticipation of freedom," promoted by Habermas. Ricoeur's connection of critique and emancipation with a long-standing tradition of liberation permits tenable thoughts, suggesting that Habermas's normative ideal is also bound up with the message of the Christian tradition (Exodus and Resurrection)—perhaps an intolerable position for him who strives to present the anticipation of freedom in nonreligious, nonmetaphysical, "materialist" principles of Reason. This conclusion reiterates my position in the sixth chapter, referring to Habermas's idea of nondistorted, idealized dialogue and its anticipation.

Thus, for Ricoeur, all the strongly antithetical positions in the debate should be seen rather as "false antinomies" that, instead, open up the way for a *dialectic* which concentrates between the "recollection of tradition" and the "anticipation of freedom," each pole represented by Gadamer and Habermas respectively. No doubt the debate is open to such an interpretation. However, there are some further points to be mentioned. My intention is to see the debate in the wider context of the two philosophical standpoints involved. I wish to oppose the idea that Gadamer's position can be reduced to a mere "recollection of tradition," as Ricoeur suggests. As I have mentioned elsewhere, Gadamer's philosophical project turns to tradition in order to recover that "Truth" which has been lost through the restricted vision and the alienation of the modern "Method"; such "truth" is essential for the realization of *phronesis* and for the ideals of humanist tradition including the notion of a "good and just life." This was his intention in *Truth and Method*, although his book has been received and interpreted in many different ways as some suggesting, for example, that it shows "truth" to be totally opposed to the methodological disciplines. Instead, I wish to attribute to Gadamer's position the role of a *project* for humanist ideas and a *critical attitude*—realized through philosophical reflection—not been appreciated so far. In agreement with Ricoeur I would say that the debate is underlined by the common aim of emancipation and the humanist ideas about a universal project of freedom. On the other hand, the antinomies to which Ricoeur points refer to two distinct parts of our cultural heritage (truth from tradition and critique of the ideological), which appear essential for any project toward freedom or an emancipated dialogic society. In this respect, the two poles of the antinomies, the "critique of ideology" and the "recollection of tradition," or "critical consciousness" and "hermeneutic awareness," must be retained in dialogue. Besides their differences, both writers belong to the tradition which sees liberation from technological rationality as an essential step for the promotion of humanism and especially of the aim of "the unfinished project of modernity."[10]

Heidegger's Critique of Technology and Humanism

We have seen how both Gadamer and Habermas have battled against technology and technocratic rationality viewing it as the major obstacle to emancipation. Technocratic rationality has been identified as the major element for the rationalization of the whole spectrum of life in terms of technological orientations. I proceed now to the third level of my review by introducing a different course of thought which opposes the views of Habermas and Gadamer. Such a contrast could, in the end, provide some valuable points for questioning their projects. I will start with a short account of central theses in Heidegger's philosophical position on technology and humanism, as it is treated by Gianni Vattimo in *The End of Modernity*.[11] My interest will focus on the way Heidegger considers humanism and technology as parts of the tradition of Western metaphysics, so that setting one against the other does not solve any of the present problems as the critics of technology imply. By humanism Heidegger is basically suggesting that humanity is at the "centre" of reality and all projects undertaken, or all values adopted, aim at securing and strengthening this position. However, for Heidegger, humanism is also *synonymous* with Western metaphysics. For him, every humanism, since it develops within the perspective which considers the human subject able to determine its role as central and exclusive, is either metaphysical or the ground of a metaphysics. The result is that the essence of man is determined through this perspective, a humanistic one, without reference to Being. Thus humanism does not allow the recognition of Being, neither its understanding.[12]

Heidegger views the *crisis of humanism*, preoccupying the "historical consciousness" of the last and the present centuries, as a *crisis of metaphysics*. Nevertheless, such an equation needs further explication, especially of understanding of the role technology plays in this crisis. Heidegger believed that Western metaphysics (which gives priority to the *ontic* aspect of being, as an assembly of entities, and which forgets the *ontological* questions) can survive as long as it conceals its "humanistic" side. If its (unsustainable) position, concerning the human subject as the "center" upon which everything could be reduced is revealed, then metaphysics is in decline. This has hap-

pened already in the work of Nietzsche who saw the decline of metaphysics and of humanism in the "death of God." Any metaphysics, in
order to keep the human subject in its central position, appeals to a
foundation or "ground." Such a foundation (always an "imaginary"
one), provided by the presence of God, has been lost with "the death
of God."13

In this century, the crisis of humanism has been mostly identified
as the outcome of technology which constitutes a general process of
dehumanisation. Technology excludes humanist cultural ideas and
convictions, instead basing everything upon scientific projects. In
this respect, the decline of humanism is seen as the collapse of the
value of humanity. Thus, Vattimo considers the debate developed
between the natural sciences and the "sciences of Mind" (*Geisteswissenschaften*) to be of a defensive character. This debate represents an
effort to save those values of the human subject that are under threat
by the advance of technology. The ideas of choice, free will, and
unpredictability of human decision are stressed since they are basic
elements in traditional humanism. Hence, the philosophical defense
against the technological threat in this century is organized around
two lines. The first line of defense seeks to differentiate what is
specifically human from what constitutes the world of "scientific
objectivity," thus preserving the unique qualities of the human subject. The second defensive line promotes attempts, by the subject, for
the reappropriation of its own central position. That is, the human
subject strives to redefine itself upon new theories (or grounds) that
would once more guarantee its role in the "center" of reality. However, are these defensive attempts capable of escaping Heidegger's
critique?

To this end, I will now consider the ways in which Heidegger
thinks of the crisis of metaphysics and the relation of technology to
metaphysics. He regards technology to be the end of metaphysics
and its culmination. As metaphysics relies upon its ontic preoccupations, technology is based upon similar assumptions. Metaphysics
directs itself toward the entities that constitute our surroundings and
attempts to relate them in predictable and controllable ways so that
(technological) reason can assure its domination. Thus technology,
thought of in these terms (as relying on similar assumptions as those
of metaphysics), does not represent a threat to humanism, because
humanism is also part of metaphysics. To express it differently,
humanism cannot persuade us any longer that its project and values
are a viable alternative to technological values. By merely placing
the human subject in the center of our preoccupations does not liberate us from the damaging aspects of technology. Nevertheless, as

technology represents the fulfillment and the end of metaphysics, we can say that we have reached the crisis of metaphysics. In Heidegger's terms this crisis has to be thought of as a call to *Verwindung* (overcoming and healing, overcoming and recognition of belonging).[14] Technology as *GeStell* (the totality of the technological "setting")[15] carries with it a call for the *Verwindung* of humanism and of metaphysics, an event which, if pursued, will bring Being beyond the limits that had been set by the forgetfulness of metaphysics.[16]

There is a further crucial relationship of humanism and Being which is bound to change in the act of *Verwindung*. In a metaphysics which had seen the ontic sides of Being, humanity and Being are related as subject and object. This relationship can be revealed if we question the position of the subject (*hypokeimenon*) in modern philosophy. The subject has started from the notion of *substratum* (it lies underneath any process and secures its unity) to finally become *consciousness*. We can observe here a *reduction* of the subject from (the larger category of) *substratum* to consciousness, or self-awareness, which is the unique quality of humanity itself. In the Cartesian philosophy, consciousness turns out to be defined as "subject" via-à-vis the "objects" of the world; consciousness becomes the "subject of an object." In this way we can understand this relationship of humanity and Being, sharing the roles of subject and object respectively, that is, humanity corresponds to subject and Being to object. In looking more closely at this connection we meet again the forgetfulness of Western metaphysics toward Being, since the former devotes itself exclusively to "objectivity" and "simple presence." This attention to "objectivity" (Being as an "object") constitutes, of course, the ideal of the sciences. However, this particular relationship of humanity and Being that metaphysics imposes has further consequences; the subject, as the subject of an object, can itself become an object, as a matter-of-fact, an object that can be manipulated as any other object. But what are the consequences of such a line of reasoning? The subject (humanity) which has to be protected from the dehumanization caused by technology is itself the agent that promotes its own manipulation in terms of technology. Therefore, Heidegger concludes that a *radical critique* of the subject/object relationship in modern philosophy and of present "historical consciousness" is required, as well as a move beyond it.

This Heideggerian critique of technology and humanism constitutes a philosophical reflection which goes much beyond the immediate picture one receives from empirical considerations. It presents a powerful approach to what technology and humanism possibly stand for in relation to Western metaphysics and therefore undermines the theoretical vision and expectations of the Enlightenment. I would argue that Heidegger's views have already become part of the present "historical consciousness" and thus cannot be ignored; instead, if taken seriously, they form the questioning points of the validity of any universal project to emancipation. Nevertheless, the critique of technological civilization and technocratic rationality (as ideology) does not lose its importance in the way it has been followed by Habermas and Gadamer inasfar as it does not seek its legitimacy in projects of *universal* liberation or in *teleological* views of history. Such a critique is capable of revealing alienating features of (social) Being imposed by technology and could represent a partial critical route in comparison to a more radical Heideggerian critique (which would wish to register and alter the subject-object relationship we exhibit with respect to Being).

During the presentation of the philosophical views of each writer, as well as through the examination of their opposing views in their debate, it became evident that, at several points I needed to deal with two different discourses unable to meet each other entirely. On the one hand there was Gadamer's philosophical discourse stressing the philosophical reflection provided by his theory. On the other hand, Habermas's discourse underlined the need for a scientific critique of ideology. My view is that these two positions cannot be merged; instead each can provide its particular critical stance. However, in view of Heidegger's position, one senses the shortcomings of the Gadamerian philosophical reflection. Although it has reinstated the "subject" to its own historicity and linguisticality in areas of understanding and knowledge, Gadamer's philosophy fails to question it. The "subject" remains coherent and with the possibility of self-transparency the hermeneutic reflection provides. Similarly, the notion of "meaning" is taken for granted. Meaning exists in the text in order to be approached and understood in the hermeneutical effort—although a different meaning will be reached in each particular "situation." Yet the presence of meaning and an (always possible) arrival at its understanding has not been challenged or seen to present any problems. The same could apply to the position of Habermas on the notion both of the "subject" and of "meaning."

The radical critique of Heidegger exercises a severe questioning of the notion of emancipation and the existence of an emancipatory interest which Habermas attributed (in an a priori fashion) to Reason itself. How could one justify an interest in emancipation if this proves to have metaphysical connotations? If such an interest does not exist in the way Habermas attempts to ground his "critical theory," what makes a critical attitude toward society possible? Should we rather view such a critical attitude as a *permanent critique* of our historical era built up as a philosophical ethos since the Enlightenment? This is the position of Michel Foucault, who thought that this *ethos* (as modernity) describes the thread that connects us with the tradition of the Enlightenment.[17] Thus it could be possible that a critical attitude does not necessarily need to be founded on an ambiguous a priori emancipatory interest; it could be seen as a stance, attitude, or *ethos,* formed and adopted in a particular historical era.[18]

Apart from Foucault's position, there is another strong thesis, concerning the foundations of critical reasoning. We met it earlier in a suggestion by Ricoeur, who considers the *interest in communication* as being able to support claims for a critical attitude, or for a critical theory. Ricoeur however, belonging in the same tradition, sees this interest in communication as the ground for a project to freedom in the humanist spirit of the Enlightenment. I interpreted the interest in communication not on the anthropological level of the survival of the species, but on the claim that solutions for practical life need to be found, adopted, or rejected in dialogue rather than in monological impositions of power. Yet, as Habermas has argued, dialogue is suspected of carrying in it ideological aspects, beliefs, and convictions of which participants are unaware. Thus, the critical theory of Habermas, as critique of ideology or critique of distorted communication, contributes to the direction of unveiling ideology and its causes (both part of the life history of the species). Nonetheless, we should not overlook the fact that the introduction of a scientific method for examining systematic distortions is accomplished when based upon certain presuppositions (of what is distorted) which necessarily restrict the range of the critique. Therefore, although interest in communication presents a very potent thesis permitting the foundation of critical reasoning, such a thesis must not be assimilated as another humanist narrative of the Enlightenment, or as part of a restricted scientific approach to language.

Reaching the end of these comments, it seems to me important to pay attention to two specific voices that we constantly meet in the philosophical projects of Gadamer and Habermas, but this time I will identify them as two specific "narratives" which are in crisis, a notion developed by Jean-François Lyotard. The first "voice" represents the theme of the "emancipation of humanity." I attempted to study it either in Heideggerian terms as part of a long-lasting metaphysical humanism, or in its recent expression, at least as part of the Enlightenment tradition. It corresponds to "the narrative of emancipation" which (until now) was capable of legitimizing scientific enterprises and justifying scientific knowledge. Nevertheless, according to the critics of modernity, this "narrative" has collapsed and cannot offer its services.

The second "voice" is (particularly on the part of Habermas) the appeal to Reason, which can promote the project of modernity, either as guarantor of a free *rational* communication, or when Reason itself is implemented, in an "evolutionary programme of self-development." Recently, Habermas has supported the idea that, in modern technocratic societies the domains of art, knowledge, and morality have been severely separated and decisions in these areas have been surrendered to specialized experts.[19] The main question is whether the unity of all the spheres he proposes can be achieved by an appeal to a unifying Reason, that is, a rationality which draws its norms from an idea that there is a permanent unity of Reason guaranteeing the unity of all experience, as in the tradition of German speculative philosophy. The appeal to Reason, in this particular fashion, has been called into question by Lyotard, who identifies this trend as "the speculative narrative," or the narrative of the "speculative unity of all thought" so characteristic of Hegel. In this way total plans of history can be envisaged, or similarly, all knowledge of the disciplines could be unified in an "illusive coherence" of some total program.[20] I consider it important to level these latest criticisms against Gadamer and Habermas since it is vital to make clear the grounds (and aims) on which the debate took place and how these grounds have been called into question today. Habermas, nevertheless, cannot only be judged along these lines; we must attribute to him a *critical* project and a language of *resistance* within the logic of the present consumerist society, even if he continues to maintain both of these narratives. As I argued earlier, his theory, devoted to the study of certain features of (social) Being, does not logically contradict a Heideggerian critique, but lies at a plane of critical scientific analysis different from a philosophical ontological perspective. Yet, Habermas is unprepared to associate his project with a critique of humanism (considered here as a total program of emancipation), since, for him, humanism constitutes a valuable alternative to technological rationality.[21]

I have endeavored to illustrate the terms in which Habermas conceived of *knowledge as critique* and the presuppositions that accompany his project of "critical theory." Such a theory still needs to be informed by the *hermeneutic understanding*, the hermeneutic experience and the "recollection of tradition" for which we are indebted to Gadamer. However, both positions, in affirming the continuation of the modernity project, cannot escape the "voice" of Heidegger and the present "historical consciousness" that struggles to unveil and do away with the narratives that have accompanied our traditions for a long time (perhaps identified as Western metaphysics, perhaps only as parts of the Enlightenment). These narratives themselves have become, explicitly, the locus of domination and "distorted communication." Therefore, if we seriously believe that a critique of technological civilization is necessary, then our usual critique and understanding of it must be rethought.

To this end, should we stop that kind of critique which, although it aims at technology, finally reintroduces "humanism," that is, an aspect of metaphysics? Or should we rather direct our critique toward the (ontic) metaphysical aspects of technology and the metaphysics of humanism (which in Heidegger's view is an obstacle to human freedom), in order to recover the ontological features of Being and further "truth" about ourselves (as part of this Being)? According to Heidegger, we could conceive of ourselves as always being at the destining of revealing, in which a freeing claim (our freedom at the proximity of Being) develops. However, one particular revealing, like that of technology, has taken over and has led us to the kind of life we experience at present. Through technology, and its "enframing," we loose the possibilities of other modes of revealing, such as "poiesis" (bringing forth); in Heidegger's words "enframing blocks poiesis."[23] If there is a way out for Heidegger, it should be through other modes of revealing of Being and disclosure of truth. Art is one such domain, where revealing can take place, and also a confrontation with technology. Nevertheless, Heidegger's vision is expressed in a poetic language. If we are going to gain from it, his thought should be rendered concrete and clear, within particular (social/historical) possibilities of truth, care, and overcoming/healing. Should we, then, abandon technology (which sounds unthinkable considering the needs of present societies)? Should technology be transformed, in order to avoid its disastrous effects—a naive thought, given the nature of technology—or should it be rethought, redistributed, and reexperienced in different forms, so that we all have access to its present form as information/technology[24]—overcoming its course as "an aimless consumption of beings?"[25] Inevitably, such thoughts would sound vacuous, if they are allowed to stand on their own. Instead, they are tightly connected to, and open up to a horizon of urgent ethical/political priorities and decisions.

Undoubtedly, these options are not necessarily the only alternatives. The subjects of critical understanding of our situation and of critical intervention remain quite open to discussion and cultural debate. It appears that no one has a concrete vision which can overcome the present, but at least the conditions and will for polyphony, dialogue, and critical resistance I have maintained as valuable considerations throughout should not, on the strength of this study, be abandoned.

Notes

In the following notes I use the abbreviations *T&M* and *KHI* for *Truth and Method* and *Knowledge and Human Interests* respectively.

Introduction

1. Jürgen Habermas's two recent major works translated into English are *Reason and the Rationalization of Society*, and *Lifeword and System: A Critique of Functionalist Reason*, vol. 1 (1984), and vol. 2 (1987), respectively, of *The Theory of Communicative Action*, trans. T. McCarthy (Boston: Beacon Press), and *The Philosophical Discourse of Modernity* (1987), trans. F. G. Lawrence (Cambridge: Polity Press). They have consequently attracted considerable attention and discussion.

2. Although Habermas would not consider the epistemological support of a "critical social theory" as his primary task today, he nevertheless does not dismiss his early efforts. In an interview in 1984 he said that

> the theory of cognitive interests I more or less shared with my friend Karl-Otto Apel—he has written further on it—and I continue to think that it's basically sound. But I would be a bit more cautious now. We have all the new arguments on the table from the post-empiricists. If only for that reason one would have to reformulate the account more carefully and leave room for historical change. Nevertheless, I hold by the fundamental idea that there are constitutive relationships between scientific enterprises and everyday orientations.

Peter Dews (1986), ed., *Autonomy and Solidarity: Interviews with Jürgen Habermas* (London: Verso, *New Left Review*), 197.

3. According to Martin Jay (1982) "Should Intellectual History Take a Linguisic Turn? Reflections of the Habermas-Gadamer Debate" in *Modern European Intellectual History: Reapraisals and New Perspectives*, eds. D. LaCapra and S. L. Kaplan (Ithaca, N.Y.: Cornell University Press), there are two tendencies in modern hermeneutics. One continues the task of earlier hermeneutics as "a recollection of primal meaning", and the second is "an exercise in suspicion to demystify illusion" (Nietzsche, Marx, and Freud belong to this trend). The terms were introduced by Paul Ricoeur who, in addition, characterizes the hermeneutics of Gadamer as a "recollection of tradition."

4. Such defensive accounts can be traced in Habermas, *Philosophical Discourse of Modernity*, which includes four lectures delivered at the College de France in Paris in

1983, and in his article (1983) "Modernity—An Incomplete Project" in *Postmodern Culture*, ed. Hal Foster (London: Pluto Press). Gadamer's defensive accounts of his philosophical hermeneutics can be found in *Dialogue and Deconstruction: The Gadamer–Derrida Encounter*, eds. Diane P. Michelfelder and Richard E. Palmer (1989) (Albany: State University of New York Press).

5. I will discuss Jean-François Lyotard's position on the "narratives of modernity" at the end of the last chapter.

6. The context of the conflict between sciences and humanities is evoked by Roy J. Howard (1982) in his *Three Faces of Hermeneutics: An Introduction to Current Theories of Understanding* (Berkeley: University of California Press), i–xvii.

7. I refer mainly to the social political, and historical disciplines (including economics, psychology, archaeology, etc.) as distinct from the natural sciences and in line with Gadamer's use of the term. For further distinction see note 3 in the second chapter.

8. The defensive position of the humanities might not be a universally acceptable opinion but it has become a widespread belief and stance in the last few decades. See Howard, *Three Faces of Hermeneutics*, xi.

9. See, for example, Hans-Georg Gadamer (1981), *Reason in the Age of Science*, trans. F. G. Lawrence (Cambridge: The MIT Press), 165.

Chapter 1. The Critique of "Scientism"

1. Critical views on positivism, as articulated by Habermas can be found in his articles in the collection, T. W. Adorno, et al, *The Positivist Dispute in German Sociology* (London: Heinemann Educational Books, 1976). This collection records the exchange which took place in the Sixties between Karl R. Popper and the Frankfurt school on the topic of the logic of the social sciences. Secondly, further views of Habermas on positivism exist in his article (1963), "Dogmatism, Reason and Decision: On Theory and Praxis in our Scientific Civilisation" in Habermas (1974), *Theory and Practice*, trans. J. Viertel (London: Heinemann Educational Books).

2. Max Horkheimer (1937), "Traditional and Critical Theory," in *Critical Theory, Selected Essays*, trans. Mathew J. O'Connell and others (New York: Herder & Herder, 1972).

3. Ibid., 207.

4. Ibid., 208.

5. Paul Connerton (1976), ed. *Critical Sociology* (Harmondsworth, England: Penguin Books), 16. Connerton actually refers to two notions of critique: one denoting *reflection* on the conditions of possible knowledge in the way it is used by Kant, and the other referring to Hegel's concept of *self-reflection* in the *Phenomenology of the Spirit*, as the process of consciousness overcoming the initial illusions and constraints it meets in its ascent to Absolute Knowledge.

6. For a comprehensive view of the way the Frankfurt school was inspired by and utilized Marx's ideas which it received through Lukács, as well as their critical absorption of German Idealism, see David Held (1980), *Introduction to Critical Theory: Horkeimer to Habermas* (London: Hutchinson).

7. Ibid., 65. Held refers in particular to Max Weber (1970), *From Max Weber: Essays in Sociology*, trans. and ed. by H. H. Gerth and C. W. Mills (London: Routledge and Kegan Paul).

8. Max Horkheimer (1946), *Eclipse of Reason* (New York: Seabury Press), 20.

9. Ibid., 21.

10. Habermas considers the term *self-constitution of the species* through labor to be the key concept Marx employs in his critical reading of Hegel's *Phenomenology*. It is a materialist concept, since the species is no longer the vehicle for the unfolding of the *Idea* but produces itself through social labor. Nevertheless, Habermas wishes to emphasize the instrumentalist nature of the concept. He states that the constitution of the self is reduced to labor only and he interprets Marx's comments "[Hegel] grasps the essence of labour and comprehends objective man, who is true man because of his reality, as the result of his own labour" (*KHI*, 43) in a similar way. However (as we will see), according to Habermas, Marx, at the same time, presented another version of the self-constitution of the species occurring at the level of interaction among individuals. This version is much closer to Habermas's attempts. As a matter-of-fact, Habermas tries to preserve this materialist approach to the history of the species by founding the constitution of the self upon more complex evolutionary patterns, which make justice to present scientific convictions (see his article, "Towards a Reconstruction of Historical Materialism," in Habermas [1979], *Communication and the Evolution of Society*, trans. T. McCarthy [London: Heinemann Educational Books].)

11. I use the term *Spirit* instead of *Mind* according to the translation of G. W. F. Hegel (1977), *Phenomenology of Spirit* by A. V. Miller (Oxford: Oxford University Press).

12. Habermas (1968), *Knowledge and Human Interests*, trans. Jeremy J. Shapiro (Boston: Beacon), 10.

13. Ibid., 15.

14. In a quotation from Marx's *Capital*, labor is a "condition of human existence that is independent of all forms of society, a perpetual necessity of nature in order to mediate the material exchange between man and nature, in other words, human life." (*KHI*, 27).

15. Habermas identifies his approach to the epistemological significance of labor with a similar orientation evident in Marx's "Theses on Feuerbach," *KHI*, 27.

16. This definition of "instrumental action" occurs in his essay Habermas (1968), "Technology and Science as 'Ideology'" in Habermas, *Toward a Rational Society*, trans. Jeremy J. Shapiro (London: Heinemann Educational Books, 1971), 91.

17. This second case of reflection as critique is closer to the original Hegelian notion of "self-reflection."

18. *KHI*, 44.

19. In this footnote I wish to provide a more expanded understanding of the difficult equation of reflection and production Habermas alludes to. If, for Hegel, consciousness is moving from one stage to a "higher" one through reflection, for Marx the abolition of one form of life and the movement to another (e. g., from feudalism to capitalism) happens through the development of the forces of production (and their subsequent contradictory relationship to the relations of production). Thus, reflection for Marx is no longer identified with the act of self-consciousness, characteristic of the Fichtean "absolute ego." As long as Marx (in Habermas's view) has transformed Fichte's "absolute ego" to the historically self-generated human species "self-reflection" as such does not appear; its position, as a motive force in history is reduced to the level of instrumental action: the level of the forces of production. Hence, the nature of this "deformed" reflection is labor. In my opinion, Habermas attempts to demonstrate the affinity between the idea of self-reflection (and its stages) in German Idealism, and the idea of the historical phases of production in Marx. Perhaps, his comments could also be seen as an attempt to allude to Marx's arrival at the concepts of "historical materialism."

20. When Habermas talks of epistemology (or epistemological justification) he has

in mind the theory of knowledge starting with Kant, and not with the methodological norms of the current philosophy of science.

21. "Communicative action": it refers to all forms of communication and social interaction that prevail in everyday life. Habermas distinguished "communicative action" from "discourse" after 1973. In the former the individuals uncritically accept the norms, social practices, and beliefs of everyday life. In "discourse" the underlying norms, ideological beliefs, and values are subjected to criticism. See Rick Roderick (1986), *Habermas and the Foundations of Critical Theory* (London: Macmillan), 82.

22. He means to "rationally reconstruct" the universal rules, patterns, and competences that govern the self-constitution of the species. I will refer again to the notion of "rational reconstruction" in the fourth and fifth chapters.

23. Habermas undertook this task in his book, *Zur Reconstruction des Historischen Materialismus* (Frankfurt am Main: Suhrkamp Verlag, 1976), published in English as *Communication and the Evolution of Society*.

24. *KHI*, 63. "Self-reflection" here means reflection of the subject upon itself, which is the basic Hegelian idea of the "self-reflection" of consciousness, as I mentioned in note 5n of this chapter.

25. This point is indicative of Habermas's conflation of the two notions of "reflection," Hegelian and Kantian that I have already mentioned in 5n and 24n. Here, he has in mind the Kantian notion of reflection on the "necessary conditions of possible knowledge." Habermas accepted this conflation later in his "A Postscript to *Knowledge and Human Interests*" (1973), *Philosophy of the Social Sciences* 3.

26. *KHI*, vii.

27. Ibid., 4.

28. I borrow this widely used concept from Thomas S. Kuhn (1962), *The Structure of Scientific Revolutions* (Chicago: University of Chicago Press), since it gives a fairly good initial approximation to the social "area" in which science "evolves" and is also practiced as research.

29. The term *social evolution* occurs in Habermas's *Communication*, in which he attempted to rewrite the basic concepts of Historical Materialism. In his article "Does Philosophy Still Have a Purpose?" (1971), in Habermas, *Philosophical Profiles*, trans. F. G. Lawrence (London: Heinemann Educational Books), science is considered as a productive force. A more extensive argument of this view, that science has turned into the most important productive force, is presented in his essay, "Science and Technology". In this article, the transformation of science into a productive force, Habermas believes, is one of two important changes which have occurred since Marx's writings on liberal Capitalism.

30. In his article, "Does Philosophy Still Have a Purpose?" 15.

31. In both Habermas, "Science and Technology," and Habermas (1976), *Legitimation Crisis*, trans. Thomas McCarthy (London: Heinemann Educational Books).

32. Thomas McCarthy (1984), *The Critical Theory of Jürgen Habermas* (Cambridge: Polity Press), 39.

33. Habermas, "Science and Technology," 113.

34. Roderick shares a similar view. He says that Habermas attempts "to formulate a concept of reason capable of a more differentiated critique of instrumental reason and of providing a more satisfactory normative justification for a critical theory of society." (Roderick, *Habermas*, 50.)

35. I will refer to Dilthey's division of sciences into two groups and the way in which Habermas draws from him in the fourth chapter.

36. *KHI*, 68.

37. The "observer's paradigm": it indicates the usual philosophical paradigm used

in the philosophy of science (especially in the empiricist tradition) where the subject is supposed to be "an observer" and the knowledge arrived at afterward, is based upon her initial observations. The term represents a recent terminology Habermas uses in his book, *Philosophical Discourse of Modernity*. The other pole of the pair is the "participant's paradigm," where the subject of knowledge starts its cognitive role already immersed in communication and language as a participant in dialogue; language, communication, and dialogue include already the initial presuppositions for the approach to any object of knowledge.

38. Husserl's early critical views on the sciences which adopt the *natural standpoint* (the commonsense belief in an external world always "present" to consciousness) can be traced in Edmund Husserl, *Ideas: General Introduction to Pure Phenomenology*, trans. W. R. Boyce-Gibson (London: George Allen and Unwin Ltd., 1967). However, his full-scale criticism of *naturalism* and *historicism*, connected with his views on the crisis of philosophy and the crisis of European man, appear in his article "Philosophy as a Rigorous Science" in Edmund Husserl, *Phenomenology and the Crisis of Philosophy*, trans. Quentin Lauer (New York: Harper and Row, Publishers, 1965), and in Edmund Husserl, *The Crisis of European Sciences and Trancendental Phenomenology. An Introduction to Phenomenological Philosophy*, trans. David Carr (Evanston, Ill.: Northwestern University Press, 1970). This is the last book written by Husserl to which Habermas mainly refers in his appendix to *KHI*. It is worth mentioning that Habermas charges Husserl with a mistaken conception of philosopny as pure theory, and consequently rejects Husserl's phenomenology, which is directed along similar lines. On the other hand, however, he borrows from Husserl the latter's critique of the objectivism of the sciences, since it coincides with Habermas's own target for the critique of scientism. So, phenomenology breaks away from the naive objectivist attitude, but, simultaneously, it reintroduces the concept of pure theory of classical philosophy. This does not allow any relation between theory and interest that Habermas wishes to present.

Such an emphasis on the notion of philosophy as pure theory constitutes a Habermasian reading of Husserl, which, although correct, does not analyze Husserl's phenomenological project, or the philosophical priorities of Husserl for the recovery of transcendental consciousness and its intentionality.

39. *KHI*, 89.

40. The two terms *objectivation* and *objectification* which I will employ at certain times, correspond to the verbs *to objectivate* and *to objectify*. To *objectivate (objektivieren)* something is to give it a form in a symbolic system (e. g., within language) so that it can be communicated and understood. To *objectify (vergegenständlichen)* something is to transform it into an object, so that instrumental action, or the statements of natural sciences, can apply to it. Objectification in this way amounts to the "constitution" of this object (in a Kantian approach). See also translator's note in *KHI*, 323.

41. "*Life-world*" is the translation of the Husserlian concept *lebenswelt*. It refers to the everyday surrounding world we are all immersed in and which is taken as the starting-point of any inquiry. Any science, any consciousness, starts from this rich, pregiven, cultural milieu which many times in various theoretical expositions is left unaccounted and unnoticed. The notion of the "life-world" is there to remind us that knowledge and understanding do not start from a "consciousness" entirely devoid of content, or point of reference. For later Husserl the concept of "life-world" serves not only as the initial ground of all sciences, but it also reveals our basic ontological condition of being with others. In this way, he avoids the solipsistic picture of a transcendental consciousness, which appears in his earlier work. "It [the "life-world"] is pregiven to us all quite naturally, as persons within the horizon of our fellow men, i. e., in every actual connection with others, as 'the' world common to us all." (Husserl, *The Crisis of*

European Sciences, 122.) The Gadamerian concept of "horizon" (which I will introduce in the second chapter) seems to be close to the notion of "life-world," although the latter comprises the *totality* of what we live and experience daily.

42. Habermas's inaugural lecture at the University of Frankfurt am Main appears as "Knowledge and Human Interests: *A General Perspective*," and forms the appendix to *KHI*. Written in 1965, it presents a short review of Habermas's beliefs at that time, as well as his first exposition of the idea that specific human interests produce and shape knowledge.

43. Habermas calls these sciences "hermeneutic," because of their interpretative character, apparent in their orientation and the methodological model they adopt in their effort to understand "meaning." At the moment it suffices to get a general idea of interpretation by considering the case of a text. In this case, the understanding of what the text "says," or what it means, or what we think it means, does not depend upon the observations of some of its physical properties; instead, we orient ourselves toward the capturing of the possible meaning(s) embedded in the text by giving possible interpretations (as in translation).

44. The early representative of the neo-Kantian controversy separating the natural and the cultural sciences is Rickert, at the beginning of the century. Dilthey continued along similar lines and Weber was also influenced in his own concept of "meaning."

45. *KHI*, 309.

46. As a matter-of-fact Habermas initially believed that "historical materialism can be understood as a theory of society conceived with practical intent" (Habermas, *Theory and Practice*, 3), and therefore his early efforts for a "critical theory" were shaped in the context of "historical materialism."

47. Habermas says that although he thought of a "systematic investigation into the relationship between theory and practice," he did not progress much, and that in later investigations he attempted to clarify three aspects of this relationship:

> (1) the empirical aspect of the relationship between science, politics, and public opinion in advanced capitalist social systems; (2) the epistemological aspect of the relation between knowledge and interest; and (3) the methodological aspect of a social theory which aims at being capable of assuming the role of a critique. (Habermas, "Some Difficulties in the Attempt to Link Theory and Praxis," 1–3).

48. McCarthy, *Critical Theory*, 2–4. Even though Habermas does not elaborate on these subjects when talking of the early Greek *theoria* in his appendix, one can find further discussion on the change of the classical doctrine of politics in the nineteenth century, in his article, "The Classical Doctrine of Politics in Relation to Social Philosophy."

49. Habermas introduces the term *monological* in opposition to *dialogic*. A monological science depends upon its descriptive propositions and its causal-analytic explanatory account which it provides for the understanding of its object of study. It excludes any form of dialogue which could enlarge the processes for the establishment of the "truth" of its propositions. It cannot cover the dialogue between different participants as well as the form of consensus prevailing between them.

50. The idea which Hobbes put forward was to discover the laws of "human nature," so that practical knowledge could be gained in a form of social theory. Such a theory could "scientifically" establish the necessary conditions for the running of human societies. In other words, as long as there is a matrix of the laws of "human nature," practical knowledge could accurately direct itself to seek solutions on a universal, scientific pattern.

We can therefore understand McCarthy saying that (with the scientisation of politics) the problems of practical life and the classical doctrine of politics are transformed into a new stage of technical problems of ordered and smooth conditions for the conduct of social agents as citizens of the state (McCarthy, *Critical Theory*, 4).

51. The notion of *praxis* refers exclusively to moral political action, in its Aristotelian meaning, and therefore it must be distinguished from other activities, such as *poiesis*, which covers the activity for the creation of artifacts and is related to *techne* (the acquisition of skills for creating artifacts).

52. *KHI*, 305.

Chapter 2. Text and History

1. *T&M*, xi.

2. Ibid., xii.

3. Gadamer refers to the *Geisteswissenschaften*, which include all the social and historical disciplines as distinct from the natural sciences. He follows the development of the above concept from its introduction in German in the translation of J. Stuart Mill's *Logic (A System of Logic, Rationcinative and Inductive, Collected Works*, vol. 7, and vol. 8, ed. J. M. Robson [Toronto: University of Toronto Press], 1973) up to Dilthey's use of it in defense of the epistemological independence of the human sciences (see *T&M*, 5–10). In the fourth chapter I use the term *cultural sciences* for *Geisteswissenschaften* as it has been rendered by the translator of Habermas's *Knowledge and Human Interests*. However, the translator (see 13n in the fourth chapter) thinks of Geisteswissenschaften in its wider meaning, including literature, philosophy and the arts (i. e., whatever springs from the mind). In Gadamer's use of the term, philosophy, the arts, and literature are kept apart.

4. *T&M*, xiii.

5. Ibid., xiv.

6. Ibid., xvi.

7. This view of the development of hermeneutics originates in Dilthey's *Die Entstehung der Hermeneutik, Gesammelte Schriften*, V, 317–31 (Leipzig und Berlin, B. G. Teubner, 1924), and it is shared by Gadamer (*T&M*, 153).

8. *T&M*, 156.

9. Ibid., 164.

10. Schleiermacher actually imposed a Romantic notion of the individual suggesting that the hermeneutical problem extends from the text to speech as well. Thus, the interpreter must not only understand the meaning of the text or the speech of the speaker, but also the individuality of the speaker and therefore of the author. The reason for this is the Romantic notion of the individual who is now seen as possessing unconscious part as well, and his speech or written text is seen in the light of "artistic production," as an "aesthetic construct." Correspondingly, understanding of this production is art, that is, understanding is an art. Therefore, interpretation is a reconstruction of this (artistic) production or construct of the individual. Moreover, the interpreter, almost certainly, is going to understand the author "better" than the author himself, since the former is going to reveal a meaning of which the author was unconscious.

11. The historians who developed a clear concern for the understanding of universal history form the Historical school. Its best-known representatives are Droysen and Ranke.

12. See Joseph Bleicher (1980), *Contemporary Hermeneutics: Hermeneutics as Method, Philosophy and Critique* (London: Routledge and Kegan Paul), 20–22.

13. We are faced here with a problem: how do we arrive at historical knowledge from the experiences of the individual? Dilthey presents all the steps, including how the individual, through his experiences, forms a continuity of life which is reexperienced and approached by the members of his community via biographical knowledge. In this way a unity of life is created around significant experiences. After that, Dilthey presents the move from the continuity of life of the individual to historical continuity; a transition which never attained adequate clarity in Gadamer's view (see *T&M*, 197–98).

14. *T&M*, 213.

15. Gadamer states that this conclusion is almost an half-affirmation of Hegel's philosophy of Mind (*T&M*, 213).

16. Rudiger Bubner argues that "*Wahrheit und Method* essentially builds on the insights of the later Heidegger, but translates his sometimes cryptic allusions into rather more accessible philosophical language and definitely gives added strength to the conception [of hermeneutics] with its historical, philological, and aesthetic studies." (Bubner [1981], *Modern German Philosophy*, trans. E Matthews [Cambridge: Cambridge University Press], 51.)

17. Martin Heidegger (1962), *Being and Time*, trans. J. Macquarrie and E. Robinson (Oxford: Basil Blackwell), 61–62. I retain here the translation from Bubner, *Modern German Philosophy*, 27.

18. Bubner, ibid., 29.

19. Heidegger, instead of accepting "phenomenon" as "appearance," insists on another meaning of "the Greek word *phainomenon*: that which shows forth itself in itself or the manifest"; see Bubner, *Modern German Philosophy*, 27, and Heidegger (1987), *An Introduction to Metaphysics*, trans. R. Manheim (New Haven: Yale University Press), 101–5.

20. Paul Ricoeur (1983), "On Interpretation," in *Philosophy in France Today*, ed. Alan Montefiore (Cambridge: Cambridge University Press), 190. For further study of Heidegger's philosophical views on the notion of *Dasein*, one must follow the unfolding of the "existential analytic" of *Dasein* in his *Being and Time*. Invaluable insights and commentary on Heidegger's work can be found in Hubert L. Dreyfus (1991), *Being-in-the-World: A Commentary of Heidegger's Being and Time. Division I* (Cambridge: MIT Press).

21. Bubner claims that Heidegger, because of serious misunderstanding of the reception of his *Being and Time*, as in the case of Sartre, is forced to make clear his position against any form of anthropology or empirical analysis of the "human essence." Such a need brought about his "Letter to Humanism" in 1947. (Bubner, *Modern German Philosophy*, 46–47.)

22. Heidegger (1978), "Letter to Humanism," in Heidegger, *Basic Writings, From Being and Time (1927) to The Task of Thinking (1964)*, ed. F. Krell (London: Routledge and Kegan Paul), 189–242.

23. *T&M*, 234.

24. Ibid., 236.

25. Although "horizon" is a widely used concept in a metaphorical sense, for Gadamer it acquires further importance in the context of his hermeneutics as we will see later in this chapter.

26. *T&M*, 238.

27. It is worth mentioning here that Gadamer talks of tradition" in the singular form. He studies the concept of "tradition" without examining traditions in their multiplicity and overlapping, even in single societies. Traditions, also, should not be considered as homogeneous entities but as "spaces" which can include opposing or contradictory views and aspects either arising from the past or formed in new conditions of life.

Nevertheless, notwithstanding these remarks, Gadamer's philosophical examination of "understanding" and "tradition" does not lose its significance and his conclusions could be applied to actual, nonhomogeneous, examples of traditions. Throughout this work I will use the concept of "tradition" in the singular, following Gadamer's style.

28. *T&M*, 268.

29. Ibid., 267.

30. Ibid., 268.

31. Ibid., 269.

32. Ibid., 269.

33. Ibid., 271.

34. Ibid., 273.

35. Ibid., 274.

36. Ibid., 275–76.

37. *Situational* meaning: it depends on the historical situation of the interpreter and the particular interpretation that has been performed.

Chapter 3. Linguisticality and "World"

1. This expression, to "have world," is the translation of "*Welt haben*," a neologism used by Gadamer to illustrate the difference between the human world and simple habitat, as I will explain later on in this chapter.

2. When Gadamer refers to "agreement," he does not mean that partners in discussion agree (have the same opinion) on the subjects they discuss. The term *agreement* indicates a common basis (the sharing of conceptions that they understand and participate in) which makes the dialogue possible.

3. I refer here to two works: T. Kuhn's *Structure of Scientific Revolutions* (Chicago: The University of Chicago Press, 1962) and Karl R. Popper's *Conjectures and Refutations: The Growth of Scientific Knowledge* (London: Routledge and Kegan Paul, 1963) which, in the philosophy of science, suggest approaches that could be seen favourably from Gadamer's viewpoint. It must be added, that in Popper's case, he has insisted that his account does not entail any relativism. Although a theory may be falsified, the scientific aim is guided by the classical normative idea of a final, absolute, objective truth. My reference to Popper intends to show that his views—even though they rely on a different perspective than that of Gadamer's—invite a multiplicity of competing theories. On this issue see Joseph Margolis (1991), *The Truth About Relativism* (Oxford: Basil Blackwell), chapter 1.

4. An extensive bibliography accompanies this subject. In relation to this present work I would mention the anthology *Understanding and Social Inquiry*, eds. Fred R. Dallmayr and Thomas A. McCarthy (1977) (Notre Dame, Ind.: University of Notre Dame Press).

5. *T&M*, 360.

6. Gadamer discusses Habermas's objections concerning Piaget's research in his article "To What Extent Does Language Preform Thought?" (1973), published as a supplement to *T&M*, 491–98.

7. *T&M*, 363.

8. Ibid., 363.

9. Ibid., 401.

10. Ibid., 402. In the original text, *Wahrheit und Methode Grundzüge einer Philosophischen Hermeneutik* (J. C. B. Mohr [Paul Siebeck], Tübingen, 1965), 419,

Gadamer uses the same expression "Welt haben" throughout his discussion of world and habitat. In this quotation the translator has rendered this expression as "to have a world" and in the next one as "to have world." This could be confusing, although I believe the translator's intention was to soften the intentional neologism of Gadamer into readable English.

11. *T&M*, 402 (German edition, 420).

12. Ibid., 401.

13. Ibid., 408.

14. The full sentence of this quotation reads: "Language is the house of Being in which man ek-sists by dwelling, in that he belongs to the truth of Being, guarding it." (Heidegger, "Letter to Humanism," in Heidegger, *Basic Writings*, 213.) In Heideggerian philosophy Being presents itself in language, sometimes revealing, sometimes concealing itself. "Language is the lighting-concealing of the advent of Being itself." (Op. cit., 206.) Such metaphors acquire their full meaning in Heideggerian language as it is unfolding in his writings. The term *ek-sistence* "means standing out into the truth of Being" (op. cit., 206). It is written in this way in order to signify the essence of man, "thought in terms of *ecstasis*," when he is near the truth of Being. *Existence*, in this context, does not refer to the usual meaning of the word as existing in space or in actuality, as Sartre transported Heidegger's thought to his own philosophy (for example, refer to J. P. Sartre's famous phrase [for human beings] "existence precedes essence" in his *Existentialism and Humanism*, trans. P. Mairet [London: Methuen, 1989]).

15. *T&M*, 408.

16. On the concept of "homogeneity" between "concept" and "reality" in Hegel's philosophy see Lucio Colletti (1973), *Marxism and Hegel*, trans. L. Garner (London: New Left Editions) and Gabris Kortian (1980), *Metacritique: The Philosophical Argument of Jürgen Habermas*, trans. F. Raffan (Cambridge: Cambridge University Press).

17. Ludwig Wittgenstein (1961), *Tractatus Logico-Philosophicus*, trans. D. F. Pears and B. F. McGuiness (London: Routledge and Kegan Paul).

18. *T&M*, 406.

19. There is no doubt that the case is different in formalized disciplines, such as in mathematics, where statements such as "1+1=2" stand for analytic "truths."

20. I do not consider it necessary to expand on the Saussurian theory of language which has been the main foundation of French structuralism. My intention, in the present context, is to juxtapose Saussure's theory as another major paradigm which opposes the Gadamerian connection of "word" and "object" as metaphysical.

21. An extended discussion on the "referent" and its position within the Saussurian theory can be found in Vincent Descombes (1980), *Modern French Philosophy*, trans. L. Scott and J. M. Harding (Cambridge: Cambridge University Press).

22. The views of Gadamer on the "Emergence of the Concept of Language in the History of Western Thought" and Plato's role in it, are presented in *T&M*, 366–97.

23. *T&M*, 410.

24. Ibid., 409.

25. Ibid., 432.

26. Ibid., 404.

27. This quotation comes from Apel K.-O. et al. (1971), *Hermeneutic und Ideologiekritik*, Frankfurt and can be found in Bubner, *Modern German Philosophy*, 57.

28. *T&M*, 447.

29. Richard J. Bernstein (1983), *Beyond Objectivism and Relativism: Science, Hermeneutics, and Praxis* (Oxford: Basil Blackwell), 152.

30. In the Hegelian philosophy, the goal of consciousness is Absolute Knowing, or Spirit that knows itself as Spirit, as a complete self-consciousness. The *identity* of con-

sciousness and reality occurs after Spirit has recognized itself in reality (history and nature), when the unfolding of reality comes to coincide with its notion (concept), produced and perfected by Spirit. By mentioning the Hegelian project here, we can disassociate it from Gadamer's views. (See in particular Hegel's *Phenomenology of Spirit*, and the accompanying analysis of text by J. N. Findlay.)

31. *T&M*, 319.

32. This affinity with Heidegger's notion of "truth" is also suggested by Georgia Warnke in her *Gadamer: Hermeneutics, Tradition and Reason* (Cambridge: Polity Press, 1987), 57–58.

33. Bernstein, *Beyond Objectivism*, 152.

34. Ibid., 154.

35. When Kuhn introduces the idea of "normal science" as the accepted "paradigm," he indicates the epistemological reasons for this acceptance. "Normal science" can solve problems which are the model for further research. However, it is finally a matter of the "scientific community" to uphold and retain something as "true" or valid, by argument. Thus, apart from the epistemological reasons that the "paradigm" satisfies, its acceptance relies upon the shared values, beliefs, and arguments of the scientific community. This is the case until a "crisis" arrives as a result of the inability of "normal science" to solve accumulating "anomalies". A shift then to another "paradigm" occurs which, in Kuhn's terms, constitutes a *scientific revolution*.

36. It is evident that the players carry on the tasks of the game in their individual ways and movements; the same game, if repeated, will never be exactly the same. But all their aspirations and individual talents are set to the tasks of the game.

37. According to Warnke this "self-contained structure" of the play is able to represent a world independent of the beliefs and intentions of any individual, the author included. On one hand, we observe a difference from the notion of the "game"; on the other hand Gadamer's position is in direct conflict with other theories which would find the meaning(s) of a play relying upon the intentions of the author. Warnke discusses these topics in *Gadamer*, 48–56.

38. To transfer the authority of the game upon its players, by analogy, to the authority of the play upon its actors and finally upon its audience, can present certain problems; especially when Gadamer insists that a play or a work of art or a book need an *audience* in order to fully realize their meaning. Further discussion on these topics (*T&M*, 91–146), which are beyond my immediate concern in this work, can be found in Warnke, *Gadamer*, 48–56.

39. Warnke, *Gadamer*, 58.

40. The notion of *language game* may bear some similarity with the Wittgensteinian term, which we will meet in the next chapter, used by Habermas. In the present context Gadamer simply evokes the similarities between language and a play or a game, so our understanding of "truth," brought in language, can be facilitated.

41. *T&M*, 446.

42. Ibid., 446.

43. Ibid., 445.

44. Ibid., 446.

45. Gadamer believes that our technological civilization can be seen to be based on *techne* (referring to the acquisition of skills); he also believes that its employment of the means-ends rationality has become central to the human aspirations and to the life of societies. Simultaneously, the conception of *praxis* has been pushed to the periphery of our civilisation.

46. When Gadamer talks of Being, saying that "language is the house of Being," he has in mind the Heideggerian *Being*. He is not concerned with the *ontic* Being (which

refers to things with specific qualities, such as "extension," in the Cartesian philosophy), but with the *ontological* Being. Truths about the ontic being can be dealt with by the sciences. Truths about Being may lie beyond the scientific enterprise in many other areas of culture. In order to decide whether a Heideggerian reading of Gadamer can be applied to the notion of "truth," one needs to investigate both the connections and distance that unite and separate Gadamer and Heidegger. This is beyond the scope and the aims of the present work.

47. When Gadamer gives examples of understanding, of an ethical principle, or of the "truth" of a mathematical proposition, he stresses the fact that this understanding involves knowledge and insight into the "subject-matter"; it is an understanding of *Die Sache*.

48. For an extensive analysis of the concept of *Bildung* before and after the Enlightenment, see *T&M*, 10–19.

49. Richard Rorty (1980), *Philosophy and the Mirror of Nature* (Oxford: Basil Blackwell). Rorty proposes the concept of edification, but I must note here that for him the discourse of hermeneutics is incommensurable with the discourse of science. Gadamer would disagree emphatically with this position (see Rorty, *Mirror of Nature*, 360ff).

50. Ibid., 359.

51. Gadamer, "Hermeneutics as a Theoretical and Practical Task," in *Reason in the Age of Science*, 114.

52. Gadamer, "Historical Transformations of Reason", in *Rationality Today*, ed. T. Geraets (Ottawa: University of Ottawa Press), 8.

53. Gadamer, *Reason in the Age of Science*, 112.

54. Ibid., 90.

Chapter 4. From Cognitive Interests to Depth Hermeneutics

1. Habermas accepted his conflation of the two notions of reflection in his "Postscript to *Knowledge and Human Interests*", which he wrote in 1971, after numerous criticisms against his positions. His acceptance of this conflation appears also in a new Introduction to *Theory and Practice*, under the title "Some Difficulties in the Attempt to Link Theory and Practice," which he also wrote in 1971. Since then he has always presented two types of sciences, the "reconstructive" ones depending on the Kantian notion of reflection, and the "critical sciences" employing the Hegelian notion of reflection. (See also note 30n in this chapter.)

2. *KHI*, 91.

3. David Hume, "An Inquiry Concerning Human Understanding," in *Enquiries Concerning Human Understanding and Concerning the Principles of Morals*, ed. L. A. Selby-Bigge (Oxford: Clarendon Press, 1975).

4. According to Peirce there are two types of (synthetic) inference, "abduction" and "induction," and both are distinguished from "deduction." We are familiar with the case of "induction," when we infer a "law" from a number of particular cases. On the other hand, through "abduction" we come to establish a working hypothesis about a result (by describing its cause), which our theories are unable to predict. In fact this case has been called "retrospective method," permitting the establishment and discovery of new explanatory hypotheses that were not available before.

5. See note 40 in the first chapter.

6. *KHI*, 112.

7. Ibid., 116.

8. This is a quotation from Peirce's "Lectures on Pragmatism," cited in *KHI*, 120.

9. *KHI*, 120.

10. Ibid., 133.

11. Ibid., 134.

12. Ibid., 135.

13. I use the term *cultural sciences* for Geisteswissenschaften, as the translator of *KHI* has proposed (see *KHI*, 337). There is a lack of an equivalent term in English which could simultaneously express the humanities, the social and political sciences, the historical sciences, and the arts, that is, areas which can be thought of as the outcome of *Geist* (Mind, Spirit). However, Gadamer has used the term exclusively for the "human sciences"; see 3n, second chapter.

14. Quotation from Dilthey's work cited in *KHI*, 338.

15. "Expressions of life" are all acts of which the individual is capable. They can be linguistic expressions, gestures, bodily movements, works of art, and so forth. For Dilthey all of them present externalizations and objectivations of the individual's mind.

16. *KHI*, 171.

17. Ibid., 173.

18. Quoted from Dilthey, *KHI*, 173.

19. The employment of hermeneutic understanding in such cases follows the familiar steps employed in the hermeneutic tradition. They are based upon the major paradigm of understanding the text, as already mentioned in the second and the third chapters.

20. See Rüdiger Bubner (1975), "Theory and Practice in the Light of The Hermeneutic-Criticist Controversy," *Cultural Hermeneutics* 2 and Bubner, *Modern German Philosohpy*; and Fred R. Dallmayr (1972), "Critical Theory Critisised; *Knowledge and Human Interests* and its Aftermath," *Philosophy of the Social Sciences* 2, who oppose such a view as an explicit "decisionism."

21. *KHI*, 176.

22. It appears to me that both Habermas (following Dilthey) and Heidegger begin with the very empirical notion of *communication* and understanding each other, that involves hermeneutic understanding. However, Heidegger leads the way beyond this basic phenomenon, in order to include the picture of *Dasein* that always is in an ecstatic position interpreting its surroundings and itself, as it is caught up in the process of understanding. For Habermas (and Dilthey), this empirical notion of intersubjectivity demonstrates an interest in communication which is "a condition of survival." His position has more to do with an evolutionary Darwinian view of humanity than with the philosophical view about Being provided by Heidegger.

23. Habermas has named "universal pragmatics" that part of his scientific efforts to reconstruct the universal rules and conditions which make communication and understanding possible. See "What Is Universal Pragmatics?" in Habermas, *Communication*.

24. *KHI*, 192.

25. Ibid., 192. Aspects and insights of "how the linguistic and logical structures are related" can be found in Jean Piaget (1971), *Stucturalism*, ed. and trans. C. Maschler (London: Routledge and Kegan Paul), chap. 5 on "Linguistic Structuralism."

26. *KHI*, 194.

27. Ibid., 195.

28. Ibid., 197.

29. Ibid., 196.

30. Dallmayr reaches a similar conclusion especially by following Habermas's later idea on the existence of two kinds of reflection (calling the Hegelian one "self-

reflection," and the Kantian one "rational reconstruction"). For Dallmayr, "self-reflection" has to do with individual experience and personal awareness, while "rational reconstructions" can uncover deeply rooted regulatory mechanisms, or anonymous sets of rules (e. g. logical or linguistic) that all members of society follow. (Dallmayr, "Critical Theory Criticised," 220–21.)

The concepts of "phylo-genesis" and "onto-genesis," concerning developmental stages of the individual, can be traced in the works of Piaget.

31. "Autonomy" and "responsibility" is a translation of *Mündigkeit* which can be found in Kant's "What is Enlightenment?", in Immanuel Kant, *Critique of Practical Reason and Other Writings in Moral Philosophy*, ed. and trans. by L. White Beck (Chicago: Chicago University Press, 1949).

32. *KHI*, 198.

33. I refer here to the notion of "class-consciousness" and to the possibility of the "working-class" to *raise its consciousness* for the emancipation of society in a classless social formation, as a modified form of self-reflection.

34. These words appear in Kant's *Critique of Practical Reason*.

> Pure practical reason cannot at all be expected to be subordinate to speculative reason and thus to reverse the order, because all interest is ultimately practical, and even that of speculative reason is only conditioned. It is complete only in its practical employment. (Quoted by Habermas, *KHI*, 203.)

35. For Fichte, a "dogmatic consciousness" comprehends itself as a consequence, or as a product of the things surrounding it: as a product of nature. Such a consciousness in order to attain "freedom" and elevate its will to emancipation, has to liberate itself from the clutches of dogmatism.

36. *KHI*, 208.

37. Ibid., 211.

38. Ibid., 214.

39. Herbert Marcuse (1962), *Eros and Civilisation: A Philosophical Inquiry Into Freud* (Boston, Beacon Press). Basing himself on the interplay of the "reality principle" and the "pleasure principle" of Freud, Marcuse attempted to provide the vision of a society which could rely upon the latter principle and project it as society's main aim. Marxist categories for the ending of exploitation and alienation must also be incorporated in this process.

40. The notion of the "text" applies to any area that involves meaning investigated by psychoanalysis. It may be a dream (nonpathological case); everyday life (speech, writing, and action); the neurotic life of the individual; the memory of the individual; or the reconstructed life-history of the patient. Also, the notion of "corruption" or "disturbance" has to be based on what has been accepted as a normal situation.

41. *KHI*, 218.

42. Parapraxes which indicate errors, refer to cases of forgetting, slips of the pen and tongue, misreadings, and similar events that happen in everyday life. They are not accidental at all, even if the "author" (of the everyday life-text) is unaware of them.

43. The interpretation of dreams, Habermas argues, goes beyond the usual hermeneutic procedures of textual understanding. In the dream the meaning of the "text-distortion itself" must be understood. The analyst must understand and show the "dream-work," that is, the transformation through which a latent dream-thought results in a manifest dream. Simultaneously, a process of reflection occurs revealing the genesis of the dream-text and complementing the dream-work.

44. From Freud's vol. 7, *The Standard Edition of the Complete Psychological Works of Sigmund Freud*, quoted in *KHI*, 229.

45. In Freud's "'Wild' Psychoanalysis," vol. 11, *Standard Edition*, quoted in *KHI*, 229.

46. *KHI*, 255.

47. Ibid., 259.

48. Like all interpretations, "general interpretations" remain within ordinary language. They can actually be regarded, in Habermas's account, as systematically generalised narratives. They have a narrative character, since they represent a series of events that are general elements of life-histories. Another difference is that there are no criteria for the failure or success of the hypotheses provided by the "general interpretation." Even in the case in which the patient does not accept them this could mean two things: they were either false, or the resistances of the patient were extremely strong. A failure here does not correspond to the way "failure" is considered in the natural or in the social sciences. The only criterion for success or failure of hypotheses seems to be the *completion* of self-reflection (not necessarily followed by the disappearance of symptoms, which could be replaced by other symptoms).

49. For example, see Howard, *Three Faces of Hermeneutics* and John B. Thompson (1981), *Critical Hermeneutics: A Stydy of the Thought of Paul Ricoeur and Jürgen Habermas* (Cambridge: Cambridge University Press).

50. Freud's *Civilisation and Its Discontents* (1930), trans. J. Riviere (London: Hogarth Press, 1979), or *The Future of an Illusion* (1927), in *Standard Edition*, vol. 21 (1927–1931), trans. J. Strachey (London: Hogarth Press, 1961), represent such a direction in his work.

51. By "civilization" Freud means all those assets that distinguish human life from animal life, and include all knowledge and capacity to control nature as well as all regulations that human beings adopt in their relation between themselves for the conduct of life, and especially the distribution of wealth. For him there is no difference between culture and civilization.

52. *KHI*, 287.

53. Ibid., 289.

54. Many criticisms were directed against Habermas after the publication of his *KHI*. They mainly concentrated on the following areas: (a) the role and existence of cognitive interests, (b) the identification of knowledge and emancipatory interest in a critical science, and (c) the transfer of the psychoanalytic model to the social/historical sciences.

A large number of criticisms came from the Marxist camp, showing that Habermas had abandoned any class-position and class-distinction; also that his conception of "human interests" was not based upon class-differences. (See Dallmayr, "Critical Theory Criticized.")

Bubner as well criticizes Habermas for the latter's a-prioristic presentation of the interests; they are shielded against any further inquiry. Bubner argues that this is the outcome of "certain distrust in speculative thought" by the Frankfurt school, and "the unwillingness to express critical premises to comprehensive philosophical reflection." (Bubner, *Modern German Philosopy*.)

Other criticisms forced Habermas to differentiate between "reconstructive" and critical sciences, as already mentioned. He even went so far as to suggest that "even moral philosophy will achieve the status of a reconstructive science to the degree that it can derive the universal rules of a communicative ethic from the basic norms of rational speech." (Habermas, [1973], "A Postscript to *Knowledge and Human Interests*," *Philosophy of the Social Sciences* 3:183.)

Habermas still "sticks to the distinction" between the two kinds of science and to the view that there cannot be any critical theory without an emancipatory interest.

(Interview 1984, in Dews, *Autonomy and Solidarity,* 198). However, he wishes to reintroduce some sort of *critical stance* within the reconstructive sciences, as this would enable them to separate what is *normal* from what is *deviant.* (Habermas [1983], "Interpretive Social Science vs Hermeneuticism," in *Social Science as Moral Inquiry*, eds. N. Haan et al. [New York: Columbia University Press].)

Chapter 5. Tradition and Authority versus the Critique of Ideology

1. The views of Habermas developed in *KHI* were already known to the German public by 1965 through his inaugural lecture at the University of Frankfurt am Main; the article is included as an appendix to *KHI*. This strongly suggests that Habermas's *KHI* was conceived prior to his article "A Review of Gadamer's *Truth and Method.*"

2. Ibid. It was published in 1970, in Habermas's study, *On the Logic of the Social Sciences* (English edition, 1988; the article in this edition appears as "The Hermeneutic Approach," 143–49). Originally it was published in the periodical *Philosophische Rundschau*, in 1967.

3. Habermas, "Hermeneutic Claim to Universality"; it can be seen as a critique to the arguments of *T&M* but also as an answer to Gadamer's earlier paper "The Universality of the Hermeneutic Problem" (1966), in Gadamer, *Philosophical Hermeneutics*, trans. D. E. Linge (Berkeley: University of California Press).

4. Gadamer's counterpositions can be traced mainly in Gadamer, "Universality of Hermeneutic Problem," and in Gadamer, "On the Scope and Function of the Hermeneutic Reflection." The second article has appeared under different headings in different translations and recently (under its original title), as "Rhetoric, Hermeneutics and Critique of Ideology" in *The Hermeneutic Reader: Texts of the German Tradition from the Enlightenment to the Present* (1986), ed. K. Mueller-Vollmer (Oxford, Basil Blackwell). (Originally published in *Kleine Scrifte*, I, Tubingen, 1967.)

5. For example Gadamer's article "To What Extent Does Philosophy Preform Thought?" and "The Hermeneutics of Suspicion"; also, Habermas's "Interpretive Social Sciences vs Hermeneuticism."

6. The articles of Jay "Should Intellectual History," and Dominick LaCapra "Habermas and the Grounding of Critical Theory," in LaCapra (1983), *Rethinking Intellectual History* (Ithaca N.Y.: Cornell University Press), belong to these new tendencies and concerns. By "postmodernity" I have in mind Jean François Lyotard's position in his book, *The Postmodern Condition: A Report on Knowledge* (1984), trans. J. Bennington and B. Massumi (Manchester: Manchester University Press), referring to the present era of theory (science) and the crisis of its legitimation because of the death of modern narratives that had sustained it.

7. Umberto Eco (1989, Interview, BBC2 ("The Late Show"), 1989.

8. Jack Mendelson (1979), "The Habermas–Gadamer Debate," *New German Critique* 18 (Fall): 44.

9. For example, the articles of Paul Ricoeur (1973), "Ethics and Culture: Habermas and Gadamer in Dialogue," *Philosophy Today* 17, Dieter Misgeld (1977), "Critical Theory and Hermeneutics: The Debate Between Habermas and Gadamer," in *On Critical Theory*, edited by John O'Neill (London: Heinemann Educational Books), and Mendelson, "The Habermas–Gadamer Debate" belong to the first trend. The articles of Jay, "Should Intellectual History" and LaCapra, "Habermas and the Grounding," belong to the second tendency. "Radical hermeneutics" is identified mainly with the work of poststructuralist French philosophers and especially with Jaques Derrida.

10. *T&M*, 241.
11. Gadamer, "On the Scope and Function," 33.
12. *T&M*, 250.
13. Gadamer, "On the Scope and Function," 29.
14. *T&M*, 252–53.
15. Ricoeur, "Ethics and Culture."
16. Habermas, "A Review," 357.
17. Ibid., 359.
18. *T&M*, 420.
19. Gadamer, "On the Scope and Function," 29.
20. Habermas draws here from Marxist and sociological views of society that enhance early Marxist conceptions on power and domination imposed through language. The whole conception retains the basic theme of ideology (or language in our case) as concealing "real" relations.
21. *T&M*, 420. I have chosen the translation of the term *happening*, following the same quotation in Bleicher's translation of Habermas, "A Review," instead of the term *event* in *T&M*.
22. *T&M*, 420.
23. Habermas, "A Review," 359.
24. As mentioned in the first chapter, it is Marx with his theory of history, who ensured such a change in our appreciation of the idealistic positions of Hegel.
25. Habermas, "A Review," 360.
26. Habermas believes that this is rather impossible for Gadamer to appreciate because of the ontological differences which exist between himself and Gadamer. In my view, this is unfair to Gadamer who has always tried to show the connection between the "real" and language; a subject treated in the third chapter.
27. Gadamer, "On the Scope and Function," 31.
28. Ibid., 32.
29. Ricoeur (1970), *Freud and Philosophy, An Essay on Interpretation*, trans. D. Savage (New Haven: Yale University Press), 20–36.
30. Gadamer, "Philosophical Foundations of the Twentieth Century," 117.
31. Paul Ricoeur talks about the philosophical tradition he follows in his article, "On Interpretation," which was published in *Philosophy in France Today*, ed. Alan Montefiore (1983). In the same article he describes how the notion of *Verstehen* is introduced in "the phenomenological question *par excellence*, namely the investigation of the intentional sense of noetic acts." Later on, in the hands of Heidegger, *Verstehen* acquires an ontological signification (the response of a being thrown into the world). In this way the subject-object relationship in the Husserlian thinking, becomes now "an *ontological* link," which, according to Ricoeur, is much stronger than any relationship sought within knowledge. (Ricoeur, 190).
32. Ricoeur, "Ethics and Culture," 164.
33. Ibid., 161.
34. Such an orientation has been proposed by Lyotard, *The Postmodern Condition*.
35. Ricoeur, "Ethics and Culture," 165.
36. Ibid., 165.
37. *Reflection* is the translation of the noun *Besinnung* in the works of Martin Heidegger, that means recollection, reflection, consideration, and deliberation. Also the verb that corresponds to it can be translated as "to call to mind, to remember, to think on, or to hit upon." (See translator's note in Heidegger (1977), *The Question Concerning Technology and Other Essays*, trans. W. Lavitt [New York: Harper], 155). For the distinction between the Kantian use of reflection as inquiry and the Hegelian use of it as a phenomenological category, I have referred to the first chapter.

38. Heidegger, *The Question Concerning Technology*, 180. Heidegger also distinguishes reflection from intellectual education (*Bildung*), and from the knowledge that is applicable to the sciences.

39. Ricoeur, "On Interpretation," 188.

40. "Reflection" with the meaning to bend back (from the Latin *reflectere*) is closer to Heidegger's *vorstellen* (to represent, to set before) and could mean "the mind's observing of itself." See translator's note, Heidegger, *The Question Concerning Technology*, 155.

41. I must add here a question concerning the *motive* for reflection which forms the basic activity of all phenomenology. Husserl was presented with the problem of what triggers philosophical reflection. How can the naive consciousness in the "life-world" start to reflect upon itself while it has no motives for this process? According to Bubner, Husserl initially had no answer to this question. Heidegger, nevertheless, insisted that there is a *motive* for reflection that is based on *existential experiences*. The motive accompanies our thinking or anticipation of death which in effect makes us confront the notion of "nothingness." Although this is such a strong argument to refute, it appears to me that Gadamer does not follow it, nor does he explicitly ask the question on the motive for reflection. Instead he is closer to Husserl who in the end believed that reflection is activated because of historical reasons. For Husserl, "the crisis of science" must be viewed as the primary ground which has created further connections that disturb a prephilosophical naïveté. Gadamer, in my opinion, would insist on a similar path looking for historical reasons. His question is usually: how do we justify our predicament before the sciences and their rationality that dominate our life today, and before the technological civilization to which they give rise? This is one of the main reasons behind the writing of his *T&M*. The question of the *motive* for reflection is surely an extremely broad one, but it seems legitimate to allow for its formation by historical reasons. For example, we could argue that historical reasons have imposed the "need" to reflect upon ourselves and to *redefine* our lives in view of new developing structures of life, particularly when the latter exhibit inefficiencies, contradictions, or repressions that do not coincide with our moral convictions. (For comments on Husserl and Heidegger see also Bubner, *Modern German Philosophy*, 39–40).

42. Gadamer, "On the Scope and Function," 40.

43. Ibid., 40.

44. Ibid., 38.

45. On this issue Bubner believes that the notion of reflection is Hegelian in its origin, at least in the way it is used by philosophical hermeneutics and its critics. However, there is an inner ambiguity in the concept which stems from the Hegelian notion. Reflection is directed either to an object (an "other-directedness"), or toward itself ("self-directedness"). According to Bubner this duality is always present and there is no priority of one aspect over the other. For Bubner, philosophical hermeneutics and critical theory have exchanged arguments on the topic of reflection which are primarily due to the delicate balance between these two aspects of reflection. If we follow Bubner's suggestion, the Freudian concept is attached to the "self-directedness" of reflection; the Gadamerian concept (for the transparency of prejudices) to the "other-directedness." Although, in my opinion, this distinction does not do justice to the phenomenological character of hermeneutics and the importance it attaches to self-awareness, Bubner's comments confirm that there is a distinction between the two uses of reflection. (For his argument see Bubner, "Theory and Practice," 340–42.)

46. Gadamer, "Hermeneutical Problem," 5.

47. Ibid., 8.

48. *T&M*, xxv.

Chapter 6. The Universality of the Hermeneutic Problem

1. Jay, "Should Intellectual History," 93.

2. Saussure had divided language (le langage) into two related sides, *la parole* and *la langue*. *La parole* refers to what we consider as speech and represents the executive side of language; it is concerned with the individual "speech acts." *La langue* refers to the system of signs (a code) which compose language and is the social part of it.

3. Habermas, "Hermeneutic Claim," 182.

4. See note 40 in the first chapter.

5. For further study of the problems involved, refer to Habermas, "Hermeneutic Claim," 186–87.

6. Habermas, ibid., 191.

7. Habermas, ibid.

8. Habermas borrows this term from A. Lorenzer who has also investigated the depth-hermeneutical deciphering of meaning in the psychoanalytic context. (See Habermas, "Hermeneutic Claim," 192).

9. See Habermas, ibid., 192–94.

10. Habermas mentions three sets of theoretical assumptions and presuppositions that guide scenic understanding. The first set includes the analyst's theoretical preconceptions of what is normal speech or normal everyday communication. The second set refers to the way in which the analyst traces the observed distortions upon the confusion of prelinguistic and linguistic organization of symbols appearing (as two different stages) in the developmental process of the individual. The third set informs us of how the analyst explains the observed speech distortions and deformations upon a theory of deviant socialization, which even includes patterns of infant interaction within the formation of personality.

11. With the term *causal explanation* I have in mind the broad idea that there is a source, or a structure that generates the symptom. It coincides with Habermas's view that explanations answer to "how" (something happens), as distinct to "what" (it is).

12. Habermas, "Hermeneutic Claim," 201.

13. Habermas believes that it is possible (because of attempts made in the field of "general linguistics") to construct a general theory of natural languages, or as he calls it, a "rational reconstruction" of a regulative system that defines our linguistic competence. Actually, if any element in the natural language can be met by a theoretical description in the reconstructed system, then the latter can replace the hermeneutic understanding of meaning. He presents this as an indisputable claim and does not inquire into the presuppositions underlying such a "rational reconstruction." Any theory must always begin with a particular "view" of language and of linguistic competence. Thus, it could only be a hypothetical reconstruction, a theory, and not an *absolute* knowledge of how natural languages perform, or how they are employed. It is possible that our linguistic competence might also depend upon different matrices to the ones Habermas has in mind.

14. Both quotations from Habermas, "Hermeneutic Claim," 205.

15. This is actually the view of A. Wellmer who believes that, with this addition, "the universal claim of the hermeneutical approach can be maintained." Habermas also quotes Wellmer, however, in order to support his own argument that a dialogue and its consensus can be a context and source of domination. (Habermas, "Hermeneutic Claim," 204–5).

16. Habermas, "Hermeneutic Claim," 205.

17. Ricoeur, "Ethics and Culture," 159.

18. Ibid., 206.

19. Ricoeur describes the position of Habermas as "an eschatology of non-violence, akin to Ernst Bloch's 'principle of Hope'." It constitutes the "ultimate horizon" of a philosophy based on an interest in anticipation rather than in reminiscence. (Ricoeur, "Ethics and Culture," 159).

20. Habermas recognized the need to secure "truth-claims." Later in his Habermas, "A Postscript to Knowledge," he said that

> while the conditions of experiencing something objectively can be clarified in a *theory of the constitution of objects,* the conditions of argumentative reasoning can be clarified in a *theory of truth* designed as a logic of discourse. The two are not the same. (170) (Habermas's italics.)

He differentiated between statements (declarative judgments), prescriptions (normative judgments), and evaluations (evaluative judgments). All of them "express an objective content of experience," but they require different criteria for evaluation (see Habermas, ibid., 171).

21. This course has been followed by Habermas in his latest writings in *Theory of Communicative Action.* Regarding the way in which Habermas combines ethics, social theory, and the philosophy of social sciences, using his communicative model of reason and action, see Stephan K. White (1988), *The Recent Work of Jürgen Habermas* (Cambridge: Cambridge Universsity Press).

22. Gadamer, "On the Scope and Function," 42.

23. Ibid., 42.

24. Habermas, "Hermeneutic Claim," 209.

25. Bernstein, *Beyond Objectivism.*

26. Ibid., 11.

27. The concept "situational" is in accordance with the notion of "situation" which "represents a standpoint that limits the possibility of vision" (*T&M*, 269). In Gadamer's terms we must accept the fact that we always belong in a situation (a historical and hermeneutic situation) which allows us to "see" the world and, at the same time, it presents its own limits.

28. Bernstein, *Beyond Objectivism,* 1.

29. Gadamer (1982), "A Letter by Professor Hans-Georg Gadamer," 262.

30. Gadamer, "Hermeneutic Claim," 1.

31. Gadamer (1975), "Hermeneutics and Social Sciences" and "Summation," *Cultural Hermeneutics* 2: 311. He also acclaims Charles Taylor's article (1971), "Interpretation and the Sciences of Man," *Review of Metaphysics* 25, for the appreciation of the hermeneutical phenomenon in the foundations of the social sciences.

32. Ibid., 311.

33. Gadamer, "Letter," 264.

34. Gadamer, "Hermeneutics and Social Science," 316.

Chapter 7. Critical Theory or Recollection of Tradition?

1. Ricoeur (1981), *Hermeneutics and the Human Sciences,* trans. J. B. Thompson (Cambridge: Cambridge University Press), 87. Ricoeur complemented his essay on the Habermas–Gadamer debate mentioned in the fifth chapter, Ricoeur, "Ethics and Culture," by another essay, "Hermeneutique et critique des idéologies," in *Démythisation et Idéologie* (1973), ed. E. Castelli (Paris: Aubier Montaigne). In this essay he has attempted to go beyond his earlier thoughts. The essay appears as "Hermeneutics and the Critique of Ideology" in Ricoeur, *Hermeneutics and the Human Sciences.*

2. Ibid., 93.

3. Ricoeur also reaches a similar conclusion: "a depth-hermeneutics is still a hermeneutics, even if it is called meta-hermeneutical" (Ricoeur, *Hermeneutics and the Human Sciences*, 97). However, he arrives at this conclusion by trying to bridge the gap which appears between pathological or ideological distortion that depth-hermeneutics analyzes, and the "misunderstanding" that textual hermeneutics tries to overcome.

4. Gadamer, *Reason in the Age of Science*, 165.

5. This is the main theme of Habermas's article, "Technology and Science as 'Ideology'."

6. Ricoeur has always called Gadamer's philosophical hermeneutics romantic hermeneutics. Now, this becomes clear considering the emphasis Gadamer has placed upon the "truths" and their recollection from tradition. Nevertheless, I think this could prove to be misleading if we recall how Gadamer disassociated his approach from the romantic hermeneutics of Schleiermacher (and others), reviewed in the second chapter.

7. Ricoeur, *Hermeneutics and the Human Sciences*, 99.

8. Ibid., 100. I believe the Exodus and Resurrection apply as a "memory" to the Western tradition and cannot be so easily universalized as a "memory of the mankind." Instead, they should be seen as part of a more open, collective memory that includes other traditions as well.

9. Fredric Jameson (1984), Foreword to Lyotard, *Postmodern Condition*, vii–xxi.

10. Habermas, "Modernity."

11. Gianni Vattimo (1988), *The End of Modernity, Nihilism and Hermeneutics in Post-modern Culture*, trans. J. R. Snyder (Cambridge: Polity Press). The main aim of his book is to present, in Heideggerian terms, the end of Modernity as the end of Metaphysics, as well as to provide an interpretation of Heidegger's call for overcoming/healing (*Verwindung*) the final form of metaphysics (technology, and humanism).

12. Heidegger, "Letter to Humanism," 202.

13. Vattimo, *End of Modernity*, 32–33.

14. For the different meanings of this term see tranlator's note, in Heidegger (1975), *The End of Philosophy*, trans. J. Stambaugh (London: Souvenir Press Ltd.), 84, and in Vattimo, *End of Modernity*, 39–41. *Verwindung* as overcoming something would mean to leave it behind. In Heideggerian use it also means that if something is *verwunden*, it is also incorporated. It is similar to those cases in which one attempts to overcome an illness, although one does not get entirely rid of it; one has to come to terms with it, and learn to live with it. In social terms, according to Vattimo, overcoming humanism can be seen as "a recognition of belonging and an assumption of responsibility."

15. *Gestell*, or "enframing." It refers to the technological framework aiming at enclosing all beings to a specific ordering (that of "standing-reserve," in which beings are available for use and manipulation).

16. The Nietzschean "death of God," and the Heideggerian views on the anihilation of Being (since, instead of living at its proximity, we have transformed it into sets of values) indicate a pessimistic nihilism. Vattimo welcomes nihilism, however from a different perspective, and in line with the Heideggerian notion of "overcoming." He believes that nihilism (announced by Nietzsche and Heidegger) does not necessarily lead to a total anihilation, but it is "the only chance" for rethinking and rebuilding a world based on the present postmodern condition of existence, where Being can be seen and appropriated differently. Nevertheless, Vattimo's proposals for a "rhetorically persuasive," "unified view of the world," which philosophy can supply, remain vague, especially when it is not clear what constitutes a postmodern existence in concrete social/historical terms, and what form "overcoming" may assume amid present conditions. (See Vattimo, *End of Modernity*.)

17. Michel Foucault (1984), "What Is Enlightenment?" ("Was ist Aufklärung?"), in *The Foucault Reader*, ed. Paul Rabinow (New York: Penguin Books).

18. It should be added that Foucault disassociates the tradition of the Enlightenment from the concept(s) of humanism. Although his view is correct (and in accordance with Heidegger's conception of humanism, as a long lasting orientation of Western thought), I believe that particular notions of humanism are articulated within the Enlightenment, in order to sustain the two meta-narratives (of "total emancipation," and "absolute reason") to which Lyotard refers. Even the genealogical analyses of the numerous constellations of power/knowledge, or of the repressive articulations of our social environment, which Foucault proposes as our task at present (that is, the task of carrying out an *historical ontology of ourselves*), should show the inextricable bond between the Enlightenment and its own particular conceptions of humanism. Enlightenment, in its appeal to reason and the adulhood of mankind (Kant), has always been associated with humanism. Otherwise, one is inclined to accept that modernity, the ethos developed within the Enlightenment, could be preserved without recourse to humanism, an ambivalent position implied by Foucault in his article "What is Enlightenment?"

19. See Habermas, "Modernity" and *Philosophical Discourse*.

20. See Lyotard, *Postmodern Condition*.

21. For an evaluation of Habermas's efforts to found a way of legitimating the project of human emancipation, see David M. Rasmussen (1990), *Reading Habermas* (Oxford: Basil Blackwell). Through Robert C. Holub's *Jürgen Habermas: Critic in the Public Sphere* (London: Routledge, 1991), one can aslo follow Habermas's most significant intellectual contributions. Holub offers an appraisal of the role of Habermas in shaping critical thinking in social and political issues, and he evaluates Habermas's critical interventions in philosophical debates, in critical discussions concerning the social sciences, and in public disputes.

22. Not only Heidegger, Foucault, as well, warns us that in the name of "humanism," through its particular configurations in the twentieth century, we have put forward projects of total liberation with disastrous concequences. This practice "has led to the return of the most dangerous traditions." (Foucault, "What is Enlightenment?", 46.)

23. Heidegger, *The Question Concerning Technology*, 311.

24. For this particular demand, relying upon the notion of "justice," refer to Lyotard, *Postmodern Condition*.

25. Heidegger, *End of Philosophy*, 106–7.

Bibliography

I have arranged the majority of Habermas's and Gadamer's works according to the date of their initial (German) publication.

Adorno, Theodor W., H. Albert, R. Dahrendorf, J. Habermas, H. Pilot, K. R. Popper (1976). *The Positivist Dispute in German Sociology*. Translated by G. Adey and D. Frisby. London: Heinemann Educational Books Ltd.

Apel, K.-O., C. Bormann, R. Bubner, H.-G. Gadamer, D. Giegel, J. Habermas (1971). *Hermeneutik und Ideologiekritik: Theorie-Diskussion*. Frankfurt: Suhrkamp, Verlag.

Bernstein, Richard J. (1983). *Beyond Objectivism and Relativism: Science, Hermeneutics, and Praxis*. Oxford: Basil Blackwell.

———, ed. (1985). *Habermas and Modernity*. Oxford: Basil Blackwell.

Bleicher, Josef (1980). *Contemporary Hermeneutics: Hermeneutics as Method, Philosophy and Critique*. London: Routledge and Kegan Paul.

Bubner, Rüdiger (1975). "Theory and Practice in the Light of the Hermeneutic-Criticist Controversy." *Cultural Hermeneutics* 2: 337–52.

——— (1981). *Modern German Philosophy*. Translated by E. Matthews. Cambridge: Cambridge University Press.

Colletti, Lucio (1973). *Marxism and Hegel*. Translated by L. Garner. London: New Left Editions.

Connerton, Paul ed. (1976). *Critical Sociology*. Harmondsworth, Middlesex: Penguin Books Ltd.

Dallmayr, Fred R. (1972). "Critical Theory Criticised: *Knowledge and Human Interests* and Its Aftermath." *Philosophy of the Social Sciences* 2: 211–29.

Dallmayr, Fred R., and Thomas A. McCarthy, eds. (1977). *Understanding and Social Inquiry*. Notre Dame, Ind.: University of Notre Dame Press.

Descombes, Vincent (1980). *Modern French Philosophy*. Translated by L. Scott-Fox and J. M. Harding. Cambridge: Cambridge University Press.

Dews, Peter ed. (1986). *Autonomy and Solidarity: Interviews with Jürgen Habermas*. London: Verso, *New Left Review*.

Dilthey, Wilhelm (1900). *Die Entstenhung der Hermeneutik. Gesammelte Schriften*, V (317–31). Leipzig und Berlin, B. G. Teubner, 1924.

Dreyfus, Hubert L. (1991). *Being-in-the-World. A Commentary on Heidegger's Being and Time. Division I*. Cambridge: MIT Press.

Eco, Umberto (1989). Interview, BBC2, "The Late Show," 1989.

Foucault, Michel (1984). "What Is Enlightenment?" in *The Foucault Reader*. Edited by Paul Rabinow. Harmondsworth, Middlesex: Penguin Books Ltd.

Freud, Sigmund (1927). *The Future of an Illusion* in *Standard Edition,* vol. 21 (1927–1931). Translated under the editorship of J. Strachey, in collaboration with Anna Freud, and assisted by A. Strachey and A. Tyson. London: The Hogarth Press, 1961.

—— (1930). *Civilisation and Its Discontents*. Translated by J. Riviere. London: The Hogarth Press. 1979.

Gadamer, Hans-Georg (1960). *Truth and Method*. Translated by Garrett Barden and W. Glen-Doepel. Edited by John Cumming. London: Sheed and Ward Ltd., 1975.

—— (1963). "The Problem of Historical Consciousness." In *Interpretive Social Science*. Edited by P. Rabinow and W. M. Sullivan. Berkeley: University of California Press.

—— (1965). *Wahrheit und Methode. Grundzünge einer Philosophischen Hermeneutik*. J. C. B. Mohr (Paul Siebeck), Tübingen.

—— (1966). "The Universality of the Hermeneutical Problem." In *Philosophical Hermeneutics*, by H.-G. Gadamer. Berkeley: University of California Press.

—— (1967). "On the Scope and Function of Hermeneutical Reflection." In *Philosophical Hermeneutics*, by H.-G. Gadamer. Berkeley: University of California Press.

—— (1971). "Reply to My Critics." In *The Hermeneutic Tradition: From Ast to Ricoeur*. Edited by Gayle L. Ormiston and Alan D. Schrift. Albany: State University of New York Press, 1990.

—— (1972). "The Philosophical Foundations of the Twentieth Century." In *Reason in the Age of Science*, by H.-G. Gadamer. Cambridge: MIT Press.

—— (1973). "To What Extend Does Language Preform Thought?" In *Truth and Method*, by H.-G. Gadamer. London: Sheed and Ward.

—— (1975). "Hermeneutics and Social Science" and "Summation." *Cultural Hermeneutics* 2: 307–16, 329–30.

—— (1976). *Philosophical Hermeneutics*. Translated and edited by D. E. Linge. Berkeley: University of California Press.

—— (1977). "On the Origins of Philosophical Hermeneutics." In *Philosophical Apprenticeships*. Translated by R. R. Sullivan. Cambridge: MIT Press, 1985.

—— (1978). "Hermeneutics as a Theoretical and Practical Task." In *Reason in the Age of Science*, by H.-G. Gadamer. Cambridge: MIT Press.

—— (1979). "Historical Transformations of Reason." In *Rationality Today*, edited by T. Geraets, Ottawa: University of Ottawa Press, 3–14.

—— (1980). "Practical Philosophy as a Model of the Human Sciences." *Research in Phenomenology* 9: 74–85.

—— (1981). *Reason in the Age of Science*. Translated by F. G. Lawrence. Cambridge: MIT Press.

—— (1982). "A Letter by Professor Hans-Georg Gadamer." In *Beyond Objectivism and Relativism*, by R. Bernstein, 261–65. Oxford: Basil Blackwell.

—— (1984). "The Hermeneutics of Suspicion." In *Hermeneutics, Questions and Prospects*, edited by G. Shapiro and A. Sica, 54–65. Amherst: University of Massachusetts Press.

—— (1987). "Interview with Hans-Georg Gadamer; a Conversation on Hermeneutics and the Situation of Art." *Flash Art* 136: 78–80.

Giddens, Anthony (1985). "Jürgen Habermas." In *The Return of Grand Theory in the Human Sciences*. Edited by Quentin Skinner. Cambridge: Cambridge University Press.

Habermas, Jürgen (1963). "The Classical Doctrine of Politics in Relation to Social Philosophy." In *Theory and Practice*, by J. Habermas. London: Heinemann Educational Books Ltd.

——— (1963b). "Dogmatism Reason and Decision: On Theory and Praxis in our Scientific Civilisation." In *Theory and Practice*, by J. Habermas. London: Heinemann Educational Books.

——— (1965). "Knowledge and Human Interests: *A General Perspective*", appendix to Habermas, *Knowledge*. Inaugural lecture at the University of Frankfurt am Main.

——— (1967). "A Review of Gadamer's *Truth and Method*." In *Understanding and Social Inquiry*. Edited by F. R. Dallmayr and T. A. McCarthy, 335–63. Notre Dame, Ind.: University of Notre Dame Press.

——— (1968). *Knoweledge and Human Interests*. Translated by Jeremy J. Shapiro. Boston: Beacon Press, 1971.

——— (1968b). "Technology and Science as 'Ideology'." In *Toward a Rational Society*, by J. Habermas. London: Heinemann Educational Books Ltd.

——— (1970). "The Hermeneutic Claim to Universality." In *Contemporary Hermeneutics: Hermeneutics and Method, Philosophy and Critique*, by J. Bleicher. London: Routledge and Kegan Paul.

——— (1970b). "Summation and Response." *Continuum* (Chicago) 8: 123–33.

——— (1971). "Some Difficulties in the Attempt to Link Theory and Praxis." In *Theory and Practice*, by J. Habermas. London: Heinemann Educational Books Ltd.

——— (1971b). "Does Philosophy Still Have a Purpose?" In *Philosohical Political Profiles*, by J. Habermas. London: Heinemann Educational Books Ltd.

——— (1971c). *Toward a Rational Society*. Translated by Jeremy J. Shapiro. London: Heinemann Educational Books Ltd., 1971.

——— (1973). "A Postscript to *Knowledge and Human Interests*." *Philosophy of the Social Sciences* 3: 157–89.

——— (1974). *Theory and Practice*. Translated by J. Viertel. London: Heinemann Educational Books Lted.

——— (1976). *Legitimation Crisis*. Translated by Thomas McCarthy. London: Heinemann Educational Books Ltd.

——— (1979). *Communication and the Evolution of Society*. Translated by Thomas McCarthy. London: Heinemann Educational Books Ltd.

——— (1979b). "Hans-Georg Gadamer: Urbanising the Heideggerian Province." In *Philosohical Political Profiles*, by J. Habermas. London: Heinemann Educational Books Ltd.

——— (1983). "Interpretive Social Science vs Hermeneuticism." In *Social Science as Moral Inquiry*. Edited by N. Haan, R. N. Bella, P. Rabinow, and W. M. Sullivan. New York: Columbia University Press.

——— (1983b). "Modernity—An Incomplete Project." In *Postmodern Culture*. Edited by Hal Foster. London: Pluto Press.

——— (1983c). *Philosophical Political Profiles*. Translated by F. G. Lawrence. London: Heinemann Educational Books Ltd.

——— (1984). *The Theory of Communicative Action*. Vol. 1, *Reason and the Rationalization of Society*. Translated by Thomas McCarthy. Boston: Beacon Press.

——— (1987) *The Theory of Communicative Action*. Vol. 2, *Lifeworld and System: A Critique of Functionalist Reason*. Translated by Thomas McCarthy. Boston: Beacon Press.

——— (1987b). *The Philosophical Discourse of Modernity*. Translated by F. G. Lawrence. Cambridge: Polity Press.

——— (1988). *On the Logic of the Social Sciences*. Translated by S. W. Nicholsen and J. A. Stark. Cambridge: Polity Press.

Hacking, Ian, ed. (1981). *Scientific Revolutions*. Oxford: Oxford University Press.

Hegel, G. W. F. (1956). *The Philosophy of History*. Translated by J. Sibree. New York: Dover Publications.

——— (1977) [First German publ. 1807]. *Phenomenology of Spirit*. Translated by A. V. Miller. Oxford: Oxford University Press.

Heidegger, Martin (1962). *Time and Being*. Translated by J. Macuarrie and E. Robinson. Oxford: Basil Blackwell.

——— (1975). *The End of Philosophy*. Translated by J. Stambaugh. London: Souvenir Press (Educational and Academic) Ltd.

——— (1977). *The Question Concerning Technology and Other Essays*. Translated by W. Lovitt. New York: Harper and Row.

——— (1978). "Letter to Humanism." In *Martin Heidegger, Basic Writings, From Being and Time (1927) to The Task of Thinking (1964)*. Edited by F. Krell. London: Routledge and Kegan Paul.

——— (1987). *An Introduction to Metaphysics*. Translated by R. Manheim. New Haven: Yale University Press.

Held, David (1980). *Introduction to Critical Theory: Horkheimer to Habermas*. London: Hutchinson.

Holub, Robert C. (1991). *Jürgen Habermas. Critic in the Public Sphere*. London: Routledge.

Horkheimer, Max (1937). "Traditional and Critical Theory." In *Critical Theory, Selected Essays*. Translated by M. J. O'Connell and others. New York: Herder and Herder, 1972.

——— (1946). *Eclipse of Reason*. New York: Seabury Press, 1974.

Howard, Roy J. (1982). *Three Faces of Hermeneutics: An Introduction to Current Theories of Understanding*. Berkeley: University of California Press.

Hoy, David Couzens (1978). *The Critical Circle: Literature, History, and Philosophical Hermeneutics*. Berkeley, University of California Press.

Hume, David (1777). "An Inquiry Concerning Human Understanding," in *Enquiries Concerning Human Understanding and Concerning the Principles of Morals*. Edited by L. A. Selby-Bigge. Oxford: Clarendon Press, 1975.

Husserl, Edmund (1911). "Philosophy as A Rigorous Science," in Husserl, Edmund, *Phenomenology and the Crisis of Philosophy*. Translated by Quentin Lauer. New York: Harper and Row, Publishers, 1965.

——— (1913). *Ideas: General Introduction to Pure Phenomenology*. Translated by W. R. Boyce-Gibson. London: George Allen and Unwin Ltd., 1967.

——— (1936). *The Crisis of the European Sciences and Transcendental Phenomenology. An Introduction of Phenomenological Philosophy*. Translated by D. Carr. Evanston, Ill.: Northwestern University Press, 1970.

Jameson, Fredric (1984). Foreword to *The Postmodern Condition: A Report on Knowledge*, by J.-F. Lyotard, vii–xxi. Manchester: Manchester University Press.

Jay, Martin (1982). "Should Intellectual History Take a Linguistic Turn? Reflections on the Habermas–Gadamer Debate." In *Modern European Intellectual History: Reapraisals and New Perspectives*. Edited by D. LaCapra and S. L. Kaplan. Ithaca, N.Y.: Cornell University Press.

Kant, Immanuel (1949). "What is Enlightenment?" in *Critique of Practical Reason and Other Writings in Moral Philosophy*. Edited and translated by Lewis White Beck. Chicago: Chicago University Press.

———— (1953). *Prolegomena to Any Future Metaphysics that Will Be Able to Present Itself As a Science*. Translated by P. G. Lucas. Manchester: Manchester University Press.

———— (1965). *Cririque of Pure Reason*. Translated by Norman Kemp Smith. New York: St. Martin's Press.

Kortian, Gabris (1980). *Metacritique: The Philosophical Argument of Jürgen Habermas*. Translated by F. Raffan, with an introductory essay by C. Taylor and A. Montefiore. Cambridge: Cambridge Univerity Press.

Kuhn, Thomas S. (1962). *The Structure of Scientific Revolutions*. Chicago: The University of Chicago Press.

LaCapra, Dominick (1983). "Habermas and the Grounding of Critical Theory." In *Rethinking Intellectual History*, by D. LaCapra. Ithaca: N.Y.: Cornell University Press.

✓ Lyotard, Jean-François (1984). *The Postmodern Condition: A Report on Knowledge*. Translated by G. Bennington and B. Massumi. Manchester: Manchester University Press.

Marcuse, Herbert (1962). *Eros and Civilisation: A Philosophical Inquiry into Freud*. Boston: Beacon Press.

Margolis, Joseph (1991). *The Truth About Relativism*. Oxford: Basil Blackwell.

Marx, Karl (1971). *A Contribution to the Critique of Political Economy*. London: Lawrence and Wishart.

———— (1973). *Grundrisse. Foundations for the Critique of Political Economy*. Translated by M. Niçolaus. The Pelican Marx Library in association with *New Left Review*. Harmondsworth, Middlesex: Penguin Books Ltd.

———— (1974). "Theses On Feuerbach." in Karl Marx, *The German Ideology*. London: Lawrence and Wishart.

———— (1976). *Capital*. Vol. 1. Translated by B. Fowkes. The Pelican Marx Library in association with *New Left Review*. Harmondsworht, Middlesex: Penguin Books Ltd.

Marx, Karl, and Frederick Engels (1974). *The German Ideology* (Pt. 1). Edited by C. J. Arthur. London: Lawrence and Wishart.

McCarthy, Thomas (1984). *The Critical Theory of Jürgen Habermas*. Cambridge: Polity Press.

Mendelson, Jack (1979). "The Habermas–Gadamer Debate." *New German Critique* 18 (Fall): 44–73.

Michelfelder, Diane P., and Richard E. Palmer eds. (1989). *Dialogue and Deconstruction: The Gadamer-Derrida Encounter*. Albany: State University of New York Press.

Mill, John Stuart (1973). *Collected Works*, vol. 7 and vol. 8, *A System of Logic, Ratiocinative and Inductive*. Edited by J. M. Robson. Toronto: University of Toronto Press.

Misgeld, Dieter (1977). "Critical Theory and Hermeneutics: The Debate between Habermas and Gadamer." In *On Critical Theory*. Edited by John O'Neill. London: Heinemann Educational Books.

Mueller-Vollmer, Kurt, ed. (1986). *The Hermeneutics Reader: Texts of the German Tradition from the Enlightenment to the Present.* Oxford: Basil Blackwell.

Outhwaite, William (1985). "Hans-Georg Gadamer." In *The Return of Grand Theory in the Human Sciences.* Edited by Q. Skinner. Cambridge: Cambridge University Press.

Palmer, Richard E. (1969). *Hermeneutics: Interpretation Theory in Schleiermacher, Dilthey, Heidegger, and Gadamer.* Evanston, Ill.: Northwestern University Press.

Piaget, Jean (1971). *Structuralism.* Edited and translated by C. Maschler. London: Routledge and Kegan Paul.

Popper, Karl R. (1963). *Conjectures and Refutations: The Growth of Scientific Knowledge.* London: Routledge and Kegan Paul.

Rabinow, Paul, and William M. Sullivan, eds. (1979). *Interpretive Social Science.* Berkeley: University of California Press.

Rasmussen, David M. (1990). *Reading Habermas.* Oxford: Basil Blackwell.

Ricoeur, Paul (1970). *Freud and Philosophy: An Essay on Inerpretation.* Translated by D. Savage. New Haven: Yale Universtity Press.

———— (1973). "Ethics and Culture: Habermas and Gadamer in Dialogue." *Philosophy Today* 17: 153–65.

———— (1981). *Hermeneutics and the Human Sciences.* Translated by J. B. Thompson. Cambridge: Cambridge University Press.

———— (1983). "On Interpretation." In *Philosophy in France Today.* Edited by Alan Montefiore. Cambridge: Cambridge University Press.

Roderick, Rick (1986). *Habermas and the Foundations of Critical Theory.* London: Macmillan.

Rorty, Richard (1980). *Philosophy and the Mirror of Nature.* Oxford: Basil Blackwell.

Sartre, Jean-Paul (1946). *Existentialism and Humanism.* Translated by Philip Mairet. London: Methuen, 1989.

Skinner, Quentin, ed. (1985). *The Return of Grand Theory in the Human Sciences.* Cambridge: Cambridge University Press.

Taylor, Charles (1971). "Interpretation and the Sciences of Man." *Review of Metaphysics* 25: 3–51.

Thompson, John B. (1981). *Critical Hermeneutics; A Study in the Thought of Paul Ricoeur and Jürgen Habermas.* Cambridge: Cambridge University Press.

Thompson, John B., and David Held, eds. (1982). *Habermas: Critical Debates.* London: The Macmillan Press Ltd.

Vattimo, Gianni (1988). *The End of Modernity: Nihilism and Hermeneutics in Postmodern Culture.* Translated by J. R. Snyder. Cambridge: Polity Press.

Wachterhauser, Brice R., ed. (1986). *Hermeneutics and Modern Philosophy.* Albany: State University of New York Press.

Warnke, Georgia (1987). *Gadamer: Hermeneutics, Tradition and Reason.* Cambridge: Polity Press.

Weber, Max (1970). *From Max Weber: Essays in Sociology.* Translated and edited by H. H. Gerth and C. W. Mills. London: Routledge and Kegan Paul.

White, Stephen K. (1988). *The Recent Work of Jürgen Habermas.* Cambridge: Cambridge University Press.

Wittgenstein, Ludwig (1961). *Tractatus Logico-Philosophicus.* Translated by D. F. Pears and B. F. McGuinness. London: Routledge and Kegan Paul.

Index

Phylogenetic process, 104
Physics, 69, 70, 78
Piaget, Jean, 59
Plato, 68, 73
Play, 75, 77, 79; authority of, 75
"Poiesis," 188
Polis, Greek, 21
Political judgment, 81, 82
Popper, Karl R., 55, 197 n.3
Positivism, 3, 6, 7, 8, 11, 14, 15, 168
Power, 62, 63, 107, 116, 129; relations, 10
Practical interest 97; cognitive character of, 97; for preservation of communication, 98. *See also* Interest: in communication
Practical knowledge, 20, 83
Practical life, 20
Practical reason, primacy of, 105
Practical reasoning, 81, 82; and the *Polis,* 83
Practical wisdom. See *Phronesis*
Praxis, 21, 79, 82, 83, 199 n.45; deformation of, 83, 179
Preconceptions. *See* Prejudices
Prejudices, xviii, 37–39, 42, 46, 47, 120, 121–22, 124, 125, 132, 139, 141; and authority, 125; evaluation of, 132; philosophical importance of, 40; productive, 41, 131; put at risk, 42; rehabilitation of, 23; and text, 39, 40; transparency of, 125; unproductive, 41
Prelinguistic experiences, 58; and reason, 59
Prescientific world, 16
"Prison of language," 71; escaping the, 60, 64
Private language, deformed, 110
Production, 10
Prohairesis, 83
Pseudocommunication, 148, 149, 150 151, 156, 157, 159, 163
Psychoanalysis, xvii, 107–14, 116, 120, 161; as critical social theory, 162, 163; as critique, 111
"Psychological interpretation," 29
Pure theory, illusion of, 18, 22

Rationality: "means-ends," 5; technological, of sciences, xxi; technocratic, 13, 14, 20, 119, 179, 182, 185. *See also*

Consciousness: technocratic
Rationalization, Weber's concept of, 5
Rational reconstructions, 207 n.13
Realist approach, naive, 54
Reality: constitution of, 87, 88; as interpretation, 101; objectified, 87
Reason, 59, 104, 106, 116, 160, 180, 187; and its interest, 106, 107 (*see also* Interest: emancipatory); Kantian, 82; and language, 59, 60; lost autonomy of, 5; and the species, 117; as Spirit, 74; as source of authority, 38, 122; unity of, 82, 117; unifying, 187. *See also* Practical reason, primacy of; Prelinguistic experiences: and reason
Reasoning, practical, 81, 82
"Recollection of primary meaning," 189 n.3
"Recollection of tradition," xix, 180, 181
Reconstruction, of linguistic rules, 147, 150. *See also* Sciences: reconstructive
Reconstruction, of the history of the species, 10, 192 n.22
"Reduction of reflection," 9
Reflection, xix, 9, 11, 86, 105, 125, 126, 130, 131, 205 n.37, 206 n.45; epistemological, 11, 168; Hegelian, 86, 200 n.1; and ideology, 130, 131; Kantian, 86, 200 n.1; loss of, 3; motive of, 206 n.41; "other-directedness" of, 206 n.45; in phenomenology, 138, 139; power of, 125, 127; psychoanalytic, 131, 162; "self-directedness" of, 206 n.45. *See also* Hermeneutic reflection; Liquidation of reflection; Self-reflection
Reflectivity, self-, 40
Reflexive philosophy, 134, 139. *See also* Philosophical hermeneutics
Relations of production, 9
Relativism, 67, 164, 197 n.3; absolute, 69, 164; versus objectivism, 165
Religious rules, interpretation of, 49, 50
Representation, of world in language, 64, 65, 66, 67, 76
Resistances, critical resolution of, 111
Retrospective method, 200 n.4. *See also* Hume, David; Induction; Universal and particular, relation of
Revealing, destiny of, 188; of technology, 188